In my kitchen

food for family and friends

Annie Bell   Photography by Lisa Linder

First published in 2004
by Conran Octopus Limited,
a part of Octopus Publishing Group,
2–4 Heron Quays, London E14 4JP
www.conran-octopus.co.uk

This paperback edition published in 2007

Publishing Director: Lorraine Dickey
Senior Editor: Katey Day
Art Director: Chi Lam
Designer: Victoria Burley
Assistant Production Controller: Natalie Moore
Photographer: Lisa Linder
Home Economist: Jacque Malouf

British Cataloguing-in-Publication Data
A catalogue record for this book is available from the British Library.
ISBN 978-1-84091-497-9

Printed and bound in China

CONTENTS

RECIPE INDEX

GRAZING
Bits with Drinks
Cocktail Sausages with Mustard Dip

Fruit and Nuts

Cheese Straws

Cocktail Puffs

Chicken Livers and Mango Chutney

Quails' Eggs with Saffron Salt

Devils on Horseback

Sausage Rolls

Cocktail Prawns

Smoked Salmon with Keta

Red Pepper Purée

Avocado Purée

Olive Swirls

Manchego with Membrillo and
  Pickled Chillies

Almost a Starter
Potted Crab

Prawns with Chorizo and Sherry

Squid and Tomato Stew

Mackerel Rillettes

Red Peppers Stuffed with
  Gorgonzola

Portobello Mushrooms Wrapped
  in Parma Ham with Goat's Cheese

WEEKDAY SUPPERS
Soup
No-nonsense Chicken Stock

Pea Soup with Bacon

Chilled Courgette Soup

Rocket and Potato Soup

Spinach Soup with Ricotta

Broccoli and Almond Soup

Lentil, Lemon and Ginger Soup

Lentil, Potato and Rosemary Broth

Chicken Noodle Soup

Favourite Cuts
Cheat's Chicken Kiev

Almond Chicken Breasts 'Levant'

Chicken Saltimbocca

Toad-in-the-Hole

Ragú with Conchiglioni

Macaroni Shepherd's Pie

Stuffed Tomatoes Campagnardes

Frankfurter and Potato Goulash

Moussaka

Lasagne al forno

Pot-au-Feu

Beetroot Bouillon with Steak

Corned Beef Hash

Greek Beef Casserole with Feta

Kleftiko

Fish Suppers
Saffron Mussels

Stew of Monkfish, Chickpeas and
  Spinach

Smoked Haddock Pie

Mussel and Monkfish Romesco

King Prawns and Mussels with
  Basil Purée

Smoked Haddock and Potato
  Chowder

Spanish-style Tuna and Potato Stew

Mussel, Cod and Tomato Pie

Skate and Potato Pie with
  Tomato Salsa

Pasta
Conchiglie with Butternut Squash
  and Sage Butter

Orecchiette with Avocado and Bacon

Spagettini Napoletana

Spaghetti with Truffles

Trofie with Sprouting Broccoli
  and Pancetta

Macaroni Cheese with Prawns

Sepia Pasta with Prawns and Chilli

SUNDAY LUNCH
The New Roast
Chicken and Red Pepper Roast

Chicken and Sweet Potato Roast
  with Rosemary

Roast Chicken with Garlic, and
  Macaroni Cheese

Chicken in Tahina Sauce

Chicken in a Herb Crust

Thyme and Lemon Roasted Chicken

Pork Loin Chops with Parsnip,
  Carrot and Beetroot

Pork Cooked in Milk

Savoy Cabbage with Almonds

Roast Beef, Chips and Aïoli

Fillet Steak with a Turnip Gratin

Fillet Steak en Croute

Sausage and Onion Roast with
  Mustard Sauce

Lamb Chops with Aubergine,
  Peppers and Mint Sauce

Whole Plaice Roasted with
  Rosemary and Lemon

Maryland Crab Cakes

Roast Salmon with Citrus Fruits

Red Mullet with a Rose Harissa

Vegetarian
Aubergine Gratin with Mozzarella
  and Olives

Flat-cap Mushrooms with Garlic,
  Lemon and Chilli

Swiss Chard, Mozzarella and
  Tomato Gratin

Gruyère and Wild Mushroom
  Gratin

Shortcrust Pastry

Spinach and Gruyère Tart

Onion Tart

Pea, Feta and Basil Tart

Fondue-filled Butternut Squash

SUMMER EATING
Barbecues
Grilled Figs with Bayonne Ham
  and Rocket

Chicken Drumsticks with
  Pomegranate Molasses

Honey and Thyme Grilled Quail

Arthur's Barbecued Sausages

Sesame-seared Sirloin

Spiced Lamb Cutlets

Bread and Tomato Brochettes

Saffron Sardines

Green Peppercorn Tuna

Alfresco
Crab Mayonnaise

Salad of Rump Steak with
  Carpaccio Dressing

Grilled Chicken, Lentil and
  Lemon Salad

Cold Lemon Chicken

Chicken Tonnato

Introduction

I've always felt enormously lucky to be able to combine the two things I enjoy doing most in the world: bringing up my children and cooking. In fact I'm not sure that I can separate the two, given that they've always gone hand in hand. Most days are a hazy mist of cosy domesticity: from my stove I have a bird's-eye view, one eye on whatever is cooking, and the other on Louis and Rothko at play. Occasionally we venture into each other's space, but it is not unknown for Louis (aged six) to mutter 'Back in the kitchen cooker' when I do. And the pleasure of cooking is having someone to eat it, so without my testers, big and small, I'd be nowhere.

My kitchen is as personal as another person's art studio or writing hut at the end of the garden; it is my den, where I think, dream, potter and muse as well as cook and wash up. And in its extended role it is pivotal as the space that defines home. During the course of a day, the table becomes sectioned into internet and paperwork, homework, and general miscellany like cottonreels and nametapes and early artworks that don't have any other home. Clearing a space for supper midweek is something like the parting of the Red Sea. And then there are those rare serene days of calm when the decks are cleared and we honour whatever occasion is at hand: Christmas, a birthday tea, Sunday lunch, or a barbecue on a balmy summer's day, when we momentarily aspire to blissful clarity of purpose. That lasts until Monday morning and then we're off again.

There are few rights and wrongs in kitchen design or paraphernalia – it's too personal and complex for there to be one solution for all. I am very fortunate to have two completely different kitchens from which to work: a steel and glass box in London, where space is at a premium and measured in square centimetres, and a cavernous crumbling country kitchen in Normandy. But the backbones of the two are identical: they are held together by a common thread dictated by the ease of cooking and living in them. Paramount is having just enough and not too much equipment. A stove of generous proportions, a big sink, a few good knives, pots and pans and one solid chopping board, and I'm well on the way to fine food.

These recipes are geared towards being a family, and all the occasions throughout the year to which that pertains. Not least for my own use, I wanted to gather together all the fallback recipes I rely on: come Christmas a reminder of how to roast a turkey (twelve months is quite long enough to forget), how to cook the ham, how to make a great bread sauce, a suitably indulgent orange trifle and homemade mincemeat. There is a call for a foolproof recipe for pancakes, a spiced peach crumble that can be thrown together in twenty minutes, macaroni cheese to silence the young that will also appease any adults if it's dished up with roast chicken and caramelized garlic cloves – the need for occasion-based recipes is endless.

There are two schools of thought as to whether we need recipes at all, but personally I've always found comfort and reassurance in the smaller details that guide you towards a particular end. Even after years of cooking, I still prefer to consult a recipe telling me exactly how long I need to roast my potatoes or how much cream to add to my mash, because sadly I don't have an encyclopedic memory and see no point in leaving good results to chance. Fine details also provide a good springboard for improvising recipes; if you can look up exactly how something should be done, you have the foundation to go on and create a dish in the way you want. In short, better too much than too little detail.

Home Comforts

Objects have to work hard these days to justify their presence in our lives. I look back with some nostalgia to how my mother had sets of glasses for best, and silver coffee spoons with filigree tips, tarnished from lack of use, that were polished up on their occasional outing. We no longer expect to lock away our goods for special occasions: the luxury of having two different sets is a waste of space. But this puts pressure on the objects that we do have, demanding that they be neither too elegant nor too delicate for everyday use, while beautiful to boot.

Central to the kind of kitchen you live in are a table and chairs. In London we have to consider carefully how every inch of space in our flat is used, and the main dilemma in the kitchen is dining. Sometimes we are two, sometimes four, and at other times eight or ten, but patience escapes me when it comes to tripping over all those chair legs on a daily basis for the sake of the occasional full house. Stackable chairs instantly free up half the room. Ron Arad's Fantastic Plastic Elastic chairs are a masterful design: they curve sinuously, are ethereal in presence but virtually indestructible, and can be wiped down.

As to a table, my perfect design is oval. Apart from being more discreet in terms of the number of people it can seat *vis à vis* the space it takes up, an oval table is much friendlier and more social – you don't have that thing of being stuck in conversation with your designated partner on either side. Eero Saarinen's table for Knoll, designed in the fifties, for me has never been surpassed, and with just one central pedestal you're not faced with having to squeeze yourself either side of a table leg.

In the garden the ideal is a table that can be set up wherever you want to be. I have two basic trestles (bought from the local ironmongery), with a door blank on top, on which I throw an antique linen sheet that doubles as a tablecloth. A coloured glass vase filled with cow parsley, and the scene is set.

I've always loved coloured glass, and five or six jelly-hued votives see me through most lighting scenarios. And using nightlights saves having to scrape the wax off the table the following morning. We also favour coloured fairy lights, largely at the whim of Louis, who was appalled one year by the apparent good taste of the white lights used to deck a local street, which were, he pronounced, 'boring, boring, boring'. The average five-year-old, to whom Christmas rightly belongs, wants an Aladdin's cave hung with jewelled strings of red, purple, yellow and green lights.

I like to buy up old hand-blown glasses. They vaguely match, but their charm is their individuality. They are chunkier than average – I have a horror of spindly stems, having snapped one too many with a vigorous swipe of the tea towel. A set of tumblers is also essential: I love Kaj Franck's Kartio tumblers and flask for iittala, which do for kiddies, as well as for water and wine. Another essential is water itself, and I would far rather look at Alberta Meda's water jug, which comes with a funnel and filter, than at the average bottle. Freshly filled with water, this jug encourages everyone in the family to drink more than they might otherwise.

Plain white crockery underpins any food type or occasion, and the plainer the better. I have stacks of small, cupped, rimless bowls that get used for everything from eating to storing and serving, and dinner plates that double as serving plates. Cutlery too can be rationalized: I have just one size of knife and fork, and a spoon that bridges the gap between soup and dessert. Luxury comes in having lots, though, to allow for a full dishwasher and a full house.

Pots 'n' Pans

Just at the point when I needed a crucial drop of white wine to lighten the base of a watercress soup, my trusted corkscrew, which had serviced more than one generation of *bon buveur*, twisted its last and died. In a state of mild panic my first port of call was the local supermarket, where I was met by a variety of colourful cutting-edge helical screws and pumping mechanisms, all apparently seeking to outwit each other. Plumping for what looked like the simplest, I managed to lacerate my finger some minutes later – and I am still looking for a replacement, scanning the aisles of every kitchen outlet I visit in frustration that it's no longer possible to buy that particular design.

Such crises have big implications for a cook. I quickly feel lost without the comfort of familiar tools, so much so that I have almost identical equipment in London and France, nearly all tried and tested classics that go back decades, if not hundreds of years, and that even when new have a well-honed feel in the hand. Towering creamy-white stacks of pudding basins in three sizes do for everything from food prep to storage, as well as the intended steamed puds. A handful of oval white china dishes sit inside each other like Russian dolls, taking care of puddings, gratins, and cold summer fare of every persuasion. Nor would I choose to be without my cane-weave mixing bowl and wooden spoons, or my seasoned riveted knives that to hold are as comfortable as slipping on a soft leather glove.

There is an intrinsic beauty about such equipment that predates the fashion for pretending we're running quasi-restaurants out of our homes and equipping them as such; it's domestic through and through. Town or country, it sits naturally in both, and, most importantly, it doesn't date. A fair deal of new equipment is driven by fashion, which is all very well if you're planning on changing your baking tins and potato peelers on a seasonal basis. But it's not the best investment: anything too avant garde is likely to please the senses today and rankle them tomorrow. Ideally it's going to stick around for a long time, and with that in mind it needs to be visually discreet, as well as sensible. Do we really need a spot in the middle of a saucepan that changes colour to tell us when it's hot?

Hardware stores are great hunting grounds, and I never visit a foreign country without scouring the shelves of the local ironmongery, full of collectable treasure that paints a telling picture of the eating habits of that particular region. Often this is where you will find the really honest, down-to-earth stuff, fashioned from wood, tin and enamel. Would that the latter came back into fashion: heavy-gauge enamelled steel roasting tins that weigh a fraction of cast iron, and perform just as well, did our grannies proud. Any chips sustained when they're dropped are a part of their charm, and give them a well-loved look that is what home kitchens are all about.

When it comes to electrical equipment, the byword is 'retrograde'. The more knobs, programmes and attachments, the more confusion (I'm still trying to learn how to programme the video). I used to think that my granny in her terraced cottage in Kensal Rise was carbon-dated by her Teasmade, which shuddered into action at the same time that the Roberts radio emitted the pips on the hour of seven. But today, having been through every type of espresso machine and requisite frother, I measure progress in terms of filter coffee machines that come with a timer. *Et plus ça change.*

GRAZING

In France the hour of the aperitif is alive and well, and rarely does a day go by in Normandy when we don't at some point sit to attention round a kitchen table, raise a glass and collectively chant 'santé'. And beneath the chinking glasses there will always be a few little somethings on which to graze. Having studied the form, I reckon my French friends have it down to a fine art, not least because with that degree of regularity ambition doesn't really come into it.

So let us start with C for Convenience: salted almonds, cashews and macadamias, pistachios and toasted sunflower seeds, which probably give way to olives further south. Next on the list come crudités and something to dip them into, as nearly everyone can almost always amass a goodly selection from the proceeds of the salad box in the fridge and the vegetable rack, or cocktail sausages (they do a great line in mini frankfurters in France). And if the occasion calls for something a little more fancy, then it's some warmed puff pastry bouchées, which the French aren't averse to buying as well, but given the buttery yellow rolls wrapped in waxed paper that loll in the chill cabinets of supermarkets there I feel almost obliged to make my own. Frankly, though, any shopbought will do, the point is ready-for-the-rolling and for once frozen is just as good as fresh. To their credit, such pastries can be prepared several days in advance and reheated for a few minutes before serving. The bottom line, playing things the French way, is that any drinks occasion is painlessly catered for with just one homemade appetiser, the rest a crafty buy-up of nibbles.

In the same spirit, the pressure of lunch or supper can be eased a hundredfold by opting for tasters that lie halfway between a cocktail nibble and a formal first course: a few oysters, some salami and gherkins, quails' eggs, or chicken livers on toast with chutney. I think formal first courses must have a lot to do with many people's dread of sit-down dinners (not least the cook), spinning the occasion into a lengthy event without allowing you to socialise as freely as you might like. I have all but given up on them, unless it's a dig-in scenario of something fingerlickingly messy plonked in the middle of the table that banishes any notion of good manners. And I would add chilled soups to that list for sheer ease. Otherwise an old-fashioned butler's tray with a stand is the most adaptable contrivance for moveable feasting, as it can be laid with a pile of small plates, forks and napkins, and food that can be handed round.

Cocktail Sausages with Mustard Dip

With a mixed bag of ages to satisfy, I head any list of nibbles with cocktail sausages and take it from there. And if it's borderline suppertime for any kiddies present, as early evening drinks tend to be, the sausages can easily be turned into quasi-hot dogs with the addition of some mini pitta breads and a bottle of ketchup.

I find that the cocktail sausages I buy from Sid my local butcher in Blythe Road, Brook Green are worlds apart from the sorry overprocessed ones from the supermarket. Sid's caramelise to a deep brown and have that chewiness you want in a cocktail sausage.

Serves 6

500 g cocktail sausages
HOT MUSTARD SAUCE
300 ml double cream
4 heaped tsp Dijon mustard
a few drops of lemon juice
sea salt

Heat the oven to 170°C fan oven/180°C electric oven/Gas 4. Lay the sausages in a single layer on a baking tray spaced slightly apart to ensure they caramelise evenly. Roast for 35–45 minutes, giving them a stir halfway through. If cooking more than this and using two baking trays, you can switch them around if they are cooking unevenly. Leave to cool for 10 minutes before serving.

While they are cooking, gently heat the cream in a small non-stick saucepan and simmer until it reduces by about a third, thickening up in the process. Stir frequently to prevent it from sticking. Remove from the heat and whisk in the remaining ingredients. The sauce can also be made in advance and rewarmed.

Fruit and Nuts

Searching out the silver lining of the cloud that would have guests stashing their pockets full of sunflower seeds before attending a drinks party, roasted nuts would now seem to be approved by just about every dietary regime. After years of being left out in the cold for being too available, too convenient, and too calorific, these considerations no longer count. And for a few minutes' toil the fragrance and squeaky clean bite that are the domain of freshly roasted nuts are ours. This is a mixed bag of favourites – almonds, cashews and macadamias, with some dried cherries for added cheer, and a minute pixiedust sprinkling of cayenne pepper.

Serves 6–8

2 tsp unsalted butter, softened
100 g raw cashews
150 g raw almonds, skinned
100 g raw macadamias
3 tbsp coarse sea salt
cayenne pepper, for dusting
75 g dried cherries

Heat the oven to 140°C fan oven/150°C electric oven/Gas 2. Grease a baking tray with the butter and lay the cashews and almonds in a single layer on top. Bake for 10 minutes then scatter over the macadamias. Bake for another 35 minutes, by which time they should be a pale creamy gold.

Scatter the sea salt over a sheet of baking parchment. Tip the nuts on top and use a teaspoon to toss and rub the salt through them. Wrap the paper up into a package and set aside overnight (the minimum they need is 1 hour if you are doing them at the last minute). On unwrapping the nuts, dust with a generous knife tip of cayenne pepper and shake off the excess salt. Transfer to a bowl and mix in the dried cherries.

Cheese Straws

The best cheese straws taste like that crispy bit of toasted cheese on the bottom of the grill pan begging to be prized off with a palette knife, usually the choice morsel of whatever you are cooking. A mixture of Gruyère and Parmesan offers the best of both worlds, a judicious balance of flavour and crunch.

Makes 20–25 Serves 8

225 g puff pastry
25 g freshly grated Parmesan
25 g grated Gruyère
a knife tip of cayenne pepper
1 egg yolk whisked with 1 tbsp
  milk

Heat the oven to 180°C fan oven/190°C electric oven/Gas 5. Thinly roll out the pastry about 1 mm thick on a lightly floured surface into a large rectangle about 30 x 50 cm. Place the long sides facing you, and trim them. Combine the Parmesan and Gruyère with the cayenne pepper in a bowl and scatter over the top half of the pastry, leaving a 1 cm edge. Brush this with the eggwash and bring the lower edge up over it. Roll the sheet to seal the edges and compress the cheese, you should have a strip about 15 cm wide. Cut this into 1 cm straws.

Holding one end in either hand, twist each strip to give you about 5 turns, and lay them 2 cm apart on one or two baking sheets, pressing the edges well down to ensure they don't unravel as they cook. Bake for 12–15 minutes until an even gold, turning the trays round halfway through. The bottom tray may take a few minutes longer than the top.

Loosen the straws with a palette knife (any that break are cook's tips), and ideally serve while still warm, or newly cooled. I like to stack them in glasses, but you could also arrange them in a bowl or on a plate. They can be stored for several days in an airtight container, and reheated for 5 minutes in an oven heated to 150°C fan oven/160°C electric oven/Gas 3.

Cocktail Puffs

These little pastry puffs are the simplest of all biscuits to make, and melt to nothing in the mouth. If you wanted to get fancy with some soup, then any leftovers can be floated aboard as a garnish, and as with cheese straws they can be reheated.

Makes approx. 40 Serves 6

150 g puff pastry
1 egg yolk whisked with 1 tbsp
  milk
sesame, poppy and cumin seeds

Heat the oven to 200°C fan oven/220°C electric oven/Gas 7. Thinly roll out the pastry about 2 mm thick on a lightly floured surface and cut out miniature shapes about 4 cm in diameter. These could be stars, moons, trees or little fluted biscuits. Transfer to one or two baking sheets, spaced 1 cm apart. Lightly brush the surface of the biscuits with the eggwash and scatter with either sesame, poppy or cumin seeds – it's nice to have a selection of all three. Bake the biscuits for 5–7 minutes until risen and lightly golden. Loosen with a palette knife and serve straightaway. They will keep well in a covered container for several days, and can be rewarmed for 5 minutes in an oven heated to 150°C fan oven/160°C electric oven/Gas 3.

* You can also make a near instant cheese pastry by scattering a large pinch of Parmesan over each one instead of the seeds.

Chicken Livers and Mango Chutney

Slightly crusty chicken livers that are still pink in the centre, with a sweet spicy hot chutney is what things on toast are all about. And things on toast fit neatly into that halfway house between nibbles and a first course. Fried bread is mouthwateringly good here, but buttered toast shouldn't be sniffed at as a timesaving device.

Serves 4

200 g chicken livers (drained
    weight)
3 tbsp groundnut oil
4 x 7 cm squares of white bread
15 g unsalted butter
sea salt, black pepper
1 large shallot, peeled and finely
    chopped
2 tbsp Madeira
4 tsp mango chutney
1 tbsp coarsely chopped coriander

Cut the fatty membranes out of the chicken livers. Heat a tablespoon of the oil in a large frying pan over a medium heat and fry one side of the bread slices until golden and crisp, then turn them, adding another tablespoon of oil, and fry this side also. Lay these out on a plate.

Turn the heat down low as the pan will have become quite hot by this stage and you don't want the fat to spit, and add the remaining oil and the butter. Season the chicken livers and fry for about 2 minutes until tinged with brown at the edges, turning them halfway through. They should remain slightly pink in the centre, and give a little when pressed. Divide them among the toast, add the shallot to the pan, turn the heat up again and cook for a couple of minutes until softened, stirring occasionally. Add the Madeira and sizzle for about a minute until it seems rich and reduced. Spoon this over the chicken livers, dollop a teaspoon of chutney on top, and scatter with the coriander.

Quails' Eggs with Saffron Salt

Whether or not you get through these first time round they are unlikely to go to waste in the coming days. They also surprisingly appeal to children, which can only have to do with unwrapping something. Under normal circumstances wild horses wouldn't drag Louis to within a yard of a boiled egg, but he is quite happy to peel and eat quails' eggs, and even better to peel them for everyone else.

Serves 6–8

approx. 30 saffron threads
1 heaped tbsp fine grain sea salt
3 dozen quails' eggs

Grind the saffron threads in a pestle and mortar, add the salt and work it using the mortar until it has blended with the spice. Transfer to a small bowl to serve.

Bring a pan of water to the boil. It is easiest to cook the eggs in two goes, gently lower them into the water and boil for 2½ minutes. Remove them with a spoon to a sink of cold water. This is important to stop the yolk cooking – it should be set on the outside, but runny within. Serve the quails' eggs with the salt to dip into.

Devils on Horseback

No need for an introduction here – crisp rolls of bacon encasing a jammy prune soaked in tea and port. I find I get more evenly gold and crisp devils by roasting them in a hot oven rather than fussing over a grill pan.

Serves 4

12 presoaked stone-out prunes
2 tbsp port
4 tbsp tea
12 rashers rindless unsmoked
    streaky bacon
1 tbsp honey mustard*

Submerge the prunes in the port and tea in a small bowl, and leave them to soak up the flavours overnight.

Heat the oven to 220°C fan oven/230°C electric oven/Gas 8. Drain off any residual liquid from the prunes, and lay out the bacon rashers on a board. Brush a little mustard down the length of each rasher and roll it around a prune. Place the rolls spaced slightly apart in a roasting dish, and roast for 12–15 minutes until golden and crisp, turning them halfway through using a palette knife to loosen them. Leave to stand for 5–10 minutes, then skewer with a cocktail stick and serve.

* Colman's Honey Mustard is ideal here, failing that blend 2 tsp prepared English mustard with 1 tsp set honey.

Sausage Rolls

A small sliver of warm sausage roll is about as welcome as bits with drinks get. These disappear as speedily as cocktail sausages, which in my experience demand double whatever quantity you anticipate you need. They are best eaten warm from the oven, but given that you probably don't want to be tied to a rolling pin and smothered in flour when your guests arrive, they can also be made several hours in advance and rewarmed for 10 minutes in an oven heated to 150°C fan oven/160°C electric oven/Gas 3.

Serves 6

250 g puff pastry
250 g sausagemeat
1 tsp Dijon mustard
1 tsp grain mustard
1 egg yolk whisked with
    1 tbsp milk

Heat the oven to 180°C fan oven/190°C electric oven/Gas 5. Thinly roll out the pastry on a lightly floured surface into a rectangle the size of a sheet of A4 paper. Trim the long edges and cut this into two finger-long strips, about 8 cm wide. Using your hands divide the sausagemeat between the strips, rolling it into a long thin cylinder, and laying it in the centre of the pastry. Blend the mustards together and, using a knife, smear this in a line down the length of sausagemeat.

Paint one long edge of each piece of pastry with a 1 cm rim of eggwash. Fold the unpainted edge over the sausagemeat, and then the painted edge on top and press together. If necessary cut the sausage rolls in half to fit on a baking tray, but otherwise lay the two rolls on a baking sheet, sealed-side down. Score the top of the sausage rolls with diagonal slits 1 cm apart, and paint the top and sides with the eggwash. Bake for 25–30 minutes. Leave to cool for 15 minutes, then cut diagonally into 1 cm slices and serve warm as an appetiser.

Cocktail Prawns

Plump tiger prawns dipped into Sauce Marie-Rose are like a prawn cocktail without the lettuce. The means of serving them is optional, you may just like to pile them into a bowl.

Serves 8

SAUCE

1 medium organic egg yolk

1 tsp Dijon mustard

150 ml groundnut oil

2 tbsp tomato ketchup

a few good shakes of Tabasco

PRAWNS

400 g cooked tiger prawns, peeled leaving tail fan attached

a generous squeeze of lemon juice

sea salt, black pepper

2 tbsp finely chopped flat-leaf parsley

TO SERVE

2 Little Gem lettuces, base trimmed and outer leaves discarded

2 spring onions, trimmed, finely sliced lengthwise and halved

To prepare the sauce, whisk the egg yolk with the mustard in a bowl, then gradually whisk in the oil, a few drops at a time to begin with until the mayonnaise takes. Stir in the tomato ketchup, then season with a shake or two of Tabasco, I like a noticeable nip of chilli.

Refresh the prawns in a sieve under the cold water tap, then drain them on kitchen paper. Toss them in a bowl with a generous squeeze of lemon, a little seasoning and the parsley. Finely slice the Little Gem lettuces into rosettes and toss with the spring onions in a bowl.* Arrange the prawns in piles on top of the salad on one or two plates with the sauce in a bowl to the side. Cover and set aside in a cool place, or chill until required, and bring back up to room temperature 30 minutes before serving.

* This is intended as a base for the prawns but if you want to eat it, then dress it just before serving with a slug of groundnut oil, a squeeze of lemon and a little seasoning.

Smoked Salmon with Keta

A little in the way of luxury, this is a good celebratory lead into dinner. Of all the 'faux' caviars, keta (salmon roe) dolloped on to a buttered baguette was my big craving when I was pregnant. My husband always felt a shrink would have had a field day knowing that I would come home after a scan and lustily consume a whole pot of eggs.

Serves 6–8

100 g fromage frais

100 g jar of keta (salmon roe)

350 g sliced smoked salmon

½ lemon

black pepper

Spoon the fromage frais into a bowl and gently fold in the keta. Transfer to a small clean bowl. Halve each smoked salmon slice into two long strips about 5 cm wide, and arrange these on one or two plates. If not eating straightaway, cover the keta roe and salmon with clingfilm and reserve in a cool place or chill. Bring back up to room temperature 30 minutes before serving.

Just before eating, squeeze a little lemon juice over the salmon and season with black pepper. Accompany with the keta roe.

6.00pm

Crudité Dips

Sitting on the terrace of Alain Ducasse's Provençal Bastide in Moustier in the shadow of a whirring blade of a helicopter dropping off its lithe and tanned lunchees from downwind Saint Tropez, crudités couldn't seem anything but glamorous. None of your great big wedges of old carrot that have you munching monotonously as one conversation melds into another. Here, plucked from the kitchen garden that morning, were the finest slivers of young fennel, dewy cherry tomatoes and radishes, and dainty batons of young carrot. With little pots of tapenade and goat's cheese mashed up with olive oil in which to dip them. You could also add some cornichons or cocktail gherkins and pickled silverskin onions to the vegetables, and line up a bowl of shelled tiger prawns.

Red Pepper Purée

The absence of garlic and raw onion that often rasp in the wake of such dips will attract many, and this is also virtuously low in fat. Depending on the availability of herbs, you could use either coriander or mint instead of both.

Serves 6

6 red peppers
75 g pine nuts
1 slice toasted white bread
2 tbsp of Greek yoghurt
a squeeze of lemon juice
sea salt, black pepper
1 tbsp each of finely chopped
   coriander and mint
extra virgin olive oil to serve

Heat the oven to 200°C fan oven/220°C electric oven/Gas 7, place the peppers on an oven rack and roast for 20 minutes. Place them in a bowl, cover and leave to cool. Turn the oven down to 180°C fan oven/190°C electric oven/Gas 5, arrange the pine nuts in a single layer in a small baking tray and toast in the oven for 7–8 minutes until golden, then remove and leave to cool.

Reduce the toast to crumbs in a food processor, then add the pine nuts and whizz to coarse nibs. Transfer the mixture to a bowl. Skin and deseed the peppers, and, discarding any juices, place the flesh in the bowl of the food processor and purée. Transfer the purée to a bowl and stir in the Greek yoghurt, and season with a good squeeze of lemon juice and some salt and pepper. Fold in the breadcrumb and pine nut mixture, and the herbs, and taste to check the seasoning. Transfer the purée to a clean bowl, cover and leave for an hour or so for it to firm up. Just before serving, drizzle with a little olive oil.

Avocado Purée

Here you can make good use of all those imperfect avocados whose moment of perfect ripeness passed you by in the fruit bowl. Their slightly over-ripe flesh can be guaranteed to be supremely creamy, and you can cut out any blackened parts likely to otherwise disgrace them. The sauce doesn't hang around however, and needs to be made relatively close to the time of serving, but it can at least be thrown together in a jiffy.

Serves 4

3 avocados
1 tbsp lemon juice
2 spring onions, trimmed and
   cut up
sea salt
Tabasco
cayenne pepper for dusting

Halve the avocados, remove the stones and scoop the flesh into a food processor. Add the lemon juice, spring onions, a little sea salt and a dash of Tabasco and reduce to a purée. Transfer this to a bowl and dust with cayenne pepper. Serve as soon as possible.

Olive Swirls

Depending on where your imagination's heading, these dainty coiled biscuits will either remind you of terraced mountains in Thailand, or the bra cups that did so much to catapult Madonna to fame. Either way they're quite impressive.

Makes 60–80 Serves 8–10

225 g puff pastry
2 tbsp tapenade or olive paste*
paprika

Thinly roll out the pastry on a lightly floured worksurface into a rectangle 30 x 50 cm. Trim the long edges, and place them towards you. Thinly spread the pastry with the tapenade using a palette knife and halve the rectangle into two squares. Roll these up into scrolls, working away from you, then wrap each one in clingfilm and chill for at least 1 hour. They can be prepared several hours in advance.

Heat the oven to 200°C fan oven/220°C electric oven/Gas 7. Trim the end of each roll and thinly slice into circles; don't worry if these are more elliptical than round. Lay them out on baking trays, spaced 1 cm apart, and bake for 8–12 minutes until evenly gold. Serve straightaway. They will keep well for several days in a covered container, and can be rewarmed for 5 minutes in an oven heated to 150°C fan oven/160°C electric oven/Gas 3. If you like you can dust them with paprika just before serving.

* There are some excellent tapenades on the market. But to make your own, finely process 110 g pitted green olives, 15 g rinsed capers, half a garlic clove and a pinch of thyme with a grinding of black pepper and a tablespoon of olive oil in a food processor. This is more than you will need for the recipe, the rest can be covered and kept in the fridge for up to a week.

Manchego with Membrillo and Pickled Chillies

A New-Age take on cheese with pineapple, whose success had everything to do with its being on a stick. Jammy dark orange membrillo and a sliver of manchego is a combination that's even better with a chilli on top. Pickled chillies come in different sizes so you may have to trim them to fit.

Makes 12 Serves 6

100 g manchego
  (weight excluding rind)
100 g membrillo
12 slim pickled chillies

Slice the manchego into 12 slim wedges about 4 cm wide by 8 cm long. Cut thin slices of membrillo a little smaller and place on top of the cheese, and then a chilli. You can serve them as they are, or skewer them with cocktail sticks and arrange on a large plate.

Potted Crab

Peeling shrimps is a task to leave to others, however delectable they might be potted. You can make an equally delicious and buttery pot with crab for spreading on thin, crisp toast, a few salad leaves or radishes to hand. In fact this is one of the best uses for crab that I can think of, where the brown meat is as readily employed as the white.

Serves 4

110 g unsalted butter
250 g white and brown crabmeat,
    picked over
juice of ½ lemon
¼ tsp ground mace
¼ tsp cayenne pepper
sea salt
1 bay leaf

Melt 70 g of the butter in a small frying pan over a medium heat, add the crabmeat and stir until heated through. Add the lemon juice, mace, cayenne pepper and a little salt to taste. Pack this into a small bowl, cover and chill for about an hour until it firms. Melt the remaining butter in a small saucepan. Lay a bay leaf over the surface of the crab and pour over the butter. Cover and chill. This will keep well for a couple of days.

Prawns with Chorizo and Sherry

Chorizo has a great affinity with seafood – all that garlic and buttery pork fat, and of course the paprika, which it sheds into the prawns' juices. It's fingers in here, and lots of bread. Personally I'd dispense with the finger bowls, I'd rather get up and wash my hands than sit looking at something that bears marked similarities to a five-year old's attempt at 'horrid soup'.

Serves 6

extra virgin olive oil
10 thin slices of chorizo, cut into
    strips 1 cm wide
400 g (approx. 24) raw tiger
    prawns (shell-on)
125 ml dry sherry
a squeeze of lemon juice
coarsely chopped flat-leaf parsley
    to serve

Heat 2 tablespoons of oil in a large frying pan over a medium heat, add the chorizo and sauté for 1–2 minutes, stirring occasionally until lightly coloured and crisp. Add the prawns and turn until their shells change colour, then add the sherry, which will start simmering instantly, cover and cook for 3 minutes. Add a squeeze of lemon, then transfer the prawns and juices to a shallow dish, drizzle over a little more oil and scatter with parsley. Serve straightaway.

Squid and Tomato Stew

Squid makes a sublimely rich and meltingly tender stew, so it can only be its grisly looks that put us off eating more of it. There is no making fake claims that this is especially quick to prepare, but in its favour it can be made in advance, and served hot or at room temperature. It can also be spooned over rice as a main course, in which case it does for about four.

Serves 6

1 kg squid (as long as your hand)

a pinch of saffron filaments
(approx. 20)

5 tbsp extra virgin olive oil, plus a
little extra

1 Spanish onion, peeled, quartered
and thinly sliced

4 garlic cloves, peeled and
smashed with a rolling pin or
the handle of a knife

2 beefsteak tomatoes, skinned and
coarsely chopped

1 small dried red chilli, finely
chopped

sea salt

1 bay leaf

4 tbsp brandy

125 ml white wine

coarsely chopped coriander or
flat-leaf parsley to serve

To prepare the squid, firmly tug the head away from the body to separate the two. Remove the hard transparent 'pen' from the body, and the thin porphyry-coloured film that covers it. Slit the pouch open and wash both sides, removing any remaining white membranes. Slice the open pouches and halve if the slices are long. Cut the tentacles from the head above the eyes, and halve if large.

Pour a tablespoon of boiling water over the saffron filaments in a small bowl and leave them to infuse.

Heat 3 tbsp of olive oil in a large frying pan over a medium heat, add the onion and garlic and cook over a low heat for about 5 minutes until soft but not coloured, stirring occasionally. Add the tomatoes, the chilli and a little salt and sauté, pressing the tomatoes down with a wooden spoon until the juices given out evaporate.

Heat the remaining olive oil in a medium-size saucepan over a medium-high heat, add the squid, some salt and the bay leaf, and stir regularly until the squid has thrown off its liquid and is seething. Add the brandy and flambé it if you are brave. The easiest way to do this is to pour in all but a little of the spirit, warm this in a metal spoon over a flame and as soon as it ignites pour it into the pan and the rest will flare up. But this isn't essential.

Add the wine, bring to the boil and simmer for a few minutes to reduce it, then add the sauté vegetables. Bring back to the boil and simmer uncovered over a low heat for about 50 minutes, stirring regularly until the squid is tender and coated in a thick sauce. Add the saffron liquid about 10 minutes before the end. Transfer to a bowl, drizzle over a little more oil and scatter with chopped coriander or parsley.

Mackerel Rillettes

This by any other name is a pâté, billed in France as rillettes, it's that much more delicate than one made with smoked mackerel. The fillets can also be eaten as they are, with a gooseberry sauce or mayonnaise on the side. You'll want some thin crisp toast or French bread and some radishes and gherkins or little pickled silverskin onions to eat with it.

Serves 4

MARINADE

1 lemon, finely sliced

1 onion, peeled and finely sliced

1 carrot, peeled and finely sliced

5 sprigs of thyme

1 bay leaf

1 bottle white wine

3 tbsp cider vinegar

3 tbsp groundnut oil

RILLETTES

4 x 250 g mackerel, heads
   removed, gutted and washed

2 heaped tbsp mayonnaise

2 tbsp single cream

2 generous tbsp finely chopped
   chives

sea salt, black pepper

cayenne pepper

1 tsp sherry or cider vinegar

1 tbsp finely chopped shallot

Place all the ingredients for the marinade in a large cast-iron casserole, bring to a rolling boil, then immerse the mackerel in the marinade, cover with a lid, turn the heat off and leave to cool for several hours or overnight.

Remove the mackerel to a board, and carefully fillet them. Place the fillets in a large bowl and mash with a fork, then add the mayonnaise, cream and chives, and blend together. Season with salt, black pepper and a little cayenne pepper, and add the vinegar and chopped shallot and mix again. Cover and chill if not serving straightaway, and bring back up to room temperature before eating.

Red Peppers Stuffed with Gorgonzola

The sweetness of the peppers is a great match for the creamy melted blue cheese. Fourme d'Ambert would be another good candidate, as would Roquefort. Long peppers can vary hugely in size, go for average-sized ones rather than large.

Serves 6

extra virgin olive oil

1 Spanish onion, peeled and
   chopped

2 red bell peppers, core and seeds
   removed, and diced

sea salt, black pepper

1 tbsp balsamic vinegar

250 g Gorgonzola
   (weight excluding rind), diced

75 g fresh white breadcrumbs

2 tbsp coarsely chopped flat-leaf
   parsley

2 tbsp coarsely chopped mint

8 long pointed red peppers

Heat 2 tablespoons of extra virgin olive oil in a large frying pan over a medium heat, add the onion and diced peppers, season and sauté for 10 minutes until soft, stirring occasionally. Sprinkle over half the balsamic vinegar, which will evaporate almost immediately. Remove to a large bowl and leave to cool. Stir in the cheese, breadcrumbs and herbs.

Trim the stalks of the 8 pointed peppers, leaving about 2 cm, then cut the tops off but don't throw them away. Remove any seeds inside. Stuff with the pepper and cheese mixture, pushing it well down to the bottom of each pepper. Arrange the stuffed peppers with their lids in place in a roasting dish. The peppers can be prepared to this point up to a couple of hours in advance, in which case cover with clingfilm and set aside in a cool place.

Heat the oven to 200°C fan oven/220°C electric oven/Gas 7. Drizzle a little more oil over the peppers and season with salt, then roast for 25 minutes until golden in patches. Drizzle over the remaining balsamic vinegar and set aside for 15 minutes. Serve warm with the pan juices spooned over. You may like to peel off the skin as you go.

Portobello Mushrooms Wrapped in Parma Ham with Goat's Cheese

With the spotlight shining on mushrooms that have sprung up in some leafy glade or tree trunk in the wild, it is all too easy to dismiss any that are cultivated as being inferior. And this would be to miss out on velvet-skinned flat-cap mushrooms, whose dark satanic juices are every bit as rich as gravy.

Serves 4

8 portobello mushrooms

extra virgin olive oil

sea salt, black pepper

225 g chèvre log, rind removed
   and sliced

8 slices of Parma or other air-dried
   ham

Heat the oven to 180°C fan oven/190°C electric oven/Gas 5. Cut the stalks off the mushrooms level with the cups. Brush the caps on both sides with olive oil and season them. Divide the goat's cheese among the cups and wrap each mushroom in a slice of ham, placing it over the mushroom cup and tucking the sides underneath. Arrange the mushrooms in a roasting dish cup-side up, drizzle over a couple of tablespoons of oil and bake for 25 minutes until the ham has begun to crisp and the cheese is melted and golden at the edges.

WEEKDAY SUPPERS

I find cooking in the evenings helps me wind down, a kind of therapy after a stressed day, and even if I'm not hungry I'm still happy to cook for anyone else. Without that early evening ritual of chopping and stirring, chatting and enjoying a glass of wine, the day doesn't seem quite complete. If you don't enjoy cooking however then it's a neverending quest to minimise what is involved. So let's assume that like me you adore cooking and couldn't think of anything you'd rather be doing of an evening, at which point the world of suppertime dishes opens up.

Heading this category is soup, which, with a handful of exceptions, I would far rather settle to as the main focus of supper than have as a starter. Soups care for the ravenously hungry, and given the full rein of being 'all there is to eat' allow us to go back for a second bowlful without having to save space for whatever's to come. They are also one of the few foods I find I can get down my entire fussy family, for the very young they're a vehicle for dipping slices of baguette, and for the not-so-young they are the perfect occasion to enjoy a few cheeses. And soup followed by cheese and a few nuts to crack is weekday nirvana.

On from there certain 'cuts' of everyday meats scream 'suppertime', the ones you pop into the trolley without knowing quite what you're going to do with them but safe in the knowledge they'll come in handy. Top of the list is mince. Even people who aren't keen on meat love mince, its universal appeal is reflected in countries around the world. There's only one rule, and that is to buy the best on offer, worth a detour to the butcher. And while you're there you can stock up on sausages, chicken breasts and stewing beef (preferably top rump), which collectively form the foundation of suppertime cuts.

Fish pies we hold almost as dearly in our hearts as shepherd's pie, and fish stews, too, offer up a relaxed rusticity. Though in the spirit of having our cake and eating it too, the ideal is a stew loaded with character, that relies on readily available and affordable fish, that's all said and done within the hour. To this end, I will go to almost any lengths to avoid having to make fish stock from scratch, and if you can buy your fish ready filleted or prepared that's another job saved. Nor is it necessary to have ten different specimens, a little in the way of interest is commendable, but one or two types will do nicely.

No-nonsense Chicken Stock

When I was a vegetarian one of the ingredients I missed most was chicken stock. There is no better foundation for a soup, providing it is fresh. Unfortunately, many shop-bought fresh stocks leave a great deal to be desired, and a quick glance down the ingredient list reveals them to be no more than rehydrated cubes and full of hydrolysed this and that. I often end up roasting a chicken as a means to an end, you do at least get supper thrown in or the wherewithal for a salad the next day. This is as basic as broth get –, by all means chuck in a few vegetables if you have them, but it won't suffer if you don't.

1 chicken carcass, post-roast
sea salt

Place the chicken carcass in a saucepan that will hold it snugly, and cover with water by 2 cm, bring it to the boil and skim off any foam that forms on the surface. Add a good teaspoon of salt and simmer for 1 hour. Strain the stock, and if it tastes insipid return it to the pan and reduce it by up to half its volume to concentrate the flavour. Leave it to cool, then cover and chill. Skim off any fat from the surface before using it.

Pea Soup with Bacon

The greatest convenience after frozen petits pois has to be finding them ready-shelled in packets. But while celebrating our good fortune we should beware the season – the winter ones grown in the further corners of the world can tend to mealiness, which doesn't matter overly in this soup providing you cook them until they are tender.

Peas 'n ham is a winning combination whichever way up you turn them, cooked to a floury khaki mush with thick, juicy pink slabs of boiled ham, or here in pea green soup with crisp sheaths of streaky bacon to nibble between spoonfuls.

Serves 4

25 g unsalted butter
1 onion, peeled and chopped
150 ml white wine
600 g fresh shelled peas
750 ml chicken stock
sea salt, black pepper
1 tsp caster sugar
8 rashers rindless unsmoked
  streaky bacon, cut into 2 long
  strips lengthwise
10 good-sized basil leaves
chopped flat-leaf parsley to serve

Melt the butter in a large saucepan over a medium heat, add the onion, and sweat for several minutes until it is translucent and soft. Add the wine and cook until it is syrupy. Add the peas and stir, then add the stock, the seasoning and sugar. Bring to the boil over a high heat and simmer for 2–3 minutes.

While simmering the soup, heat the grill and lay the bacon strips out on the grid of a grill pan. Grill until golden and crisp on both sides. Pile on to a plate.

Place the soup with the basil leaves in a food processor and purée, then adjust the seasoning – it may well need more salt. I like a slight texture to this soup, but if you prefer it completely smooth you can liquidise it in a blender, and if necessary pass it through a sieve. Return to the saucepan, rewarm and serve scattered with parsley and accompanied by the bacon strips.

Chilled Courgette Soup

The delectably sweet savour of a mass of summer vegetables, this falls in the gazpacho league, a very handy warm weather appetiser.

Serves 6

100 g unsalted butter
1 Spanish onion, peeled and chopped
1 kg courgettes, ends removed, halved lengthwise if large, and thickly sliced
2 cucumbers, ends removed, halved lengthwise and thickly sliced
sea salt, black pepper
juice of ½ lemon
finely chopped chives and double cream to serve

You will need to cook the vegetables in two goes. Heat half the butter in a large saucepan over a medium heat, add the onion and sweat for a few minutes until it turns translucent, then add half the courgettes and cucumber, season them and sweat for 10 minutes, stirring occasionally until softened and glossy. Remove the vegetables to a bowl. Heat the remaining butter in the pan, add the remaining vegetables and cook in the same fashion. Return all the vegetables to the pan, and add 850 ml of water, which should almost cover them – there may be a few tips showing through. Add some more seasoning, bring to the boil and simmer over a medium heat for 10 minutes.

Purée the soup in batches in a liquidiser, then pass it through a sieve into a bowl or plastic container. Cover and leave it to cool, then chill for several hours or overnight. Just before serving, stir in the lemon juice and taste for seasoning. Serve with some chives scattered over, and a swirl of cream for those who want it.

Rocket and Potato Soup

It's a close-run thing whether this or leek and potato soup is better at soothing frazzled nerves. This one has lots of little comforting nibs of potato, with a mass of chopped rocket added at the end. It's great made with watercress, too, or wild garlic in the spring. And it is amenable to being made in small quantities.

Serves 4–6

50 g unsalted butter
4 onions, peeled and finely chopped
225 ml white wine
700 g potatoes, peeled and sliced
1.2 l chicken stock
sea salt, black pepper
200 g rocket, stalks trimmed
4–6 tsp crème fraîche (optional)

Melt the butter in a large saucepan over a medium-low heat, add the onions and sweat for 6–7 minutes until soft and glossy, but not coloured. Add the wine, turn the heat up, bring to the boil and reduce by two thirds. Add the potatoes, the chicken stock and some seasoning, bring back to the boil, then turn the heat back down again and simmer for 15 minutes or until the potatoes are tender when pierced with a knife. Using a potato masher, coarsely mash the potatoes into the soup. It needn't be completely smooth, small nibs of tattie are welcome. You can prepare the soup to this point in advance.

Just before eating, thinly slice the rocket and add it to the pan. Bring back to the boil, then taste for seasoning. Ladle into warm soup bowls. Drop a teaspoon of crème fraîche into the centre of each bowl of steaming soup, if wished, and serve straightaway.

Spinach Soup with Ricotta

Gently warmed by the heat of the soup the ricotta is rendered exquisitely soft and creamy, in contrast to the crispness of the bacon.

Serves 4

50 g unsalted butter

3 white onions, peeled and
   chopped

sea salt, black pepper

150 ml white wine

1 l chicken stock

500 g spinach

80 g parsley (curly or flat), leaves
   and fine stalks

8 rashers smoked streaky bacon,
   rind removed (optional)

a squeeze of lemon juice

4 tbsp ricotta

Melt the butter in a large saucepan over a lowish heat, add the onions, scatter over a teaspoon of salt and sweat for 15–20 minutes until soft and syrupy, stirring occasionally, without allowing them to colour. Add the wine, turn the heat up and cook to reduce it by half. Pour in the chicken stock, bring to the boil, then add the spinach and half the parsley. Bring the stock back to the boil, then cover the pan and cook over a low heat for 10 minutes, stirring the soup after a couple of minutes to submerge the leaves. Add the remaining parsley at the last minute, then purée the soup in a liquidiser. Season with black pepper and a little more salt if necessary.

If you choose to serve it with bacon, heat the grill and cook the rashers on both sides until golden and crisp while the soup is cooking.

Gently reheat the soup, and add a squeeze of lemon just before serving. If this is added too far in advance the soup will dull in colour.

Place a tablespoon of ricotta in the centre of four warm soup bowls, ladle the soup around it and serve straightaway. Lay a couple of rashers of bacon in the middle, if wished.

Broccoli and Almond Soup

I rate broccoli more highly for its flavour than its texture, and as such use it most in soups that capitalise on its aromatic sweetness.

Serves 6

500 g broccoli

25 g unsalted butter

1 tbsp extra virgin olive oil

1 Spanish onion, peeled, halved
   and sliced

1 celery heart, trimmed and sliced

50 g flaked almonds

1.4 l chicken stock

150 ml white wine

sea salt, black pepper

6 tsp fromage frais (optional)

Trim the broccoli stalks and finely slice them, then cut up the florets. Heat the butter and oil in a large saucepan over a medium heat, add the onion, celery, broccoli stalks and almonds and sweat for 10 minutes, stirring occasionally, until softened and lightly coloured. In the meantime, bring the stock to the boil in a small saucepan.

Add the wine to the vegetables and cook until it is syrupy and reduced. Add the broccoli florets and stir for a moment until they darken, then pour over the stock, which should come back to the boil almost instantly. Season the soup and simmer for 5 minutes, then purée it in a food processor. It should retain a slight texture, specked with the green of the broccoli.

Taste for seasoning and serve in warm bowls. Dollop a spoon of fromage frais in the centre of each bowl, if wished.

Lentil, Lemon and Ginger Soup

A recipe courtesy of chef Caroline Brett that banishes any notion of lentil soups being about Jesus sandals and long hair, with a judicious squeeze of lemon at the very end, a splash of olive oil and a few caramelised onions.

Serves 4–6

SOUP

4 tbsp extra virgin olive oil

4 carrots, peeled and sliced

1 celery heart, trimmed and sliced

2 red onions, peeled and chopped

5 cm knob of fresh ginger root,
     peeled and finely chopped

6 garlic cloves, peeled and finely
     chopped

225 g red lentils

225 g yellow split peas

2 l chicken or vegetable stock

sea salt, black pepper

GARNISH

2 tbsp extra virgin olive oil, plus
     extra for drizzling

2 white onions, peeled, halved and
     sliced as finely as possible

4 squeezes lemon juice

Heat the olive oil for the soup in a large saucepan over a medium-low heat, add the carrots, celery, red onions, ginger and garlic and sweat, stirring occasionally, for about 20 minutes until soft and aromatic. Rinse the lentils and split peas in a sieve under the cold tap, add them to the pan and cook for 4–5 minutes, stirring occasionally. Pour in the stock, bring to the boil, cover and simmer over a low heat for 1 hour, by which time the split peas should be nice and mushy.

While the soup is cooking, melt the 2 tablespoons of olive oil in a large frying pan over a very low heat. Add the white onions and cook for 40–50 minutes, stirring frequently, especially towards the end as they may catch and burn. They should by the end be a deep even gold. Transfer these to a bowl.

Liquidise the soup in batches with some salt and pepper; it should be very thick, the consistency of a thin purée. Ladle it into warm soup bowls, squeeze a little lemon juice over each serving, then drizzle over some olive oil and finally strew over the caramelised onions.

Lentil, Potato and Rosemary Broth

A great post-Christmas soup when you have litres of turkey stock in the fridge. And it hits just the right note, a warming bowlful of chunky vegetables scented with rosemary, with the faintest nip of chilli to ward off the blues. I'd plump for a nutty brown granary bread with this.

Serves 6

4 tbsp extra virgin olive oil

2 leeks, trimmed and sliced

3 large carrots (approx. 350 g),
   peeled and cut into 1 cm dice

5 small turnips (approx. 350 g),
   peeled and cut into 1 cm dice

4 x 5 cm sprigs of rosemary

200 ml white wine

1.8 l fresh chicken or turkey stock

600 g maincrop potatoes, peeled
   and cut into 1 cm dice

150 g green lentils

1 small red dried chilli, finely
   chopped

sea salt

Heat the olive oil over a medium heat in a large saucepan, add the leeks, carrots, turnips and rosemary and sweat for about 8 minutes until glossy and beginning to soften. Add the wine and cook to reduce it by half. Add the chicken stock, the potatoes, lentils and dried chilli, bring to a simmer, then cover and cook over a low heat for 40 minutes. Season generously with sea salt about 10 minutes towards the end. Give it a good stir, taste for seasoning and ladle into warm bowls.

Chicken Noodle Soup

Chicken noodle soup is pasta and roast chicken rolled into one, which may go some way to explain its popularity. And it should be as easy to prepare as it is to eat.

Serves 4

25 g unsalted butter
3 leeks, trimmed and thinly sliced
150 ml white wine
1.2 l fresh chicken stock
sea salt, black pepper
60 g filini or other soup noodles
2 chicken breasts, skinned
1 tbsp extra virgin olive oil
3 tbsp finely chopped parsley
freshly grated Parmesan to serve

Melt the butter in a medium-sized saucepan over a lowish heat and sweat the leeks for 5–7 minutes until starting to relax, stirring occasionally. Add the wine, turn the heat up and cook to reduce it by half. Pour in the chicken stock, season and bring to the boil. Add the noodles and give them a stir, then simmer the soup over a low heat for 10 minutes.

Once the soup is simmering, cut out the tendon from the lower side of the fillets and slice them into two thin escalopes. Now slice across into thin strips. Heat the olive oil in a large frying pan over a medium-high heat, add the chicken and fry for a minute or two to seal it, stirring frequently, then turn the heat up and fry for a few minutes longer until starting to colour, seasoning it towards the end.

Stir the parsley and chicken into the soup, taste for seasoning and serve straightaway in warm bowls. Accompany with the grated Parmesan.

Cheat's Chicken Kiev

For anyone who grew up in the sixties and seventies chicken kiev is an abiding memory of the local trattoria. Its essence is the river of garlicky melted butter that spills from the inside of the breast when you pierce it, but who can be bothered with all that dipping and deep-frying? This deconstructed version is more amenable to the home kitchen, but the spirit is still there. A small bunch of watercress will lap up any leftover juices.

Serves 4

BUTTER
100 g unsalted butter, softened
3 garlic cloves, peeled and coarsely chopped
zest and juice of 1 lemon
a dash of Tabasco
sea salt, black pepper
3 tbsp finely chopped flat-leaf parsley
2 tbsp finely chopped chives
1 tsp finely chopped thyme leaves
CHICKEN
4 chicken breasts
groundnut oil

Place the butter, garlic, lemon zest and juice, the Tabasco and some seasoning in the bowl of a food processor and blend at high speed until creamy and amalgamated. Add the chopped herbs and give another quick whizz to incorporate them. Do not worry if a little of the lemon juice seeps out – most of it will have been incorporated. Place the butter in a length on a strip of clingfilm, and wrap it up into a smooth cylinder, twisting both ends. Chill for at least 30 minutes.

To cook the chicken, heat the griddle on a medium heat. Cut out the white tendon on the lower side of each chicken breast, brush all over with groundnut oil and season on both sides. Grill skin-side down for 7–8 minutes, then turn and cook the other side for 4–5 minutes. Heat the grill.

Place the chicken breasts on plates, with a couple of slices of the garlic butter on top. Even though this may appear to be a lot of butter, it is mainly herbs. Flash under the grill until this melts and serve straightaway.

Other Uses For Garlic Butter
* Add just a squeeze of lemon to the butter, and use to sandwich a sliced baguette to make garlic and herb bread.
* Serve grilled white fish in lieu of chicken.
* Sauté some prawns and squid, add a knob of butter to the pan at the very end and toss.
* Omit the lemon zest and juice, and serve as a butter with grilled lamb chops or steak.
* Stuff the caps of flat-cap mushrooms and bake.

Almond Chicken Breasts 'Levant'

Nibs of flaked almonds mixed in with breadcrumbs render a coating for chicken breasts particularly crisp and crunchy. The relish and additional melted butter are both asides. The chicken can be served with any green salad or some roasted vegetables.

Serves 4

CHICKEN BREASTS

225 g unsalted butter

2 large chicken breasts, skinned

sea salt, black pepper

75 g flaked almonds

25 g fresh breadcrumbs

4 lemon wedges

RELISH

3 tbsp finely chopped flat-leaf parsley

1 garlic clove, peeled and finely chopped

½ tbsp finely chopped lemon zest

2 tsp extra virgin olive oil

1 tsp lemon juice

To clarify the butter, gently melt it in a saucepan. Skim off the surface foam and decant the clear yellow liquid, discarding the milky residue at the bottom. Slice the chicken into two thin escalopes and remove the tendons. Fold the inner tenderloins to the side so they are evenly thick and season the breasts on both sides. Place the flaked almonds in a food processor and whizz until coarsely crumbed. Combine them with the breadcrumbs in a shallow bowl. Place half the clarified butter in a shallow dish and dip the breasts to coat both sides. Then pat them in the almond-breadcrumb mixture to form a crust and set aside for 10 minutes.

Combine all the ingredients for the relish in a bowl, with a little seasoning.

Heat half the remaining butter in a heavy cast-iron frying pan over a medium heat. When the butter is hot, put the breasts in the pan, reduce the heat to medium-low and sauté for 4–5 minutes each side. The crust should be a rich golden brown.

Heat the remaining butter in a small saucepan. Serve the breasts on warm plates with some of the butter drizzled over each one, a spoonful of relish to the side. Accompany with the lemon wedges.

Chicken Saltimbocca

To enter the domain of toasted cheese without combining Parma ham with melted fontina would be to pass by one of life's most unctuous mouthfuls. It's bread for mopping, and a big salad to follow.

Serves 4

4 chicken fillets, skinned
sea salt, black pepper
8 slices Parma or other air-dried
   ham
8 sage leaves
25 g unsalted butter
1 tbsp extra virgin olive oil
plain flour for dusting
150 ml white wine
150 g fontina, sliced wafer thin

Heat the oven to 190°C fan oven/200°C electric oven/Gas 6. Cut out the white tendon from the lower side of each fillet and slice into two thin escalopes. Lay these out on a board, gently level into escalopes using a rolling pin and lightly season. Cut the ham to the same size as the escalopes and lay a slice on top of each one. Place a sage leaf on top and secure with a cocktail stick.

Heat half the butter and the oil in a large frying pan over a medium heat. Season the flour in a shallow bowl, dip the underside of a third of the escalopes in the flour and fry floured-side down for 2–3 minutes until golden underneath and the chicken on top appears almost cooked. Transfer these to a gratin or roasting dish and repeat with the remaining escalopes.

Add the wine to the pan and simmer for approximately 2 minutes until well-reduced. Whisk in the remaining knob of butter. Remove the cocktail sticks from the chicken escalopes and coat with the fontina slivers. Pour the pan juices over the chicken and place in the oven for 8–10 minutes until cooked through and the cheese is melted and bubbling. Serve straightaway, with any melted cheese that has run down into the pan and the juices.

Toad-in-the-Hole

Batter is by nature bland and, however traditionalists might have it, I like to jazz mine up with mustard. I also favour really spicy sausages or ones with the addition of leeks or bacon to give them added interest. You could of course turn to ketchup, but gravy is nicer. The real subtlety lies in heating up the dish with plenty of fat, ideally dripping, before the batter goes in. This ensures it almost fries at the edges and around the sides and comes out beautifully crisp and rich, with that particular flavour that gives it the hallmark of being British.

Serves 4

BATTER
110 g plain flour, sifted
½ tsp sea salt
2 medium eggs
150 ml milk
1 tsp Dijon mustard
1 tsp wholegrain mustard
SAUSAGES
dripping, lard or vegetable oil
450 g sausages

Whizz all the ingredients for the batter plus 150ml water in a blender until smooth, then leave to rest for 30 minutes.

Halfway through resting the batter, heat the oven to 200°C fan oven/220°C electric oven/Gas 7. Heat a little dripping, lard or vegetable oil in a frying pan and slowly colour the sausages on all sides. Try to do this as evenly as possible, turning them frequently; they should by the end be a nice golden colour, but not too dark since they will colour further in the oven. Place a couple of tablespoons of whatever fat you are using in a 35 cm oval gratin dish or one equivalent in size, and heat this in the oven for 10 minutes.

Pour the batter into the hot dish and lay the sausages on top. Place the toad-in-the-hole in the oven and cook for 30 minutes until the batter is risen and golden. Serve straightaway.

Ragú with Conchiglioni

A properly made ragú is vastly different from the bolognese sauce so often ladled over spaghetti. The real thing is that much richer courtesy of its long slow cooking, two hours minimum and even then many an Italian mamma will give it closer to five.

Serves 4

1 carrot, trimmed and peeled

1 celery stick, trimmed

1 onion, peeled

25 g unsalted butter, plus 10 g

1 tbsp extra virgin olive oil

2 tbsp fresh oregano or marjoram
  leaves

800 g minced beef

150 ml milk

150 ml red wine

1 x 400 g tin chopped tomatoes

1 small dried red chilli, finely
  chopped

sea salt

425–600 ml beef stock

250 g conchiglioni shells

freshly grated Parmesan to serve

Cut the carrot, celery and onion into chunks, place in a food processor and finely chop. Heat the 25 g of butter and the olive oil in a medium-sized saucepan over a medium heat, add the chopped vegetables and the oregano or marjoram, and sweat for about 5 minutes, stirring occasionally until softened. Add the meat, turn the heat up and cook, stirring, until it changes colour. Now add the milk, a couple of tablespoons at a time, cooking each addition until it's absorbed. Pour in the red wine and continue boiling until reduced by half, then turn the heat down. Add the tomatoes and chilli and season with salt. Bring to a simmer, then cook over the very lowest heat for about 1 hour, stirring occasionally, until all the juices have been absorbed. Keep a careful eye on it towards the end to prevent it from burning. Tip the pan and skim off any surface fat.

The ragú needs to cook very slowly for another hour. Add the beef stock about 150 ml at a time, adding more as necessary. The end result should be rich and soupy.

Bring a large pan of salted water to the boil, add the pasta, give it a stir and simmer until tender – the time it takes will depend on the pasta type. If necessary reheat the ragú. Drain the pasta shells into a colander, then return them to the pan and toss with the 10 g of butter. Serve the pasta shells on warm plates with the ragú spooned over, scattered with freshly grated Parmesan.

* Serve the ragú spooned over roasted vegetables, peppers, aubergines, carrots, courgettes or parsnips.
* Ladle it over a chicory and blue cheese salad.
* Layer the ragú with slightly undercooked pasta and fontina or mozzarella. Scatter with freshly grated Parmesan or breadcrumbs tossed with olive oil and bake until golden and bubbling.
* For a hearty winter supper, slit baked potatoes, score the flesh and dot with melted butter, then spoon the ragú over.
* Add cooked kidney beans and cayenne pepper to taste, and serve the ragú Mexican style with tortillas, guacamole and salsa.

Macaroni Shepherd's Pie

I first heard of this pie from a New Yorker when it was doing the rounds of Manhattan as chic comfort food. A good one for when you can't choose between macaroni cheese or shepherd's pie.

Serves 6

MINCE

2 tbsp groundnut oil

3 shallots, peeled and finely
chopped

1 large or 2 small carrots, peeled
and thinly sliced

1 leek, trimmed, halved and thinly
sliced

2 sticks of celery heart, trimmed
and thinly sliced

2 sprigs of thyme

750 g minced lamb

150 ml red wine

2 tbsp tomato ketchup

1 tsp Worcestershire sauce

sea salt, black pepper

MACARONI

35 g unsalted butter, plus 15 g
melted

30 g plain flour

750 ml whole milk

1 bay leaf

120 g mature Cheddar, grated

1 tbsp Dijon mustard

150 g macaroni

2 tbsp white breadcrumbs

2 tbsp freshly grated Parmesan

Heat the oil in a large saucepan and sweat the vegetables and thyme for about 8 minutes over a low heat until glossy and tender, stirring occasionally. Add the mince, turn the heat up and cook, stirring, until it changes colour and separates. Add all the remaining ingredients listed under mince, bring to a simmer and cook over a low heat for 15 minutes. There should still be some juice; if there appears to be a lot of fat on the surface, skim the excess off. Check the seasoning, then transfer the mince to a shallow ovenproof dish discarding the thyme (a 20 x 30 cm roasting pan allows for plenty of golden surface) and leave to cool for about 20 minutes. You can also prepare the pie to this point in advance, cover and chill it until required.

Heat the oven to 180°C fan oven/190°C electric oven/Gas 5. Melt the 35 g of butter for the macaroni in a medium-sized non-stick saucepan over a medium heat, add the flour and cook the roux for about 1 minute until it's floury in appearance and seething nicely. Remove from the heat and gradually work in the milk using a wooden spoon, just a little at a time to begin with. Return the béchamel to the heat and bring to the boil, stirring frequently until it thickens. Add the bay leaf and simmer over a low heat for 10 minutes, stirring occasionally. Remove the bay leaf, stir in the Cheddar and the mustard and taste for seasoning. Bring the sauce back to the boil, stirring. Now liquidise it until really silky.

At the same time as cooking the sauce, bring a medium-sized pan of salted water to the boil. Add the macaroni to the pan, give it a stir to separate the strands and cook until almost tender, leaving it slightly undercooked. Drain the macaroni into a colander, quite thoroughly, then return it to the pan. Toss the macaroni with the sauce and pour on top of the mince.

Toss the breadcrumbs and Parmesan with the melted butter and scatter them over the pasta. Bake the pie for 25–30 minutes until the top is golden and sizzling.

Stuffed Tomatoes *Campagnardes*

Ask any Frenchman about his memories of maman's cooking and he will go weak at the knees at the thought of her stuffed tomatoes. Having tried Pascal Aussignac's of Club Gascon I can see why – and as good cold as hot.

Serves 4

8 x 200–225 g ripe beefsteak
   tomatoes
sea salt, black pepper
caster sugar
600 g sausagemeat
1 medium egg
50 g fresh breadcrumbs
2 garlic cloves, peeled and finely
   chopped
2 shallots, peeled and finely
   chopped
3 tbsp chopped parsley, plus extra
   for serving
extra virgin olive oil

Remove a lid from each tomato. With the aid of a small sharp knife and a teaspoon, scoop out the insides, reserving them in the bowl of a food processor. Purée these in a food processor with a little salt, pepper and sugar. Sprinkle the inside of each tomato with a little salt and sugar, and place upside down on a double layer of kitchen paper to drain for 20 minutes while you prepare the stuffing.

Combine and thoroughly blend the sausagemeat, egg, breadcrumbs, garlic, shallots, parsley and some salt and pepper in a large bowl. Turn the tomatoes up the right way and stuff them to the top with the sausage mixture, smoothing the surface. Heat 3 tablespoons of olive oil in a large cast-iron casserole (about 25 x 30 cm) that will hold the tomatoes snugly in a single layer over a medium heat; this will help to contain their sides as they cook. Add the tomatoes stuffed-side down and cook for about 5 minutes until the stuffing colours a deep gold, then loosening them with a palette knife, gently turn them the right way up. If some colour more quickly than others, remove these to a plate, then return them once they are all done.

Spoon 400 ml of the reserved tomato purée, approximately half, around the stuffed tomatoes. Bring the purée to a simmer then cook, uncovered, over a low heat for 1¼–1¾ hours until they are sitting in a rich well-reduced sauce. The exact time this will take can vary, so keep a watchful eye that the sauce isn't drying out. Serve hot or at room temperature, drizzled with olive oil and scattered with parsley.

Frankfurter and Potato Goulash

I have a soft spot for frankfurters, the flavour of every cinema and stadium of one's childhood. Follow up with a toffee apple or candyfloss.

Serves 4

25 g dripping
3 rashers of unsmoked streaky
   bacon, sliced
3 white onions, peeled, halved
   and sliced
1 tsp sweet paprika
1 tsp caraway seeds
900 g waxy potatoes, ideally
   Charlotte, peeled
12 frankfurter sausages
325 ml chicken stock or water
TO SERVE
soured cream
coarsely chopped flat-leaf parsley

Melt the dripping in a large flameproof casserole over a medium heat and fry the bacon until it's lightly golden. Add the onions, turn the heat down a little and cook for 12–14 minutes until creamy and caramelised, stirring frequently. Add the paprika and the caraway seeds and stir, then add the potatoes and the frankfurters and gently toss to combine. Pour over the chicken stock or water, bring to a simmer, then cover and cook over a low heat for 25–30 minutes, by which time the potatoes should be tender and have absorbed nearly all the liquid. Keep an eye on it towards the end to make sure it doesn't stick. Serve the goulash with a dollop of soured cream, scattered with parsley.

Moussaka

There are endless variations of this classic Greek dish, which when it is well-made is still worthy of all the attention it has received over the years. I like a moussaka to have plenty of aubergines in proportion to the meat, and to this end layer them top and bottom. A tomato salad cuts through the richness nicely.

Serves 6

MINCE

extra virgin olive oil

2 onions, peeled and chopped

1 kg minced lamb

225 ml red wine

1 x 400 g tin chopped tomatoes

2 tbsp tomato purée

2 tsp dried oregano

1 small dried red chilli, finely chopped

½ tsp ground cinnamon

sea salt, black pepper

4 aubergines

BÉCHAMEL AND CRUST

75 g unsalted butter

60 g plain flour

700 ml milk

1 bay leaf

75 g freshly grated Parmesan

150 g feta, broken into 1 cm dice

50 g fresh white breadcrumbs

To prepare the mince, heat 2 tablespoons of olive oil in a large saucepan over a medium heat and sweat the onions for 5–6 minutes until glossy and soft, and just beginning to colour. Add the meat, turn the heat up and fry, stirring occasionally until it changes colour, then add the red wine, bring to the boil and reduce by half. Add the remaining ingredients listed under mince, except for the aubergines. Season the sauce with salt, bring to the boil then turn the heat down low and simmer for 30 minutes. Tip the pan and skim off any excess fat (it is a good idea to leave this to harden before throwing it away). There should be just a few tablespoons of juice remaining.

While the mince is cooking, slice the aubergines 1 cm thick, discarding the stalks. Heat a large dry cast iron or non-stick frying pan over a medium-high heat (or even better two frying pans), brush the top side of enough aubergine slices to cover the base with oil, season with salt and pepper and fry until golden. Brush the other side with oil, turn and grill this side too. Remove the cooked aubergine to a large bowl and repeat with the remaining slices. Try to use as little oil as possible as it will seep out again when the moussaka is baked.

Once the mince and aubergines are ready, start to prepare the béchamel. Melt the butter in a small non-stick saucepan over a medium heat, add the flour and allow the roux to seethe for about a minute until dry and floury. Working off the heat, gradually incorporate the milk using a wooden spoon. Return to the heat, and bring to the boil, stirring frequently, add the bay leaf and simmer over a low heat for 10 minutes, stirring occasionally. Remove the bay leaf, stir in the Parmesan and season to taste with salt.

Arrange half the aubergine slices on the base of a 38 x 25 cm roasting or ovenproof dish, spoon the mince on top, then arrange the remaining aubergine slices on top of this. Evenly coat the aubergine with the béchamel, and scatter over the feta. Toss the breadcrumbs with 1 tablespoon of olive oil and scatter over the top. The moussaka can be prepared to this point in advance. If you cover and chill it, you may need to allow a little extra cooking time, or take it out of the fridge an hour in advance.

Heat the oven to 170°C fan oven/180°C electric oven/Gas 4 and bake the moussaka for 55–60 minutes until the top is golden and crusty. Spoon off any excess fat around the edges before serving.

Lasagne al forno

The one we all know and love, layers of pasta with a meaty ragú sauce and béchamel in between. Parma ham gives the sauce an especially aromatic flavour, but it could just as well be unsmoked streaky bacon, in which case sauté it a couple of minutes longer.

Serves 6

100 g freshly grated Parmesan

350 g yellow or green lasagne

RAGÚ

2 tbsp extra virgin olive oil

1 large onion, peeled and finely chopped

1 large carrot, peeled and diced

2 sticks celery, trimmed and finely sliced

85 g Parma ham, diced

900 g minced beef

300 ml red wine

425 ml chicken stock

3 tbsp tomato purée

black pepper

BÉCHAMEL

50 g unsalted butter

40 g plain flour

1 l milk

1 bay leaf

freshly grated nutmeg

sea salt

To make the ragú, heat the olive oil in a large saucepan over a medium heat, add the onion, carrot and celery and sweat for 8–10 minutes until aromatic and lightly coloured. Add the ham and give it a stir, then add the mince and cook, stirring frequently until it seals and changes colour. Pour in the red wine and simmer until well-reduced. Add the chicken stock, tomato purée and a grinding of black pepper. Bring to a simmer, then cover and cook over a low heat for 45 minutes. Leave the sauce to stand for a few minutes, then skim off any oil on the surface. Taste for salt; depending on the salinity of the ham, it may or may not require any extra.

To make the béchamel, melt the butter in a medium-sized saucepan, add the flour and let the roux seethe for about a minute. Now gradually incorporate the milk using a wooden spoon; do this very slowly to begin with. Add the bay leaf, bring to simmering point, stirring constantly, then cook over a low heat for 10 minutes. Give it an occasional stir to make sure it doesn't catch on the bottom. Season with nutmeg and salt.

Select a 30 x 23 x 6 cm roasting or baking dish and layer the ingredients as follows. Cover the base of the dish with a thin layer of ragú, then drizzle over some béchamel. Scatter over a little Parmesan then cover with a layer of lasagne, breaking the sheets to fit. Repeat this until all the ingredients are used up, ending with ragú and béchamel, and finally whatever Parmesan is left over. In total you should have four layers of pasta and five of ragú and béchamel. At this point you can cover and chill the lasagne for up to 12 hours until you need it. Return the lasagne to room temperature before you put it in the oven.

Heat the oven to 170°C fan oven/180°C electric oven/Gas 4 and bake the lasagne for 30–35 minutes until golden and bubbling on the surface.

Pot-au-Feu

This takes its cue from the classic French assembly, albeit a simplified version. I love the clarity of the broth and the way the vegetables retain their colour and shape. The French would drink the soup and then eat the meat and vegetables separately, either hot with some gherkins and mustard, or cold with a vinaigrette. It makes a great soupy stew as well, with some floury buttered boiled potatoes alongside. The basil purée is optional, you can also serve it with horseradish sauce* and scattered with chopped parsley.

Serves 4

STEW

1 tbsp groundnut oil

900 g top rump, trimmed of fat, cut into 3–4 cm chunks

200 g smoked streaky bacon, rind on, cut 1 cm thick and into 2 cm pieces

sea salt, black pepper

4 leeks, trimmed and cut into 2 cm chunks

4 carrots, trimmed, peeled and sliced diagonally into 2 cm chunks

1 celery heart, trimmed and cut into 2 cm pieces

2 bay leaves

5 sprigs of thyme

BASIL PURÉE

1 garlic clove, peeled and chopped

50 g basil leaves

6 tbsp extra virgin olive oil

Heat the groundnut oil in a large cast-iron casserole over a medium heat, add half the beef and bacon and sear on all sides, then remove and cook the remainder. Return all the seared meat to the pan, add 1.8 l of water, 1½ teaspoons of salt and some black pepper. Slowly bring to a simmer, skimming off the greyish foam as it rises. Add all the remaining ingredients for the stew, bring back to a simmer, cover and cook over a low heat for 2 hours.

Place the garlic, basil, olive oil and some seasoning in the bowl of a food processor and reduce to a smooth purée. Discarding the herbs, serve the stew in warmed bowls, with a spoonful of basil purée in the centre. Remove the bacon rind as you go, it adds lots of flavour to the broth as it cooks.

* For the horseradish sauce, blend 1 x 200 g tub crème fraîche and 2–3 tablespoons finely grated horseradish together in a bowl and season with salt.

Beetroot Bouillon with Steak

This is halfway between a comforting British stew and an oriental noodle-pot. Should fresh horseradish prove hard to come by a teaspoon of grainy mustard can be stirred into the crème fraîche in lieu.

Serves 4

groundnut oil

1 red onion, peeled, halved and
   thinly sliced

2 small uncooked beetroot, peeled
   and finely sliced

150 ml red wine

600 ml beef stock

sea salt, black pepper

1 x 200 g sirloin steak 1.5 cm thick

100 g crème fraîche

1–1½ tsp finely grated fresh
   horseradish

100 g mangetouts, topped and
   tailed

Heat a tablespoon of oil in a medium-sized saucepan over a medium heat, add the onion and sauté for a few minutes until softened. Add the beetroot and sweat for a couple of minutes longer, turning it now and again, then pour in the wine and reduce by half. Add the beef stock and some seasoning, bring to the boil, then cover and simmer over a low heat for 20 minutes.

About 5 minutes into simmering the soup, heat a ridged griddle over a medium heat for 5 minutes and bring a small pan of water to the boil. Brush the steak on both sides with oil and season it. Sear for about 2 minutes each side to leave it medium-rare, then remove to a board to rest for 5 minutes.

Gently blend the crème fraîche and horseradish in a small bowl with a pinch of salt, if you stir too vigorously the mixture can thicken and curdle. Blanch the mangetouts for a minute, then drain into a sieve. Cut the fat off the steak and slice the meat across into long strips.

Divide the beetroot soup between four warm deep bowls. Place a few strips of steak to one side of each bowl and a pile of mangetouts to the other. Dollop a spoonful of the horseradish sauce in the middle and serve straightaway.

Corned Beef Hash

Corned beef appreciation tends towards those on a nostalgia trip down memory lane – school food complete with steamed puds and all that. It fries up a treat. It can either be shaped into little patties and served with a salad or more basically as a fry-up.

Serves 4

HASH

650 g maincrop potatoes

1 x 340 g tin corned beef

Tabasco

celery salt

1 large egg

SALAD

3 handfuls flat-leaf parsley leaves,
   coarsely chopped

75 g green olives, stoned and
   sliced

¼ red onion, finely chopped

extra virgin olive oil

a squeeze of lemon juice

tomato chutney to serve

Bring a pan of salted water to the boil and cook the potatoes in their skins until tender. Drain and leave them to cool, then skin them and coarsely chop on a board into small dice. Mash the corned beef in a large bowl, add the chopped potatoes, season with Tabasco and celery salt and bind with the egg. Taking a tablespoon of mixture at a time, form into round flat cakes. Store them on a plate as you make them; you should end up with about twelve.

Toss the parsley, olives and onion for the salad in a bowl with 1 tablespoon of olive oil and a squeeze of lemon. Heat a little olive oil in two frying pans over a medium-low heat and cook the patties for 3–4 minutes each side until golden and crusty on the outside. Serve them with some of the salad to the side, and a heaped teaspoon of chutney on top.

Basic Hash

* Make up the hash mixture as indicated. Without shaping it, fry it up in a little vegetable oil and serve with baked beans and a knob of butter. With or without a fried egg.

Greek Beef Casserole with Feta

Like all the most useful casseroles this can be made in advance, reheated, then given its final flourish with crumbled feta and chopped herbs just before serving. Some buttered spinach would also go down nicely.

Serves 4

300 g plum tomatoes
2 tbsp extra virgin olive oil
1 kg top rump, trimmed of fat and
    cut into 3 cm cubes
3 garlic cloves, peeled and finely
    chopped
½ tsp freshly grated nutmeg
½ tsp ground cumin
1 cinnamon stick
300 g shallots, peeled
150 ml red wine
sea salt, black pepper
300 g green and white tagliatelle
25 g salted or unsalted butter
100 g feta, coarsely crumbled
2 tbsp chopped flat-leaf parsley

Bring a small pan of water to the boil, cut out a cone from the top of each tomato, plunge them into the water for 20 seconds and then into cold water. Slip off the skins and coarsely chop them.

Heat the olive oil in a large cast-iron casserole over a medium heat. Add half the beef and sear it on all sides, then remove it and sear the remainder. Return all the beef to the pan, add the garlic and spices and stir momentarily until fragrant, then add the tomatoes, the shallots, the wine, 225 ml of water and some seasoning. Bring to the boil, cover and cook over a low heat for 2 hours, stirring occasionally. Check towards the end to make sure it isn't drying out, and add a little more water if necessary. By the end the juices should be well reduced and rich.

About 25 minutes before serving, bring a large pan of salted water to the boil. Add the tagliatelle, give it a stir and cook until just tender. Drain it into a colander, return to the pan and toss with the butter. Serve the beef scattered with feta and parsley, accompanied by the noodles.

Kleftiko

This matures in flavour and is almost better given a day between cooking and eating. In which case cover and chill it, and scrape any fat off the surface before reheating.

Serves 4

1 kg lamb shoulder
1 heaped tsp dried oregano
finely grated zest of 1 lemon
extra virgin olive oil
2 large onions, peeled, halved
    and sliced
sea salt, black pepper
1 small dried red chilli, chopped
425 ml red wine
juice of ½ small lemon
8 thin slices of haloumi
    (about 140 g)
plain flour
chopped flat-leaf parsley to serve

Cut the meat into 4 cm cubes, toss with the oregano and lemon zest in a bowl and set aside. Heat 2 tablespoons of olive oil in a medium-sized cast-iron casserole over a medium heat, add the onions and sweat for about 15 minutes, stirring frequently, until nicely caramelised. Remove to a bowl and turn the heat up high. Season and add the meat and sear to colour it all over, stirring almost constantly. Return the onions to the pan, add the chilli and the red wine, which should almost cover the meat, bring to a simmer, cover and cook over a very low heat for 1½ hours. Check to make sure it isn't drying out towards the end, and add a drop of water if needed.

Skim any fat off the surface, add the lemon juice to taste, and if necessary a little more seasoning. Cover the base of a large frying pan with oil and heat over a medium heat. Coat both sides of the haloumi slices with flour and fry on either side until golden and crisp at the edges, turning them with a spatula. Drain them on kitchen paper. Serve the stew with the haloumi on top, scattered with a little parsley.

King Prawns and Mussels with Basil Purée

There's lots of dipping and finger licking here, one of the most enjoyable aspects of eating shellfish. It's the smaller king or tiger prawns you want, not the really big ones.

Serves 4

1 kg mussels
1 beefsteak tomato
25 g basil leaves
6 tbsp extra virgin olive oil
squeeze of lemon juice
sea salt, black pepper
2 shallots, peeled and finely
   chopped
2 garlic cloves, peeled and finely
   chopped
16 (approx 250 g) raw peeled king
   prawns

To clean the mussels, soak them in a sink of cold water. Remove any beards and barnacles, then give them a second wash. To skin the tomato, cut out the central core, immerse it in boiling water for 20 seconds and then in cold water. Slip off the skin, remove the seeds and dice it. Place the basil, 5 tablespoons of olive oil, the lemon juice and a little seasoning in a liquidiser and reduce to a smooth green purée.

   Heat the remaining tablespoon of olive oil in a large saucepan over a medium heat, and sweat the shallots and garlic for about 1 minute until they soften. Add the prawns and turn them in the oil for another minute until they turn opaque, then add the mussels and diced tomato. Cover and steam over a high heat for 4 minutes, stirring halfway through to circulate the shellfish. Ladle the shellfish and juices into warm bowls, discard any unopened mussels and drizzle with basil purée.

* In theory mussel juices should be perfectly seasoned with salt. Occasionally, however, they can be lacking in flavour. If so, simply strain the mussel liquor into a small saucepan and boil to reduce it by about a third to concentrate the flavour.

Stew of Monkfish, Chickpeas and Spinach

Any converts to espinacas con garbanzos, *the Spanish tapa of lightly spiced and wilted spinach with chickpeas, will immediately be able to tune into the spirit of this dish. It's all about the contrast of the succulence of the leaves and the sweet mealiness of the peas.*

Serves 4

4 tbsp extra virgin olive oil, plus a
   little extra
2 shallots, peeled, halved and sliced
4 garlic cloves, peeled and sliced
1 x 400 g tin chopped tomatoes
1 dried red chilli, finely chopped
1 bay leaf
sea salt, black pepper
800 g monkfish
200 g young spinach leaves
4 tbsp white wine
1 x 400 g tin chickpeas, drained
   and rinsed
juice of ½ lemon
a large handful of basil leaves,
   torn in half

Heat half the olive oil in a small saucepan over a low heat, add the shallots and garlic and sweat for about 5 minutes until soft and just beginning to colour. Add the tin of tomatoes, the chilli, bay leaf and some salt. Bring to a simmer and cook gently for 15–20 minutes until you have a rich thick sauce.

   Slice the monkfish off the bone, carefully running the knife between the flesh and the membrane to remove it. It's important to get rid of all the grey skin which contracts and toughens on cooking. Slice the fillets into 2 cm medallions. Toss these in a bowl with the remaining olive oil. Heat a large frying pan over a medium-high heat, add the monkfish and sauté to seal it on all sides, seasoning it towards the end. Add the spinach and stir until it wilts, then pour in the wine, cover the pan with a lid and cook over a low heat for 3 minutes.

   Add the tomato sauce to the pan, then the chickpeas, and heat through, then stir in the lemon juice and the basil, which should wilt instantly. Taste for seasoning, and serve in warm bowls, drizzled with a little extra olive oil.

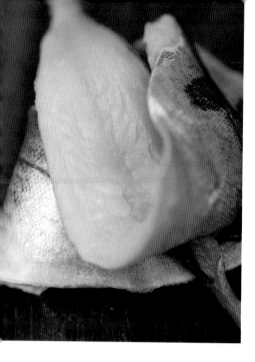

Smoked Haddock Pie

A stock favourite, not overly grand or too time-consuming. It relies on one of the most successful combinations of fish in a pie, a mixture of smoked and fresh haddock, which unlike more delicate white fish hold their own as big chunky flakes once they are cooked.

Serves 6–8

FISH

500g smoked haddock fillet
   (skin on)

500 g haddock fillet (skin on)

300 ml milk

1 bay leaf

100 g unsalted butter

450 g leeks, trimmed and sliced

sea salt, black pepper

50 g plain flour

150 ml white wine

150 ml double cream

MASH

1.5 kg maincrop potatoes, peeled,
   and halved if large

100 ml double cream

50 g unsalted butter

2 large egg yolks

Place the haddock in a large saucepan. Pour over the milk, tuck in the bay leaf and bring to the boil. Cover with a lid, leaving a gap for the steam to escape, and cook on a low heat for 5 minutes. Strain the cooking liquor into a bowl, and once the fish is cool enough to handle, flake it as coarsely as possible, discarding the skin. Melt 40 g of the butter in a large frying pan over a medium heat, add the leeks, season them and sweat for a few minutes until soft, without colouring, and stirring occasionally. Remove the pan from the heat.

To make the béchamel, melt the remaining 60 g of butter in a small non-stick saucepan over a medium heat, stir in the flour and allow the roux to seethe for a minute. Very gradually work in first the wine, then the fish cooking liquor and finally the cream. Season with black pepper. Bring to the boil, stirring occasionally, and simmer over a very low heat for 10 minutes. Stir the sauce now and again. Taste to check the seasoning, then fold in the fish, discarding any additional liquid that has been given out. Transfer the mixture to a 35 cm oval gratin or other ovenproof dish with a 2.5 l capacity, scatter the leeks over the surface and leave it to cool. This will help prevent the potato from sinking into the fish when you layer it on top.

Bring a large pan of salted water to the boil and cook the potatoes until they are tender. Drain into a sieve or colander and allow the surface moisture to evaporate for a minute or two. Pass them through a mouli-legumes or a sieve back into the pan. Heat the cream with the butter and some seasoning and beat this, then the egg yolks, into the mash. Smooth this over the top of the fish, forking the surface into furrows.

To cook the pie, heat the oven to 180°C fan oven/190°C electric oven/Gas 5 and bake it for 40 minutes until crusty and golden on the surface. You can cover and chill the pie until required for up to 48 hours, but it may take a little longer to cook.

Mussel and Monkfish Romesco

A hearty Catalan stew, thickened with a sweet, garlicky romesco.

Serves 4

12 whole skinned almonds
1 slice white bread
extra virgin olive oil
4 tomatoes, halved
3 garlic cloves, peeled
1 tsp sweet paprika
a pinch of saffron filaments
    (approx. 20)
1 tsp sherry vinegar
125 ml white wine
1 Spanish onion, peeled and
    chopped
2 red peppers, core, seeds and
    membranes removed, and thinly
    sliced
300 ml fish stock
500 g monkfish
500 g mussels
sea salt, black pepper

Heat the oven to 180°C fan oven/190°C electric oven/Gas 5, lay the almonds out in a small tray and toast for 10 minutes. Meanwhile, heat a ridged griddle over a medium heat for about 5 minutes. Brush the bread on both sides with olive oil and toast on the griddle until golden. Brush the tomatoes with oil, grill the cut-side first and then the skin-side for several minutes until striped with gold and softened.

Break the bread up, and whizz to crumbs in a food processor. Add the almonds and pulverise, then remove to a bowl. Now pulverise the garlic. Skin and add the tomatoes, the paprika, saffron, vinegar and wine, and reduce to a smooth sauce.

Heat 4 tablespoons of olive oil in a large saucepan over a medium heat, add the onion and sauté for 5 minutes until relaxed, then add the peppers and continue to cook for about 10 minutes until the onions are golden and the peppers have softened. Add the romesco sauce base and the fish stock, bring to the boil and cook over a low heat for 20 minutes, stirring occasionally.

While the soup is cooking, prepare the fish. Cut the monkfish off the bone, slicing between the flesh and the grey membrane to remove it. Cut the flesh into 1–2 cm dice. Wash the mussels in cold water, discarding any that are broken or do not close when sharply tapped. Pull off their beards and scrape off any barnacles.

Stir the crumbs into the simmering soup, season the monkfish with salt and pepper and add together with the mussels. Bring the soup to the boil, then cover and cook over a high heat for 5 minutes. Taste for seasoning and serve in warm soup bowls removing any mussels that have not opened.

Saffron Mussels

Mussels at their best are small, dark orange and imbued with copious salty sea juices. In Normandy we are spoilt, the local beaches are fringed with poles encrusted with mussels that reach the market stalls and shops within hours of being harvested.

Serves 2

1 x 1 kg bag of mussels
2 shallots, peeled and finely
    chopped
125 ml dry white wine
3 heaped tbsp crème fraîche
15 saffron filaments, infused in
    1 tbsp boiling water for
    30 minutes
1 tsp beurre manié (equal
    quantities of plain flour blended
    with unsalted butter)
a baguette and unsalted butter
    to serve

To clean the mussels, wash them in a sink of cold water, discarding any that are broken or do not close when sharply tapped. Pull off any beards and scrape off any barnacles. If they are very dirty, give them a second rinse. Otherwise place them with the shallots and wine in a large saucepan, and cover with a tightly fitting lid.

Heat the pan over a high heat for 3–4 minutes, shaking it once or twice, by which time the mussels should have just steamed open. Decant the juices into a small pan, leaving the mussels covered in the pan in which they were cooked. Boil vigorously to reduce the juices by half, add the crème fraîche, saffron and beurre manié and continue to simmer for a couple of minutes longer until you have a thin creamy sauce. Transfer the mussels to a large bowl, pour over the sauce and toss. Serve straightaway in large warm bowls, accompanied by the bread and butter.

Smoked Haddock and Potato Chowder

This is a great recipe to have up your sleeve. The technique is to cook the bacon and leeks in one pan, and the haddock, milk and cream in another, and acquaint them at the very end, which ensures perfect results.

Serves 4

40 g unsalted butter

7 rashers rindless smoked back
   bacon, cut into 1 cm strips

3 leeks, trimmed and sliced

400 ml full-cream milk

200 ml whipping cream

450 g maincrop potatoes, peeled
   and cut into 1 cm dice

1 bay leaf

450 g undyed smoked haddock
   fillet, skinned and cut into
   2 cm pieces

black pepper

coarsely chopped flat-leaf parsley

Melt the butter in a large saucepan over a medium heat, add the bacon and sauté for 7–9 minutes, stirring occasionally and separating out the pieces, until it is lightly coloured. Add the leeks and continue to fry for about 7 minutes until softened and just starting to colour.

At the same time, bring the milk and cream to the boil in another large pan with the potatoes and bay leaf, and simmer over a low heat for about 8 minutes. Add the haddock and poach for another 5 minutes until the potatoes are tender and the haddock flakes. Combine the contents of the two saucepans and season with black pepper. Serve in warm soup bowls, scattered with parsley.

Spanish-style Tuna and Potato Stew

A really earthy satisfying stew, tuna and potatoes make hearty bedfellows. Give this a final flourish with a top-hole olive oil such as Ravida.

Serves 4

extra virgin olive oil

2 red onions, peeled, halved and
   sliced

2 garlic cloves, peeled halved and
   sliced

2 tsp finely sliced red chilli

1 x 400 g tin chopped tomatoes

100 ml white wine

1 level tsp ground cumin

1 level tsp ground coriander

sea salt, black pepper

425 ml fish stock

700 g new potatoes, peeled and
   thickly sliced

700 g tuna, skin and bones removed

125 g (1 x 230 g jar) anchovy or
   pimento-stuffed green olives,
   rinsed

Heat 4 tablespoons of olive oil in a large saucepan or stove-top casserole over a medium heat, add the onions and sweat them for 8 minutes, adding the garlic and chilli halfway through. By the end the onions should be soft and silky, and the garlic just beginning to colour. Add the tinned tomatoes and the wine and cook for a few minutes to reduce the liquid, then add the spices, seasoning and fish stock, stir and add the potatoes. Bring to a simmer then cover and cook over a low heat for 15 minutes. The stew base can be prepared to this point in advance.

Slice the tuna 2.5 cm thick and then into 6 small steaks. Brush them with olive oil and season them on both sides. Heat a frying pan over a high heat and sear the tuna for 30 seconds each side to colour the surface. Do this in two batches. If the stew base has cooled at all, bring it back to a simmer, add the tuna to the pan, spooning the potatoes and sauce over the top to submerge it, cover and simmer for 5 minutes. Stir in the green olives, taste to check for seasoning and serve straightaway in warm bowls.

Mussel, Cod and Tomato Pie

A puff pastry pie filled with a rich tomato sauce set with mussels and cod, more Provence than Brixham.

Serves 6

2 kg mussels

500 g puff pastry

3 tbsp extra virgin olive oil, plus a little extra

1 small dried red chilli, finely chopped

4 garlic cloves, peeled and finely chopped

1 head of fennel, green shoots trimmed and outer sheaths discarded, diced

2 x 400 g tins chopped tomatoes

3 tbsp chopped parsley (curly or flat)

500 g cod fillet, skinned and cut into 2 cm dice

sea salt, black pepper

1 egg yolk blended with 1 tbsp milk

Wash the mussels in cold water, scraping off any barnacles and pulling off the beards. Discard any that are broken or that do not close when tapped sharply. Wash the mussels a second time then put them in a large saucepan. Cover and steam over a high heat for 4–5 minutes, shaking the pan halfway through, until the mussels have just opened. Drain the mussel liquor into a small saucepan, bring to the boil and reduce to several tablespoons of liquor. As soon as they are cool enough to handle, shell the mussels and set aside.

Heat the oven to 180°C fan oven/190°C electric oven/Gas 5. Thinly roll out half the pastry on a lightly floured worksurface to fit the base and sides of a 30 x 20 x 5 cm dish (I use a cast-iron roasting dish), leaving the excess pastry hanging over the sides. Line the pastry with foil, pressing the sides to the tin and weight with baking beans (dried pulses will do). Bake the case for 20 minutes until just starting to colour, then remove the foil and beans.

In the meantime, heat the 3 tablespoons of olive oil in a medium-sized saucepan over a medium heat, add the chilli and garlic, and moments later add the fennel and sweat for several minutes until translucent and softened. Add the tomatoes and the parsley, bring to the boil and cook at a lively simmer for about 30 minutes, stirring occasionally, until the oil separates from the sauce. It is important that it is really thick and well reduced, otherwise the base of the pastry will turn out soggy. Pour in the mussel liquor and simmer until it thickens again. Taste for seasoning.

Heat a non-stick frying pan over a high heat. Toss the cod in a bowl with a little oil to coat it and some seasoning, and sear on all sides, you may need to do this in two goes. Transfer the cod to a bowl, and discard any juices given out in the next few minutes. Stir the cod into the sauce with the shelled mussels. You can prepare the pie to this point in advance, in which case cover the fish with clingfilm and set aside in a cool place.

Heat the oven to 180°C fan oven/190°C electric oven/Gas 5 if it isn't already on. Tip the fish and sauce into the pastry case, then trim the sides, leaving a 1 cm rim. Paint these with eggwash. Thinly roll out the remaining half of pastry to fit the top of the pie and lay it in place, pressing the edges together. Trim the pastry lid, leaving a 2 cm rim bigger than the bottom to allow for shrinkage. Cut several slashes diagonally in the surface and press a fork or the tip of a knife around the edge. Brush the surface with eggwash and bake for 25 minutes until the top is golden and risen. Serve straightaway.

Skate and Potato Pie with Tomato Salsa

This is not unlike a gratin dauphinoise with a layer of skate in the centre, and a tomato salsa spooned on top. There is a huge difference in the quality of small and large skate wings; the latter promise long milky skeins, while the former tend to collapse to a mush when you cook them. It's worth a trip to the fishmonger to procure some nice fleshy ones.

Serves 6

PIE

1.1 kg large waxy potatoes

6 tbsp extra virgin olive oil

2 tbsp soft thyme leaves, coarsely chopped

sea salt, black pepper

700 g skate wings

100 ml white wine

25 g unsalted butter

4 tbsp double cream

100 g grated Gruyère

SALSA

3 small beefsteak tomatoes

1 level tbsp finely chopped shallot

4 basil leaves, finely sliced

Bring a large pan of salted water to the boil and cook the potatoes in their skins for 15 minutes. Drain them into a colander and once they are cool enough to handle, slip off the skins, using a small sharp knife to help, then slice them. Toss the potato slices in a bowl with half the olive oil, the thyme and some seasoning.

While the potatoes are cooking, place the skate in a medium-sized saucepan. Pour over the wine, dot with the butter and season. Bring the wine to the boil, then cover and cook over a low heat for 4 minutes or until the fish turns opaque, this will depend on its thickness. Using the lid of the pan, strain the cooking juices into a small pan and reduce to a couple of tablespoons of liquor. Once the skate is cool enough to handle, scrape off the skin using a blunt knife, then scrape the flesh off the bone. Place in a bowl and dress with the reduced liquor. Taste and season if necessary.

Heat the oven to 190°C fan oven/200°C electric oven/Gas 6. Layer half the potato in the base of a 2 l/33 cm oval shallow gratin or roasting dish, scatter the skate over, then lay over the remaining potato slices in overlapping rows. Drizzle over the cream, scatter over the Gruyère and bake for 35 minutes until golden and bubbling.

While the pie is baking, bring a small pan of water to the boil. Cut out a cone from the top of each tomato, plunge them into the boiling water and then into a bowl of cold water. Slip off the skins, quarter them and remove the seeds, then slice the flesh into long thin strips. Combine this in a bowl with the shallot, basil, remaining olive oil and some seasoning. Serve the pie with the salsa spooned over.

Conchiglie with Butternut Squash and Sage Butter

Here conchiglie shells are tossed into a pan of caramelised butternut squash, the roasting juices coating the pasta, with some melted butter and crisp sage leaves for good measure.

Serves 4

2 butternut squash
(approx. 800 g each)
3 tbsp extra virgin olive oil
sea salt, black pepper
4 garlic cloves, peeled and sliced
300 g conchiglie shells
100 g unsalted butter
10 g sage leaves
freshly grated Parmesan to serve

Heat the oven to 190°C fan oven/200°C electric oven/Gas 6. Cut the skin off the squashes, quarter the bulbs to remove the seeds and slice these sections into wedges. Halve the remaining cylindrical trunks lengthwise and slice 1 cm thick. Arrange the squash in a baking tray in a crowded single layer, I use one 38 x 25 cm. Drizzle over the olive oil, season and roast for about 55 minutes until nicely caramelised, turning the squash after 25 minutes. Scatter the garlic over the squash and give them another stir 15 minutes before the end.

Halfway through cooking the squash, bring a large pan of salted water to the boil. Add the conchiglie, give it a stir and cook until just tender – most dried varieties take about 10 minutes.

Five minutes before the pasta is ready, melt the butter in a medium-sized frying pan over a medium heat, skim off the surface foam, decant the clarified butter to a small bowl and discard the milky residue in the base. Return the clarified butter to the pan and heat, scattering the sage leaves over the surface. Cook until they darken in colour and crisp, then remove from the heat.

Drain the pasta into a sieve, add it to the roasting pan and gently turn it using a spatula to coat with the oil and sticky roasting juices. Spoon the butter and sage leaves on top, scatter over some more seasoning and gently toss again. Serve accompanied by the Parmesan.

Orecchiette with Avocado and Bacon

Designed to be eaten warm rather than hot, this dish is not a million miles from a pasta salad, but as with most pasta dishes it is at its best the moment it's been tossed.

Serves 3–4

200 g orecchiette
25 g unsalted butter
1 tbsp extra virgin olive oil
200 g unsmoked lardons or sliced
streaky bacon
125 ml port
sea salt, black pepper
a couple of squeezes of lemon juice
2 avocados
6 tbsp coarsely chopped flat-leaf
parsley

Bring a large pan of salted water to the boil, add the orecchiette and give it a stir.

At the same time, heat the butter and olive oil in a large frying pan over a medium-high heat and sauté the lardons, stirring frequently until crisp and golden. Remove them to a bowl and spoon off all but a few tablespoons of the fat. Carefully add the port, which will splutter, and some seasoning and simmer to reduce by half, scraping up all the sticky bits on the bottom. Add a generous squeeze of lemon juice to the pan juices. Quarter the avocados, removing the stone. Peel off the skin and slice the flesh into thin segments. Gently toss them in a bowl with a squeeze of lemon and a little salt.

Drain the pasta into a sieve, then briefly pass it under the cold tap and shake it dry. Add it to the frying pan, toss with the juices, then transfer it to a large shallow bowl or plate. Toss in the lardons, parsley and finally the avocado. Taste to check the seasoning and serve.

Spagettini Napoletana

We all know how good a simple sauce made with fresh tomatoes can be, and this is the storecupboard equivalent. One of those useful sauces where chances are you have the wherewithal to hand without having to pop to the shop. The pangratto are an optional extra rather than a must.

Serves 4

PASTA

2 tbsp extra virgin olive oil

4 garlic cloves, peeled and finely chopped

1 medium-hot red chilli, seeds and membranes removed, finely chopped

2 x 400 g tins chopped tomatoes

25 g unsalted butter

¾ tsp golden caster sugar

sea salt

300 g spagettini

PANGRATTO

1 large slice white bread, crusts removed

4 tbsp extra virgin olive oil

1 tsp thyme leaves

Heat the olive oil in a small saucepan over a medium heat, add the garlic and chilli and sauté for about a minute until the garlic is really fragrant, without allowing it to colour. Add the tomatoes and bring to a simmer, then add the butter, sugar and a heaped teaspoon of salt and simmer over a low heat for 40–50 minutes, stirring now and again until well reduced and thick. Keep a careful eye towards the end to make sure it doesn't stick.

To cook the pangratto, finely nib the bread using a sharp knife. Heat the olive oil in a large frying pan over a medium heat, add the bread and thyme and fry for 3–4 minutes, tossing frequently until golden and crisp. Transfer to a double thickness of kitchen paper to drain using a slotted spoon and leave to cool.

About halfway through cooking the sauce, bring a large pan of salted water to the boil. Add the pasta to the pan, give it a stir and cook until just tender. Drain it into a colander, without being too thorough about it, and return it to the pan, add the sauce and toss. Taste and season with a little more salt if necessary. Serve straightaway on warm plates or bowls, scattered with the pangratto.

Spaghetti with Truffles

Once familiar with the perfume of truffles it is easy enough to understand the Italians' passion for them. Summer truffles are the ones we most frequently encounter here, which can be eked out with a few drops of white truffle oil into a convincingly luxurious cloak for a plateful of spaghetti for supper.

Serves 4

350 g spaghetti

100 g freshly grated Parmesan, plus extra for the table

100 g unsalted butter, softened

sea salt, black pepper

30 g finely chopped black truffles (summer or winter)

2 tsp truffle oil

Bring a large pan of salted water to the boil, add the pasta and give it a stir to separate out the strands, then simmer until tender.

Drain it into a colander in the sink, then straightaway return it to the saucepan while there is still some water trickling off. This is all-important in creating a creamy emulsion. Toss half the cheese and then half the butter and some seasoning into the pasta, and once they have melted enough to coat the strands, toss in the remaining cheese and butter, and the chopped truffles and oil. Turn the spaghetti several times to coat it thoroughly. Serve on warmed plates with additional Parmesan at the table.

Trofie with Sprouting Broccoli and Pancetta

Trofie are slender spirals, a speciality of Genoa hand-rolled by women – no two strands are the same. They have the kind of tender pudginess that makes gnocchi so pleasing in the mouth.

Serves 4

300 g trofie

250 g purple sprouting broccoli
(trimmed weight)

200 g rindless unsmoked pancetta
or streaky bacon, sliced

4 garlic cloves, peeled and finely
chopped

4 tbsp white wine

100 g freshly grated Parmesan,
plus extra to serve

sea salt, black pepper

Bring two large pans of salted water to the boil. Add the pasta to one pan, give it a stir and cook for 18–20 minutes until tender. Cut the broccoli stems and leaves into 1 cm lengths, leaving the little heads whole. Add them to the second pan of boiling water and cook at a rolling boil for 2 minutes, then drain into a colander.

Heat the pancetta in a large frying pan over a medium heat and fry in the rendered fat for 8–12 minutes until golden, stirring frequently. Add the garlic a minute before the end. Pour in the wine, which will sizzle furiously, and simmer scraping up all the sticky bits on the bottom of the pan, until reduced by half.

Just before the pasta is ready, reheat the pancetta, add the broccoli and heat through. Drain the pasta, reserving half a cup of cooking liquid, and return it to the saucepan. Tip in the contents of the frying pan and toss, then add the Parmesan and the reserved cooking water and stir over a low heat until everything is coated in a creamy emulsion. Season to taste and serve straightaway on warm plates, with extra Parmesan at the table.

Macaroni Cheese with Prawns

I've been addicted to this combination ever since a sizzling gratin dish of macaroni dressed in cream with succulent pieces of lobster arrived at the table of La Table Du Marché, Christophe Leroy's brasserie in St Tropez. Langoustines would also go down a treat, but small prawns are that little bit more accessible.

Serves 6

300 ml fish stock

150 ml dry white wine

200 g small macaroni

350 g crème fraîche

100 g Beaufort, Comté or
Gruyère, grated

sea salt, black pepper

250 g cooked and shelled prawns

2 tbsp fresh breadcrumbs

25 g unsalted butter

Place the fish stock and wine in a small saucepan, bring to the boil over a medium-high heat and reduce to a small quantity of concentrated liquid. Discard any skin that has formed on the surface.

Bring a large pan of salted water to the boil, add the macaroni and stir to separate it. Cook until just tender, then drain it. While it is cooking heat the crème fraîche in a small saucepan and simmer vigorously for 4–5 minutes until it thickens slightly, stirring frequently to prevent it from spluttering. Add the reduced stock and the cheese, and stir over a low heat until it melts. Season to taste with salt and pepper.

Heat the grill. Add the macaroni and the prawns to the sauce and gently warm through, stirring all the time, then tip the mixture into a shallow gratin or other ovenproof dish, (I use a 30 cm 1.5 l oval china dish). Scatter over the breadcrumbs, dot with the butter and place under the grill until golden and sizzling. There's a lot of spluttering at this point, don't be bullied into thinking it's done until it's lightly tanned all over. Serve straightaway.

Sepia Pasta with Prawns and Chilli

Noodles dyed black with sepia ink relish the presence of shellfish. Here it's prawns but it could just as well be crab or squid.

Serves 4

250 g sepia noodles

8 tbsp extra virgin olive oil

3 garlic cloves, peeled and finely chopped

1 medium-hot red chilli, seeds removed and finely chopped

350 g shelled raw tiger prawns

sea salt, black pepper

3 tbsp white wine

juice of 1 lemon

8 heaped tbsp coarsely chopped flat-leaf parsley

Bring a large pan of salted water to the boil, add the pasta, give it a stir and cook until just tender. The time this will take will depend on the type of noodles, so check the packet for the ideal cooking time.

At the same time, heat 6 tablespoons of the olive oil in a large frying pan over a high heat, add the garlic, chilli and prawns and cook, turning them for about a minute until they are a nice shrimp pink, seasoning them as you go. Add the wine and cook for about a minute more until the wine reduces a little, then remove it from the heat.

Drain the pasta into a colander, but not too thoroughly, and return it to the saucepan. Tip in the contents of the frying pan and toss. Add the lemon juice, remaining olive oil and the flat-leaf parsley and toss again. Taste for seasoning and serve straightaway.

4 RUGBY UNION: ENGLAND'S TRIUMPH

The men who got

N

SUNDAY LUNCH

I recall as a child that my mother's planning of a dinner party – the phoning round, polishing of glasses and cutlery, shopping, cooking and laying the table were a weekly event. I don't know quite how she did it, in this house midweek dinner parties are not so much weekly as annual, unless the children are on holiday and we've switched to cruise control, whereby one day runs into another and weekdays no longer matter.

I find Sunday lunch accounts for most of my entertaining, not least because when you have children (or even if you don't) it makes life so easy. There are no restraints, no niggling worries about what time the alarm is going to sound the next morning, and you actually have the energy to enjoy it. I also appreciate the lack of formality. Lounging, reading the papers and chatting, good food and good wine seems to me like the perfect equation. If the weather's great then you can spill out of doors, and the greater the age span the better. There is no simpler way of keeping everyone happy.

My one niggle against the traditional Sunday lunch line-up is the number of different dishes we are expected to put on the table at once, which is enough to leave any cook frazzled. I find an all-in-one roast does away with much of the stress, without losing sight of the things that we love about a Sunday roast. A sizzling tray of vegetables caramelised at the edges, bay leaves, rosemary and thyme, whole garlic cloves and the like, with chops or a small joint on top, is every bit as yummy.

But with this kind of roast, caramelisation is everything. A good-sized roasting dish (about 38 x 25 cm) will do nicely for four people, if you want to feed more, then it's either a bigger roasting dish or two, in which case you should swap them around halfway through. And rather a sauce that can be made in advance in lieu of gravy: an aïoli to go with roast beef, a spicy apple sauce for pork chops, or a romesco with chicken.

I also like to roast fish, usually whole, a method that captures all the succulence of the flesh as well as rendering a golden skin. And for those of us fazed by the prospect of filleting a fish, the flesh is easily lifted. In addition, it takes as little as 5 minutes to assemble, and the cooking juices act as a sauce.

Chicken and Red Pepper Roast

Roasted peppers are as tasty served hot as cold, in which case you could throw over some pitted black olives and chopped flat-leaf parsley. Served hot, I'd think along the lines of a gratin dauphinois or crispy little potatoes and a big green salad.

Serves 6

6 red or orange peppers, core,
    seeds and membranes removed
2 onions, peeled, halved and sliced
8–10 thyme sprigs
2 bay leaves
5 garlic cloves, peeled and sliced
extra virgin olive oil
sea salt, black pepper
6 free-range chicken breasts
    (skin on)
1 tsp balsamic vinegar

Heat the oven to 180°C fan oven/190°C electric oven/Gas 5. Quarter the peppers and arrange them together with the onions in a crowded single layer in a baking dish or roasting pan, approximately 38 x 25 cm in size. Tuck in the herbs and scatter over the garlic. Drizzle over 4 tablespoons of olive oil and season with salt and pepper. Roast for 40 minutes, stirring halfway through. Towards the end of this time, heat a dry iron frying pan over a medium heat, cut out the tendon from the underside of each chicken breast, lightly brush all over with olive oil, season them and sear until deep golden on both sides. You will need to do this in batches.

Give the peppers a stir to baste them, and nestle the chicken breasts between them skin-side up. Roast for another 20–25 minutes until the chicken is golden and sizzling and the peppers are singed at the edges. Drip the vinegar over the peppers, vaguely stirring to mix it into the juices, and serve straightaway.

Chicken and Sweet Potato Roast with Rosemary

A showcase for sweet potatoes, where the sugars render the edges caramelised and golden in no time at all.

Serves 4

10 small sprigs of rosemary
1 head of garlic, separated into
    cloves
1 x 1.6 kg free-range chicken
extra virgin olive oil
sea salt, black pepper
1.1 kg orange-fleshed sweet
    potatoes, peeled and sliced into
    1 cm slices
4 medium-hot red chillies
rocket or spicy mix of small salad
    leaves to serve 4
a squeeze of lemon juice

Heat the oven to 190°C fan oven/200°C electric oven/Gas 6. Pop a couple of the rosemary sprigs and small garlic cloves into the chicken cavity. Using your hands, coat the chicken with a little oil and season it. Arrange the sweet potatoes and remaining rosemary sprigs in a 38 x 25 cm roasting dish, drizzle over 3 tablespoons of oil and season. Place the chicken on top and roast for 20 minutes.

Transfer the chicken to a plate, and turn the potatoes using a spatula, mixing in the chillies and remaining garlic cloves. Place the chicken back on top and roast for a further 30 minutes.

Transfer the chicken to a plate, loosely cover it with foil and leave it to rest for 15 minutes. Turn the potatoes again, and roast them for another 10 minutes while the chicken is resting.

Just before serving, toss the salad leaves with enough oil to coat them, a few drops of lemon juice and a pinch of salt. Carve the chicken and serve with the potatoes (with garlic cloves and chillies for those who want them), and a pile of salad leaves.

Roast Chicken with Garlic, and Macaroni Cheese

Macaroni cheese has as much to do with the béchamel as the pasta, I like mine to be really creamy, which means starting out with lots of sauce and a moderate amount of macaroni. This is my 'stock' recipe, the one I wheel out for family suppers, but for a real treat try it with roast chicken doused in gravy and surrounded by meltingly soft cloves of roasted garlic. You could also serve it with roast lamb, and roast some cherry tomatoes on the vine separately rather than on top of the pasta. It's a good line-up for a mixed crowd, when you're trying to keep both vegetarians and meat-eaters happy.

Serves 4–5

ROAST CHICKEN

4 heads of garlic

1 x 1.6 kg free-range chicken

50 g unsalted butter

sea salt, black pepper

90 ml white wine

180 ml chicken stock
  (or 90 ml water)

MACARONI CHEESE

65 g unsalted butter

45 g plain flour

1 l full-cream milk

1 bay leaf

150 g mature Cheddar, grated

2 tbsp Dijon mustard

200 g macaroni

2 plum tomatoes

1 tbsp freshly grated Parmesan

Heat the oven to 190°C fan oven/200°C electric oven/Gas 6. Slice the top and bottom off the heads of garlic, separate out the cloves and tuck the small unpeeled cloves inside the chicken's cavity with half the butter. Place the chicken in a roasting dish, smear the remaining butter over the skin and season with salt and pepper. Peel the remaining garlic cloves.

Roast the chicken for 30 minutes, then scatter the garlic cloves around the bird, basting them and the chicken with the juices. Roast for another 25 minutes, then transfer the chicken and garlic cloves to a warm plate, tipping any juices inside the bird back into the dish. Loosely cover the chicken with foil and leave to rest for 20 minutes.

While the chicken is cooking, prepare the macaroni cheese. Melt 50 g of the butter in a medium-sized non-stick saucepan over a medium heat, add the flour and cook the roux for about a minute until it's floury in appearance and seething nicely. Remove from the heat and gradually work in the milk using a wooden spoon, just a little at a time to begin with. Return the béchamel to the heat, and bring to the boil, stirring frequently until it thickens. Add the bay leaf and simmer over a low heat for 10 minutes, stirring occasionally. Remove the bay leaf, stir in the Cheddar and the mustard and taste for seasoning. Bring the sauce back to the boil, stirring. Now liquidise it until really silky.

At the same time as cooking the sauce, bring a large pan of salted water to the boil. Add the macaroni to the pan, give it a stir to separate out the strands and cook until almost tender, leaving it slightly undercooked. Drain the macaroni into a sieve, quite thoroughly, then return it to the pan.

Toss the macaroni with the sauce, discarding the bay leaf and tip into a 2.75 l/ 35 cm gratin or other shallow ovenproof dish. Cut out a cone from the top of each tomato and slice them, discarding the end slices, and arrange on top of the macaroni. Season them then scatter over the Parmesan and dot with the remaining butter. Cook for 25 minutes until golden on the surface and sizzling at the edges. To ensure that the chicken and macaroni cheese are ready at the same time, you will need to put the macaroni cheese in the oven 5 minutes before you remove the chicken.

While the chicken is resting and the macaroni cheese is finishing off in the oven, skim any excess fat from the roasting dish, add the wine and simmer until rich and syrupy, scraping up all the sticky bits on the bottom. Now add the chicken stock, or water and simmer for several minutes until the gravy looks and tastes nice and rich.

Carve the chicken, adding any juices given out to the gravy. Serve it with the roasted garlic, accompanied by the macaroni cheese, with the gravy spooned over.

Chicken in Tahina Sauce

A good chicken dish for spring going into summer, this can be eaten warm or at room temperature. Tahina (pulped sesame seeds) is full of goodness, with a pleasant bitterness offset by the pine nuts.

Serves 4

extra virgin olive oil

1 x 1.6 kg free-range chicken

sea salt, black pepper

300 ml white wine

4 garlic cloves, peeled

4 green cardamom pods

1 cinnamon stick

2 bay leaves

2 x 5 cm strips of lemon peel

1 tbsp lemon juice, plus a little
 extra

120 g tahina

50 g pine nuts

¼ tsp chilli flakes

SALAD

flat-leaf parsley and coriander
 sprigs for 4 small salads

4 spring onions, trimmed, halved
 and cut into thin strips

Heat a large frying pan over a medium-high heat. Pour a little olive oil into the palm of your hand, rub your hands together and coat the chicken all over. Season it with salt and pepper and colour it on all sides. Place the wine, garlic cloves, cardamom pods, cinnamon stick, bay leaves and lemon peel in a large cast-iron casserole. Add the chicken, bring the liquor to the boil, cover and cook over a low heat for 1 hour.

Remove the chicken to a plate to rest for 20 minutes, tipping any juices inside back into the pan. Strain the cooking juices into a bowl and leave them to stand for 10 minutes for the fat to rise, then skim it off. Measure 150 ml of the liquor into a jug and add a tablespoon of lemon juice. Beat this a little at a time into the tahina in a bowl, to begin with it will thicken, and then start to thin as more liquid is added. It should be the consistency of thick pouring cream. Season to taste with salt.

Heat 2 tablespoons of olive oil in a large frying pan over a medium heat, add the pine nuts and fry until lightly golden, stirring all the time, then stir in the chilli. Transfer the nuts to a bowl – you need to start removing them a little before they are fully coloured. Toss the herbs and spring onions in a bowl with enough olive oil to coat, a few drops of lemon juice and a pinch of sea salt.

Carve the chicken and lay it out on a large warm serving plate, spoon the sauce over, then scatter with the pine nuts. Accompany with the salad.

The chicken can also be served cold, in which case allow it to cool before carving and dressing it with the sauce. It can stand prepared for a few hours, though the sauce will thicken. In this case, cover with clingfilm and set aside in a cool place.

Chicken in a Herb Crust

Here the chicken is roasted in a thick green overcoat of herbs, and gravy comes in the form of a creamy mustard sauce made from the juices. Some sauté mushrooms and mashed potato go down a treat.

Serves 4

100g mixture of watercress,
 flat-leaf parsley and dill, tough
 stalks removed

2 tbsp tarragon leaves

1 x 1.6 kg free-range chicken

2 medium egg yolks

sea salt, black pepper

50 g unsalted butter

50 ml white wine

2 generous tbsp crème fraîche

1 tsp Dijon mustard

Heat the oven to 190°C fan oven/200°C electric oven/Gas 6. Place the mixture of herbs and the tarragon leaves in a food processor and finely chop. Place the chicken on a plate, paint the surface of the bird with the egg yolks and press the herbs into the skin. Transfer the chicken to a roasting dish, season and dot with the butter. Roast for 50 minutes, basting frequently to ensure the herbs don't burn.

Transfer the chicken to a plate to rest for 20 minutes, tipping any juices from inside the bird into the pan. Skim any excess fat off the roasting tray, add the wine and simmer to reduce by half, scraping up all the residue on the bottom. Stir in the crème fraîche and the mustard, and simmer for a minute or so. Taste for seasoning. Carve the chicken and serve with the sauce poured around it.

Thyme and Lemon Roasted Chicken

This is another way of saying chicken salad, but with a freshly roasted bird with deep-golden skin, eaten hot with a cooling fattoush it's a cut above leftovers for Sunday supper.

Serves 4

CHICKEN

extra virgin olive oil
4 tbsp lemon juice
½ tsp paprika
¼ tsp allspice
1 tbsp thyme leaves
1 x 1.6 kg free-range chicken
sea salt

FATTOUSH

2 pitta breads
½ cucumber, peeled, halved lengthways and thickly sliced
150 g radishes, trimmed and quartered
200 g baby plum or cherry tomatoes, halved
1 small red onion, peeled, halved and thinly sliced
a large handful each of mint and flat-leaf parsley leaves

Ideally marinade the chicken overnight, but it isn't the end of the world if you don't. Combine 2 tablespoons of olive oil with 2 tablespoons of lemon juice, the spices and thyme in a bowl. Spoon this over the chicken in a roasting dish, coating the surface of the skin. If marinading the chicken overnight, cover the dish with clingfilm and chill.

Heat the oven to 190°C fan oven/200°C electric oven/Gas 6. Baste the chicken with any juices that have run down into the pan, season it with salt and roast for 55 minutes, basting it a couple of times during roasting. Leave the chicken to rest in the pan for 20 minutes.

To make the fattoush, open out the pitta breads by slicing off one of the long edges, and slipping a knife inside. Cut each half in two and toast them, bearing in mind they cook more quickly than sliced bread, being thin and dry. Once they have cooled break them into 2 cm squares and place in a bowl. Place the cucumber, radishes and tomatoes in another bowl with the onion, separating out the strands. Tear the mint leaves in half and coarsely chop the parsley, and toss with the salad vegetables. You can prepare the salad to this point in advance, in which case cover the vegetables with clingfilm and set aside somewhere cool.

Just before eating, pour 3 tablespoons of olive oil over the bread and toss. Pour another 3 tablespoons over the vegetables with the remaining 2 tablespoons of lemon juice, season with salt and toss, then mix in the bread.

Remove the chicken to a plate, tipping any juices inside back into the pan, then skim off the excess fat. Carve the chicken, adding any juices given out to the pan. Reheat these, scraping up the sticky bits on the bottom of the pan. Serve the chicken with the juices spooned over, accompanied by the salad.

Pork Loin Chops with Parsnip, Carrot and Beetroot

Everything we love about a pork roast – crisp crackling, roast parsnips and apple sauce, here spiced with a little chilli and lemon.

Serves 4

APPLE SAUCE

600 g Bramley apples, peeled, cored and sliced

50 g golden caster sugar

finely grated zest of 1 lemon

1 tsp finely chopped medium-hot red chilli

ROAST

4 pork loin chops (rib-in)

sea salt, black pepper

600 g carrots, trimmed and peeled

600 g parsnips, trimmed and peeled

2 good-sized raw beetroot, peeled and cut into wedges

a large handful of sage leaves

4 tbsp extra virgin olive oil

Place all the ingredients for the sauce in a medium-sized saucepan with 100 ml water. Bring to the boil then cover and cook over a low heat for 15–17 minutes, mashing the apple to a coarse purée once or twice during cooking. Transfer the sauce to a bowl and leave to cool.

In the meantime, heat the oven to 190°C fan oven/200°C electric oven/Gas 6. Slice the skin off the chops and score with a crisscross pattern using the tip of a sharp knife. Heat a large non-stick frying pan over a medium heat, season and colour the chops on both sides, then sear the fat to crisp it a little. Now lightly colour the fat side of the crackling, then turn and colour the other side too.

Either halve or quarter the carrots and parsnips depending on their size, and cut in half lengthwise if necessary. Arrange the vegetables and sage leaves in a 38 x 25 cm roasting dish. Drizzle with the olive oil and season. Lay the crackling on top, rind uppermost, and roast for 20 minutes. Stir the vegetables, leaving the crackling on top and roast for another 20 minutes. Give the vegetables a final stir and arrange the chops on top, without covering the crackling, and roast for another 15 minutes. Leave to rest for 5 minutes, then serve the chops, crackling and vegetables with the apple sauce spooned over.

Pork Cooked in Milk

There are endless variations of this Italian classic where a rib roast is slowly simmered in milk that tenderises the meat and turns to a soft curdy mass.

Your butcher can prepare your joint ready for the oven. Ask for the row of chine bones at the base to be removed and either cut up or left in one piece. Ask, too, for the skin to be scored at 5 mm intervals with a crisscross pattern, and sliced off so the fat is evenly distributed between meat and skin.

Serves 6

2 tbsp extra virgin olive oil

sea salt, black pepper

1 x 2.2 kg pork loin rib roast
(see introduction, above)

25 g unsalted butter

5 garlic cloves, peeled and halved

500 ml full-cream milk

2 bay leaves

Heat the oven to 180°C fan oven/190°C electric oven/Gas 5. Heat the olive oil in a roasting dish over a medium heat that will hold the joint relatively snugly. Season the meat all over and sear to colour on all sides. Remove it to a plate, pour off the fat and add the butter. Once this has almost melted and is frothing, add the garlic and stir for a moment until it begins to colour. Return the joint, fat-side up, to the roasting dish, with the chine bones closeby. Pour in the milk, add the bay leaves, bring to the boil and place in the oven. Turn the heat down to 140°C fan oven/ 150°C electric oven/Gas 2 and roast for 2 hours, basting frequently, the milk will curdle after about 1½ hours. The joint by the end should be very golden, sitting in a pool of curds and whey. At the same time roast the crackling. Rub some salt into the pork skin, place it skin-side up in a small roasting dish and place in the oven.

Remove the roast to a plate, cover with foil and leave to rest for 20 minutes. Turn the oven up to 200°C fan oven/220°C electric oven/Gas 7 and continue to roast the crackling while the joint is resting. It should crisp and turn pale, and be set with small bubbles below the surface.

Just before the end of resting the joint, discard the bay leaves and chine bones from the roasting dish and reheat the curds and whey, detaching the skin from the sides. Tip the contents into a blender and whizz to a creamy gravy. If this seems too thick, add a drop of boiling water. Check the seasoning then transfer to a jug.

Carve the roast – you should get one slice between each rib and one with the bone-in. Add any juices given out to the gravy jug. Drain any fat off the crackling into a small bowl – it is a good idea to leave this to harden before throwing it away. Serve the roast pork with the crackling and gravy, accompanied by the cabbage.

Savoy Cabbage with Almonds

A delicious accompaniment to the roast pork.

1 Savoy cabbage

150 ml white wine

50 g unsalted butter, diced

sea salt, black pepper

50 g toasted flaked almonds*

Bring a large pan of salted water to the boil. Discard the outer leaves from the cabbage, quarter, cut out the core and finely slice. Add the cabbage to the boiling water and blanch for 2 minutes, then drain into a colander and shake dry. Return the cabbage to the saucepan, pour over the wine, dot with the butter and season. Bring the liquid to the boil, then cover and cook over a low heat for 20–25 minutes, stirring now and again until the cabbage is tender and all the wine has evaporated. Take care that it does not colour. Stir in the toasted, flaked almonds and serve.

* To toast almonds, arrange them in a small baking tray and toast for 8–9 minutes in an oven heated to 180°C fan oven/190°C electric oven/Gas 5.

Roast Beef, Chips and Aïoli

Thin slices of rare roast beef, a gutsy garlic mayonnaise and golden chips are about as good as Sunday lunch gets.

Serves 4

ROAST

1.2 kg large new potatoes, peeled

10 thyme sprigs

finely grated zest of 1 lemon

1 tbsp lemon juice

2 tbsp extra virgin olive oil

40 g unsalted butter

sea salt, black pepper

1.1 kg joint of topside

watercress to serve

AÏOLI

3–5 garlic cloves, peeled

1 large egg

200 ml groundnut oil

100 ml extra virgin olive oil

a squeeze of lemon juice

Heat the oven to 190°C fan oven/200°C electric oven/Gas 6. Slice the potatoes lengthwise 1 cm thick, then cut into thick chips. Arrange them in a 38 x 25 cm roasting dish with the thyme and lemon zest. Drizzle over the olive oil and lemon juice, dot with the butter and season. Cover with foil and roast for 20 minutes. Meanwhile, heat a frying pan over a medium heat, season the joint and colour first the lean sides, and then the fat.

Remove the foil from the roasting dish and give the chips a stir with a spatula. Settle the joint between them and roast for 17 minutes per 500g for medium-rare meat (a 1.1 kg joint will take 37 minutes).

In the meantime, make the aïoli. Place the garlic cloves in a food processor and pulse to finely chop them. Add the egg and continue to whizz, and then slowly trickle in the oils as though making a mayonnaise. Finally add a squeeze of lemon juice to taste, season with salt and transfer to a bowl.

Remove the joint to a plate, loosely cover with foil and leave to rest for 15 minutes. Give the potatoes a stir and return to the oven for another 10–15 minutes until golden and caramelised. Carve the beef and serve with the chips (discarding the thyme), with a bunch of watercress to the side. Accompany with the aïoli.

Fillet Steak with a Turnip Gratin

A thick steak, creamy gratin and some watercress is reverentially French. This is a good choice for when you don't feel like roasting a whole joint.

Serves 4

TURNIP GRATIN

1 kg turnips, trimmed and peeled

sea salt, black pepper

25 g unsalted butter

50 g fresh white breadcrumbs

100 ml double cream

freshly grated nutmeg

STEAK

1 tbsp groundnut oil

4 x 175 g fillet steaks, 2 cm thick

50 g unsalted butter, diced

3 tbsp port

watercress to serve

To make the gratin, finely grate the turnips, either by hand or using a food processor. Transfer the turnip to a bowl, sprinkle with a little salt, and set aside for 15 minutes.

Melt the butter in a frying pan over a medium heat, add the breadcrumbs and sauté, stirring for about 5 minutes until tinged with gold. Remove these to a bowl.

Using your hands, squeeze out the turnip and place it in a bowl. Add the cream, a little pepper and nutmeg and mix. Press this into the base of a round 18 cm gratin or shallow ovenproof dish and scatter with breadcrumbs.

Heat the oven to 180°C fan oven/190°C electric oven/Gas 5 and cook the gratin for 25–30 minutes until golden. About 10 minutes before the gratin is cooked, heat the oil in a large frying pan over a medium heat. If your frying pan isn't large enough to hold all the steaks then heat two, adding a tablespoon of oil to each one. Season the steaks with salt and pepper on both sides, and cook for 3 minutes, then add the butter, which will fizzle, turn the steaks and cook for another 3 minutes on the other side. Remove the steak to a plate to rest for a few minutes. Add the port to the pan, once this stops seething cook it for a moment longer scraping up any caramelised bits on the bottom. Add any juices given out by the steak.

Place the steaks on warm plates with the juices spooned over, a spoon of turnip gratin and pile of watercress to the side and serve.

Fillet Steak en Croute

There are endless reasons for wheeling this one out. It remains the chicest party piece, hot or cold, and today with the plethora of wild mushrooms available the results promise to be better than ever. Although fillet is expensive, you don't need quite as much as you would if eating another steak (sorry, that's the closest I can give you to justification). I would accompany this with buttered asparagus tips and small crispy potatoes.

Serves 4–6

300 g wild and cultivated
    mushrooms, trimmed
25 g unsalted butter
2 shallots, peeled and finely
    chopped
sea salt, black pepper
2 tbsp chopped flat-leaf parsley
a squeeze of lemon juice
750 g piece fillet steak, trimmed of
    fat and sinew (ask your butcher
    for the thick end of the fillet)
groundnut oil
350–400 g puff pastry
100 g cream cheese
1 scant tbsp Dijon mustard
1 medium egg, beaten

Finely chop the mushrooms by hand into pieces a few millimetres in size. Heat the butter in a large frying pan over a medium heat, add the shallots and sweat for a few minutes until softened, stirring them occasionally. Add the mushrooms and some seasoning and continue to fry for another 5–6 minutes until any juices given out have evaporated and they have started to colour. Transfer them to a bowl, stir in the parsley and lemon juice and leave to cool.

Heat another large frying pan over a medium heat for several minutes. Brush the fillet steak all over with oil, season it and sear for a minute each side. Transfer to a plate and leave to cool.

Thinly roll out the pastry on a lightly floured worksurface. Spread the cream cheese over the middle of the pastry the length and width of the fillet. Spread mushrooms on top. Brush the top of the fillet with the mustard and place mustard-side down on top of the mushrooms. Trim the pastry allowing enough to parcel the steak. Paint one of the long edges with the beaten egg and both of the short sides. Bring the long painted edge up over the other long edge, then tuck up the sides, trimming off any excess pastry and securing them with more beaten egg. Place sealed-edges-down on a baking tray, then use the pastry trimmings to decorate the top of the pie, fixing them with the beaten egg. You can prepare the steak to this point a couple of hours in advance, cover and chill it.

Heat the oven to 220°C fan oven/230°C electric oven/Gas 8, brush the croute with beaten egg and bake for 30 minutes until golden. Leave to rest for 10 minutes, then carve into thick slices, don't worry if this seems rather messy, there's no neat way of doing it. The end slices will be medium-rare and the centre ones rare.

Sausage and Onion Roast with Mustard Sauce

Any hearty British banger will do here, and a pot of buttery mash or some floury boiled potatoes are as welcome as ever.

Serves 4

ROAST

3 tbsp extra virgin olive oil

800 g pork sausages

4 red onions, peeled, halved and sliced

4 leeks, trimmed and thickly sliced

10 thyme sprigs

sea salt, black pepper

2 tbsp coarsely chopped flat-leaf parsley

SAUCE

150 ml soured cream

1 tbsp Dijon mustard

Heat the oven to 170°C fan oven/180°C electric oven/Gas 4. Heat a tablespoon of oil in a 38 x 25 cm roasting dish (ideally cast-iron) on the hob over a medium heat and colour the sausages on both sides. Remove the dish from the hob and transfer the sausages to a plate. Arrange the onions, leeks and thyme sprigs on the base of the pan, drizzle over the remaining oil and season. Arrange the sausages on top and roast for 1 hour, stirring every 20 minutes until the vegetables are silky and coloured, they will reduce considerably in the process of cooking.

In the meantime, blend the soured cream and mustard together in a bowl. Discarding the thyme sprigs, serve the sausages and vegetables with the mustard sauce spooned over, scattered with parsley.

2.00pm

Lamb Chops with Aubergine, Peppers and Mint Sauce

A gentle mint sauce that can be dolloped greedily onto the lamb. All herbs and a barely any vinegar, rather than the other way around.

Serves 4

ROAST

2 red peppers, core and seeds
    removed, and quartered

extra virgin olive oil

sea salt, black pepper

2 small aubergines, ends discarded
    and cut into 1 cm slices

8 lamb loin chops (125 g each)

3 bay leaves

SAUCE

2 tsp balsamic vinegar

a pinch of golden caster sugar

1 scant tsp Dijon mustard

4 tbsp extra virgin olive oil

10 g basil leaves, finely chopped

10 g mint leaves, finely chopped

Heat the oven to 190°C fan oven/200°C electric oven/Gas 6. Arrange the peppers in a 38 x 25 cm roasting dish, drizzle over 2 tablespoons of olive oil, season and roast for 30 minutes.

In the meantime, heat a large non-stick frying pan over a medium-high heat. You will need to cook the aubergine slices in batches. Brush as many as will fit into the pan with olive oil on both sides, season just one side and sear until golden either side. Remove to a plate and cook the remainder in the same fashion. Also season the chops on both sides and colour these, too, including the fat at the edges. You will need to cook these in two goes.

To make the sauce, whisk the vinegar with the sugar, some seasoning and the mustard in a small bowl, then whisk in the oil and stir in the herbs.

Once the peppers are cooked, mix in the aubergine slices and bay leaves and lay the chops on top. Roast for 15 minutes, then leave to stand for 5 minutes. Serve the vegetables and chops with the sauce spooned over.

Whole Plaice Roasted with Rosemary and Lemon

A humble fish like plaice can be exquisite when simply cooked. This method works for any flat fish, offering succulent scented flesh and a sauce of the cooking juices. Delicious with mashed potato and a salad to follow.

Serves 4

2 tbsp extra virgin olive oil, plus
    extra for brushing

sea salt, black pepper

1.3 kg plaice (trimmed weight),
    gutted and trimmed

1 tbsp rosemary leaves, plus a
    couple of sprigs

1 lemon, thinly sliced

2 garlic cloves, peeled and thinly
    sliced

150 ml white wine

Heat the oven to 200°C fan oven/220°C electric oven/Gas 7. Choose a shallow roasting dish that will hold the plaice and brush with oil. Season the fish on both sides and place dark skin upwards in the roasting tray. Pop the rosemary sprigs and a couple of lemon slices inside the fish cavity. Lay the remaining lemon slices over the surface of the flesh, discarding the ends, then scatter over the rosemary leaves and the garlic. Carefully pour over the wine without dislodging the lemon, garlic and herbs, then trickle over the oil.

Roast the fish for 20–25 minutes; if you slip a knife into the thickest part of the flesh along the backbone, you should be able to see if it is cooked through. Remove and leave the fish to rest for 5 minutes. Fillet and serve with the pan juices spooned over. I find it easiest to remove the flesh from the skin as I go.

Maryland Crab Cakes

This is a special occasion fishcake, though it does make good use of the brown meat as well as the white, whose preferential treatment few of us can afford to exploit.

Serves 6 as a starter

4 as a main course

CRABCAKES

50 g water biscuits or cream crackers

1 medium egg, beaten

2 tbsp mayonnaise

2 tsp Dijon mustard

a shake of Worcestershire sauce

1 tbsp lemon juice

sea salt, black pepper

450 g white and brown crabmeat, picked over

4 tbsp coarsely chopped flat-leaf parsley

1 tbsp groundnut oil

RELISH

6 spring onions, trimmed and finely sliced

2 tbsp capers, rinsed

1 tbsp lemon juice

4 tbsp groundnut oil

Reduce the crackers to fine crumbs, either by placing them inside a plastic bag and crushing them using a rolling pin, or by whizzing them in a food processor. Whisk the egg with the mayonnaise, mustard, Worcestershire sauce, lemon juice and a little seasoning in a bowl. Blend this with the crabmeat, then stir in the cracker crumbs. Cover and set aside in a cool place for 30 minutes for the crackers to absorb any moisture and the mixture to firm up, then stir in the parsley. Taking a tablespoon of mixture at a time, shape 12 flattened crab cakes and place on a couple of large plates or the lid of a plastic container.

Combine all the ingredients for the relish in a small bowl with a pinch of salt.

To cook all the crabcakes at once you will need to have two frying pans on the go. Otherwise cook them in two batches, and keep the first batch warm in a low oven while you cook the second. In this case there shouldn't be any need to add more oil to the pan after the first batch. Heat a tablespoon of oil in a large frying pan over a medium heat and cook the crab cakes for 3 minutes each side until lightly golden, turning them using a palette knife. Drain them on a double thickness of kitchen paper and serve with the relish.

Roast Salmon with Citrus Fruits

Some buttery spinach and new potatoes complete the classic line-up.
Any leftover salmon is delicious eaten cold with a salad the next day.

Serves 6–8

1 x 2.2 kg salmon, gutted and
    scaled, head and tail removed
sea salt, black pepper
2 oranges, scrubbed and sliced
2 lemons, scrubbed and sliced
1 onion, peeled, sliced and
    separated into rings
150 ml white wine
75 g unsalted butter

Heat the oven to 200°C fan oven/220°C electric oven/Gas 7 and heat the grill. Score the salmon flesh on both sides at 5 cm intervals and season it with salt and pepper, as well as inside the gut cavity. Lay the salmon on a baking sheet and grill for 3–4 minutes each side until the skin blisters and colours.

Line a baking dish or tray that is as long as the salmon with a double layer of foil. Lay out half the orange and lemon slices (discarding the end slices) and the onion so they overlap in a row and season them. Lay the fish on top and arrange the remaining orange, lemon and onion slices on top, again seasoning them. You may not need all of them. Cup the edges of the foil. Pour over the wine, dot with the butter and roast for 30–35 minutes. Check whether it is cooked after 30 minutes by slipping a sharp knife between the backbone and the flesh. One should come away from the other with ease; if the flesh clings to the bones, it needs a little longer.

Tip the juices and top layer of fruit into a sieve over a bowl. Slip the fish off the foil into the tray and add the remaining fruit to the sieve. Press any extra juice from the fruit. Taste the sauce, adjust the seasoning and serve spooned over the filleted fish.

Red Mullet with a Rose Harissa

A girly take on harissa, not too hot and no garlic, scented instead with
saffron and rosewater. Try it with some bread or toast drizzled with olive oil.

Serves 4

4 x 300 g red mullet, gutted,
    scaled and trimmed
1 heaped tbsp each coarsely
    chopped coriander and dill
2 heaped tbsp each coarsely
    chopped chives and parsley
sea salt, black pepper
5 tbsp extra virgin olive oil
juice of ½ lemon
HARISSA
1 red pepper
½ tsp cayenne pepper
sea salt
20 saffron filaments
2 tsp rosewater
1 tbsp tomato purée
2 medium-hot red chillies, seeds
    and membranes removed and
    coarsely chopped

To make the harissa, heat the oven to 180°C fan oven/190°C electric oven/Gas 5 and roast the red pepper on the oven rack for 20 minutes. Place it in a bowl, cover with clingfilm and leave to cool. Slip off the skin, and remove the seeds and membranes. Place all the remaining ingredients for the harissa in a food processor and whizz until smooth; this may take several minutes. Transfer to a bowl to serve.

Heat the oven to 200°C fan oven/220°C electric oven/Gas 7. Score the mullet diagonally at 2 cm intervals. Combine the chopped herbs in a bowl and stuff a generous pinch into each slit. Reserve any leftover herbs. Season the fish on both sides with salt and pepper and arrange top to tail in a roasting dish. Drizzle over the olive oil and roast for 25 minutes, then remove, trickle over the lemon juice and leave to rest for 5 minutes. Serve the mullet with the pan juices spooned over, scattered with any leftover herbs. Accompany with the harissa.

Aubergine Gratin with Mozzarella and Olives

An extravagant mass of melting aubergine and gooey mozzarella, with a tomato sauce and olives.

Serves 6

1 kg aubergines (3–4 medium ones)
extra virgin olive oil
sea salt, black pepper
250 ml tomato passata*, seasoned
   with salt and pepper
2 buffalo mozzarellas, drained and
   sliced
75 g green olives, pitted and halved
50 g freshly grated Parmesan

Heat the oven to 180°C fan oven/190°C electric oven/Gas 5. Removing the stalk from each aubergine, slice them lengthwise 1 cm thick. Heat a large dry frying pan, or even better two. Brush one side of each slice of aubergine with oil, season and fry this side until golden. Brush the top side with oil, turn and fry this side too. As the slices are cooked, arrange them in overlapping rows in a 30 x 20 cm gratin dish (ideally cast-iron).

Having covered the base with half the aubergine slices, spoon over half the tomato passata, lay over half the mozzarella and scatter over all of the olives. Now repeat with the remaining aubergine slices. Spoon over the remaining sauce, lay the remaining mozzarella over and scatter over the Parmesan. Bake for 25–30 minutes until nicely golden and gooey. Serve hot or warm.

The gratin can be successfully reheated for 20–25 minutes in a medium oven, though the mozzarella will never return to being quite as gooey.

* Even better than passata is sugocasa, a chopped tomato sauce that has a good chunky texture. Alternatively you could briefly whizz tinned chopped tomatoes in a food processor.

Flat-cap Mushrooms with Garlic, Lemon and Chilli

This delectable way of cooking flat-cap mushrooms is apt with any roast or grilled meat, bacon and fried eggs, or for vegetarians simply with some crusty bread for mopping up all the dark mushroomy juices.

Serves 4

8 medium flat-cap mushrooms
4 garlic cloves, peeled and finely
   chopped
1 medium-hot red chilli, core and
   seeds removed and finely
   chopped
grated zest of 1 lemon
3 tbsp extra virgin olive oil
25 g unsalted butter
sea salt, black pepper
1 tbsp lemon juice
2 tbsp coarsely chopped flat-leaf
   parsley

Heat the oven to 180°C fan oven/190°C electric oven/Gas 5. Trim the ends of the mushroom stalks and arrange them in a roasting dish cup-side up. Divide the garlic, chilli and lemon zest between the cups. Drizzle over the olive oil, dot with the butter, season and bake for 25 minutes.

When they come out of the oven, sprinkle the lemon juice over the mushrooms and scatter with parsley. Serve hot or warm.

Swiss Chard, Mozzarella and Tomato Gratin

After an uphill struggle that seems to have been going on for centuries, Swiss chard has finally found a place in the nation's affection, helped along by farmers' markets and other inspiring outlets. Quite why is a mystery, when it has so much more flavour than spinach. There is an organic stall in my local market in Normandy that takes enormous pride in cultivating unusual varieties of vegetable. And the stallholder frequently has ruby chard, and occasionlly rainbow, whose colours sadly wash off in the boil, but it looks great in the vegetable basket.

Serves 4

white wine vinegar
1 kg Swiss chard
500 g plum tomatoes
5 tbsp extra virgin olive oil
2 garlic cloves, peeled and finely
    chopped
sea salt, black pepper
2 buffalo mozzarellas, drained and
    sliced
50 g coarse-textured white bread,
    crusts on, broken into pieces
1 heaped tsp thyme leaves

Bring a large pan of water to the boil and acidulate it with a slug of vinegar. Cut the base off the Swiss chard and separate out the leaves, cutting out any browning bits of leaf or stalk. Halve the sheaths where the stalk turns to leaf, and wash both separately in a sink of cold water. If the stalks are more than 7–10 cm long, halve them again. Add the stalks to the pan and cook for 3 minutes, then transfer to a colander using a slotted spatula. Bring the water back to the boil, add the leaves and cook for 2 minutes, then transfer to a sieve, again using a slotted spatula. Using rubber gloves, squeeze out as much water as possible from the leaves, then place them on a board and slice.

Bring the cooking water back to the boil. Cut out the core from each tomato using a small sharp knife and plunge into the water for 20 seconds, then remove to a large bowl of cold water. Slip off the skins and slice the tomatoes.

Heat 2 tablespoons of olive oil in a large frying pan over a medium heat, add half the garlic and once this starts to sizzle add the chard stems. Season and sauté for several minutes until glossy and relaxed, turning occasionally. Remove to a bowl and repeat with the remaining garlic and chard leaves, adding another 2 tablespoons of oil to the pan. Arrange the chard stems on the bottom of a 30 x 20 cm gratin dish (ideally cast-iron). Arrange half the tomato slices and half the mozzella on top, season and repeat with the chard leaves, remaining tomatoes and mozzarella.

Whizz the bread in a food processor to small croûton-like nibs. Toss in a bowl with the thyme, the remaining tablespoon of oil and some seasoning and scatter over the top of the gratin. It can be prepared to this point up to several hours in advance, in which case cover it with clingfilm and set aside.

Heat the oven to 180°C fan oven/190°C electric oven/Gas 5 and bake the gratin for 30–35 minutes until the crumbs are crisp and golden and the cheese melted and bubbling. Serve straightaway.

Gruyère and Wild Mushroom Gratin

This is a savoury bread and butter pud that has all the charm of a sweet one. Certain cheeses are born for melting, better for having been shown an oven or grill than eaten raw. Gruyère, Emmental and Raclette are all such prime fondue cheeses, though personally I have downed the pronged forks and quenched the spirit burner in favour of other routes. Some honey roast or Parma ham alongside would go nicely.

Serves 6

2 tbsp groundnut oil

3 red onions, peeled, halved and
   sliced

200 g wild mushrooms, picked
   over and sliced

sea salt, black pepper

salted butter

6 thin slices white day-old bread,
   with crusts

275 g grated Gruyère

3 medium eggs

300 ml milk

300 g crème fraîche

50 g freshly grated Parmesan

Heat the oven to 180°C fan oven/190°C electric oven/Gas 5. Heat a tablespoon of the oil in a large frying pan over a medium heat, add the onions and fry for about 10 minutes, stirring frequently, until evenly golden. Remove to a bowl, heat the remaining tablespoon of oil in the pan, add the mushrooms and sauté for several minutes until softened and lightly coloured, seasoning them at the end. Remove the pan from the heat.

Butter the slices of bread and halve each into two triangles. Cover the base of a 2.6 l/35 cm oval gratin or other shallow ovenproof dish with half of these, setting them at an angle for even coverage, then scatter over half each of the onions, mushrooms and Gruyère. Repeat with the remaining bread, onions, mushrooms and Gruyère.

Whisk the eggs, milk, crème fraîche, Parmesan and some seasoning in a large bowl and evenly pour over the top. Place the gratin dish inside a roasting dish with warm water to come two thirds of the way up the sides and bake for 35 minutes until puffy and golden. Serve straightaway while the cheese and custard are molten and gooey.

Shortcrust Pastry for 23 cm Tart Case

Homemade shortcrust pastry is crumbly and good enough to eat on its own. That said, shopbought pastry is adequate, if you're not in the mood for making it.

These tarts benefit from 10–20 minutes standing around after they come out of the oven, for the pastry to crisp and the filling to set. And most are equally delicious at room temperature. If you chill them however, the filling firms up and you lose that wonderful creaminess. While they do reheat, there is nothing quite as fine as a tart that is fresh from the oven.

225 g plain flour
a pinch of sea salt
150 g unsalted butter, chilled
   and diced
1 medium egg, separated

Place the flour and salt in the bowl of a food processor, add the butter and reduce to a fine crumb-like consistency. Incorporate the egg yolk, and then with the motor running trickle in just enough cold water for the dough to cling together in lumps. Transfer the pastry to a large bowl and bring it together into a ball using your hands.

Wrap the pastry in clingfilm and chill for at least 1 hour. It will keep well in the fridge for up to a couple of days.

Heat the oven to 180°C fan oven/190°C electric oven/Gas 5. Knead the pastry until it is pliable. Thinly roll it out on a lightly floured surface and carefully lift it into a 23 cm tart tin with a removable base. It is quite a durable pastry and shouldn't tear or collapse. Press it into the corners of the tin and run a rolling pin over the top to trim the edges. Reserve the trimmings to patch the pastry case after it is baked. Prick the base with a fork and line it with a sheet of foil, tucking it over the top to secure the pastry sides to the tin. Now weight it with baking beans – dried pulses will do nicely.

Bake the case for 15 minutes, then remove the foil and baking beans. If any of the sides have shrunk more than they should, use a little of the reserved pastry to patch them. Remember the quiche can only be filled as far as the lowest point of the sides. Brush the base and sides of the case with the reserved egg white, then bake it for another 10 minutes until it is lightly coloured. This glaze helps to seal the pastry and prevent the custard from soaking in.

Tart Tins

I like deep tarts with a good ratio of filling to pastry, so the depth of the tin is all-important. I would recommend two depths, 4 and 6 cm, or the deeper of the two if you want just one. Failing that, you could forgo the crimped edges and use a cake tin with the right dimensions. I'd avoid china quiche dishes, which make it difficult to serve the tart without damaging it. Removeable sides let you slip the tart on to a plate with ease, or serve it straight from the base.

Spinach and Gruyère Tart

A plate of buttered spinach and melted Gruyère for lunch is my idea of heaven. Together they make one of the finest fillings for a crisp pastry case. Success here lies in squeezing every last drop of liquid from the cooked spinach, otherwise it may jeopardise the set.

Serves 6

23 cm tart case, 4 cm deep,
    prebaked (see opposite)
FILLING
800 g spinach, washed
300 ml whipping cream
3 medium eggs
sea salt, black pepper
freshly grated nutmeg
200 g grated Gruyère
120 g cherry tomatoes, halved
groundnut oil

Heat the oven to 180°C fan oven/190°C electric oven/Gas 5. You may need to cook the spinach in two pans, or in two batches. Place it in a large saucepan with just the water that clings to the leaves, cover with a lid and steam over a medium heat for 10 minutes, stirring halfway through, until it collapses. Drain it into a seive, and press out as much liquid as possible using a large spoon. Either leave it to cool, or, using rubber gloves, squeeze balls of the spinach between your hands to extract every last trace of moisture. Place the spinach on a board and slice it.

Whisk the cream, eggs, some seasoning and a little grated nutmeg in a bowl. Stir in the spinach, making sure it is evenly distributed, and then half the Gruyère. Transfer to the tart case and smooth the surface. Toss the cherry tomatoes in a bowl with just enough oil to coat them, and a little seasoning. Scatter over the surface of the tart and press into the filling so they are level with the spinach. Scatter over the remaining cheese mainly towards the centre and bake for 35–45 minutes until golden on the surface and set. Leave to cool for 10–20 minutes before serving. While it is best eaten hot or warm from the oven, it does reheat successfully.

Onion Tart

It's not hard to see why this has become a classic. Onions slowly sweated in butter to a sweet creamy mass, here married with lots of Parmesan.

Serves 6

23 cm tart case, 6 cm deep,
    prebaked (see opposite)
FILLING
40 g unsalted butter
6 Spanish onions (approx. 1.4 kg),
    peeled, halved and thinly sliced
sea salt, black pepper
300 g crème fraîche
2 medium eggs
1 tbsp thyme leaves
150 g freshly grated Parmesan

Heat the oven to 180°C fan oven/190°C electric oven/Gas 5. Melt the butter in a large saucepan over a low heat, add the onions, scatter over a teaspoon of salt and sweat for 40 minutes until creamy and soft, without allowing them to colour. Stir more frequently towards the end when they may stick a little and turn the heat down if necessary. This period of cooking is all-important to both the flavour and texture of the onions, it takes time to render them subtly sweet and silky.

In the meantime, in a large bowl whisk the crème fraîche with the eggs, some pepper, a little more salt, the thyme and half the Parmesan. Stir in the cooked onions and pour the mixture into the prepared tart case. Scatter over the remaining Parmesan and bake for 30-35 minutes until golden on the surface and set. Leave to stand for 20 minutes before serving. This tart is almost nicer eaten at room temperature (when it is supremely creamy) than hot.

Pea, Feta and Basil Tart

An early summer tart, and great way of enjoying peas. Take full advantage of the ready-shelled packs unless you have an army of idle hands around to help with the shelling.

Serves 6

23 cm tart case, 6 cm deep, prebaked (see page 96)
FILLING
25 g unsalted butter
½ tsp caster sugar
sea salt, black pepper
600 g shelled fresh peas
2 medium eggs, plus 1 yolk
300 ml whipping cream
150 g freshly grated Parmesan
150 g feta, cut into 1 cm dice
a handful of basil leaves, torn into 2 or 3
1 tbsp extra virgin olive oil

Heat the oven to 180°C fan oven/190°C electric oven/Gas 5. Place 150 ml water in a large saucepan with the butter, sugar and ½ teaspoon of salt. Bring to the boil over a high heat, add the peas and cook for 5 minutes, stirring occasionally, until tender. Drain them into a sieve. Place half the peas in a food processor and briefly whizz to break them up.

Whisk the eggs and yolk with the cream, some seasoning and half the Parmesan in a large bowl. Fold in all the peas, half the feta and the basil. Transfer the filling to the tart case and scatter over the remaining feta and Parmesan. Drizzle the olive oil over the surface and bake the tart for 35–40 minutes until golden and set in the centre. Leave to cool for 20 minutes before serving. This tart is good eaten hot or at room temperature, and can be reheated.

Fondue-filled Butternut Squash

There's very little vegetarian food that offers the ease of chucking a chicken breast on to the grill – most dishes are quite complex. This however is an exception to the rule, and you can prepare it in advance and pop the squash into the oven half an hour before you want to eat. The croûtons are an optional extra.

Serves 4

FONDUE
1 tbsp kirsch or white wine
1 tbsp cornflour
130 g Gruyère, grated
40 g crème fraîche
sea salt, black pepper
freshly grated nutmeg
SQUASH
2 x 700 g butternut squash
1 garlic clove, peeled and crushed
**   to a paste**
1 tbsp thyme leaves
25 g unsalted butter, melted

Heat the oven to 190°C fan oven/200°C electric oven/Gas 6. Blend the kirsch or wine with the cornflour in a bowl, then add the remaining ingredients for the fondue and work to a paste using a spoon. Halve the squash lengthwise, I find it easiest to slice through the bulb first, then turn the squash stalk down and cut through the trunk. Scoop out the seeds and fibrous matter from each half using a teaspoon, and score the flesh of the trunk in a crisscross pattern at 2 cm intervals, using the tip of a sharp knife.

Divide the crushed garlic among the squash hollows and, using your fingers, smear it over the surface. Fill the cavities with the fondue paste to within a couple of millimetres of the surface; there should be a little room for the cheese to bubble without overflowing. The squash can be prepared to this point in advance, in which case heat the oven just before cooking.

It's important that the squash bake level in order to contain the fondue within the hollow. Arrange the squash halves top to tail in a roasting dish, using foil loosely bundled into a ball to raise the thin end of the trunk to the same level as the bulb. Season the surface of the squash, scatter over the thyme and drizzle with the melted butter. Bake the squash for 35-40 minutes, until the fondue is golden and bubbling, and the trunk of the squash is tender when pierced with a knife. Serve straightaway, accompanied by the croûtons.

Croûtons
2 slices day-old white bread, 1 cm thick
groundnut oil

Cut the crusts off the bread and dice it, using a sharp chopping knife rather than a bread knife, which will tear the crumb. Heat several millimetres of oil in a frying pan until it is hot enough to immerse a cube of bread in bubbles. Add the croûtons to the pan and fry them, tossing occasionally until they are evenly gold and crisp. Remove them with a slotted spoon and drain on kitchen paper, then leave them to cool.

SUMMER EATING

Summer holidays in Normandy are everything you dream summer holidays should be. Open to a sky that is sometimes moody and at other times crystal blue for days on end. So hot you don't dare venture down to the beach until six at night, for a cooling evening dip, an aperitif in the beachside bar and a game of chess. Home, a log fire when the temperature drops, or dinner in the orchard when it doesn't, a big white linen cloth thrown over a trestle table. And as much seafood as the heart could desire: oysters are plentiful as is crab, and nowhere has better mussels than the local *moules de bouchot*.

None of this is to say that summer cooking in London doesn't come with its own attractions. A golden opportunity for delving into the flavour palates of Italy and the Middle East, courtesy of the many wonderful delis. But when we decamp to Normandy all that changes, and whatever I cook is inspired by what I can find locally. Ingredients from further afield seem out of place. So out go the spices and olive oil, and in comes the butter and untreated cream, herbs and cider.

The one constant is the mood of summer food. In a heatwave all I want are dishes to pass a cooling wand over my insides – chilled soups and salads, jelly and ices – and the scent of smoke drifting in on a warm air current. The advent of bags of charcoal that can be lit at the touch of a match has revolutionised barbecues insofar as they have done away with their being the domain of the male of the species. Except that most men I know enjoy roasting food over an open fire, furnace-like in its capacity to generate a thirst, and that's fine by me. I don't need much persuasion to take a back seat at the stove.

Gender aside, reams could be written about the imprecise art of the barbecue, not least because every summer returns us to the scene as novices. Added to which, food may cook more quickly if you are grilling over a fierce heat, or it's a very hot day, than if it's windy or

you're using a disposable barbecue. The golden rule is to start by underestimating how close to the coals the food should be; it can always be given a little longer on the grill or moved closer to the coals, but you can't undo those burnt bits. That said, meat and fish on the bone benefit from a longer, slower heat than say a few morsels of fillet threaded as a kebab.

And there are no tricks to be had in buying fancy equipment, the results achieved with a basic grid set over coals in a hole in the ground will be as good as the most technologically advanced. That's surely their appeal in the first place, you can rig one up on the beach or on a camping trip with a bag of charcoal, a grid and a little imagination. Though the portable barbecues that close down to a bucket and are carried by a handle, the charcoal within, are very neat affairs, and if you're a regular wanderer they're a good idea (see p220). Otherwise a palette knife for loosening the food on the grill and a pair of tongs are your two best friends.

Another piece of equipment that will do you proud is a salad spinner. When a friend inadvertently left hers in my kitchen, I cursed the sight and size of it and silently willed her to pick it up as quickly as possible. She didn't, and today it is hard to imagine life without one. Tight lettuces may need no more than their outer leaves discarded, but loose leaves such as baby spinach, rocket, watercress and lamb's lettuce need to be thoroughly dried before acquainting with any oil and vinegar.

As to the perennial or rather annual dilemma of picnics, bring on the layered salad. More usually the domain of sandwich bars, they are practical and portable. The bottom layer should contain the dressing, protecting any layers above from the usual fatigue that sets in as soon as a salad is tossed. Next a little marinated something, cubes of feta or roasted vegetables, and the layer above green beans, sliced raw vegetables or potato. And finally some herbs, baby spinach or rocket, and crisp or piquant toasted nuts, croûtons or olives. And off you go.

Grilled Figs with Bayonne Ham and Rocket

Figs with Parma ham and rocket have been doing the rounds for many years, and in Normandy we have a local artisanal ham to call on. Like Bayonne ham, it is cut into lusciously thick slices, a more robust product than its Italian cousins, and a slice is normally enough. You can dish this one up as an appetiser or starter while you're cooking the main course.

Serves 6

1 tbsp balsamic vinegar

sea salt, black pepper

6 tbsp extra virgin olive oil, plus a little extra

6 figs, stalks trimmed and halved

12 slices Bayonne ham

6 handfuls of rocket*

Whisk the balsamic vinegar with some seasoning in a small bowl, then whisk in the 6 tablespoons of oil. Brush the fig halves with oil, and barbecue flesh-side down for 3–5 minutes until caramelised, then turn and grill for another 3 minutes. Remove them to a plate and leave to cool for 5 minutes.

Lay a couple of slices of Parma ham on the side of six plates, with a pile of rocket beside. Place 2 fig halves on this side of the salad, and drizzle the dressing over the ham, rocket and figs.

Indoors

Heat a double ridged griddle over a medium-low heat and grill the figs flesh-side down for 3 minutes until caramelised, then turn and grill the other side for about a minute or until the figs feel soft when gently squeezed with a pair of tongs.

* The wild rocket that has crept into the shops as the new leaf in town is to be lauded over the ordinary. The leaves have a defined bite, but are that much more delicate in appearance.

Chicken Drumsticks with Pomegranate Molasses

Pomegranate molasses is lovely stuff, sweet, sour and sticky.

Serves 6

12 chicken drumsticks
sea salt, black pepper
coarsely chopped coriander to serve
MARINADE
4 shallots, peeled
3 tbsp pomegranate molasses or
  paste
3 tbsp lemon juice
3 tbsp extra virgin olive oil
½ tsp ground cinnamon
¼ tsp ground allspice

Coarsely grate the shallots without risking your knuckles – half of each one will do.

Blend with all the other ingredients for the marinade in an airtight container large enough to hold the drumsticks. Add these and coat thoroughly with the marinade. Cover and leave in the fridge overnight, basting them once.

Season the drumsticks and barbecue for 20–40 minutes, turning to cook them on all sides, and starting well away from the coals to ensure they cook through without burning. Transfer to a plate and scatter with coriander.

Indoors

Heat the oven to 200°C fan oven/220°C electric oven/Gas 7 and line the base of a grill pan with foil. Season the drumsticks and lay them on a rack in the grill pan. Spoon over a little marinade and cook for 20–25 minutes until golden and caramelised at the edges. Eat hot or cold scattered with chopped coriander.

Honey and Thyme Grilled Quail

Quail make good barbecue fare, sufficiently delicate to cook through, with the advantage of being cooked on the bone.

Serves 4

QUAIL
8 quail
extra virgin olive oil
juice of 1 lemon
2 tsp runny honey
1 heaped tbsp thyme leaves
SALAD
3 uncooked beetroot (about the
  size of an apple)
sea salt, black pepper
200 g curly kale, tough stalks
  removed
juice of 1 lemon
200 g feta, broken into 1 cm dice

Spatchcock the quail by halving and opening them out using a large sharp knife, leaving them joined at the breastbone. Blend 3 tablespoons of oil, the lemon juice, honey and thyme in a large bowl, add the quail and coat them with the marinade. You can cover and chill them for a couple of hours or overnight if wished.

Heat the oven to 220°C fan oven/230°C electric oven/Gas 8. Cut the shoots and whiskery root off each beetroot and place them in a small roasting dish. Drizzle over a little olive oil, season with salt and roast for 45 minutes. Leave to cool.

Bring a large pan of salted water to the boil, add the kale and cook for 8 minutes. Drain into a sieve and press out as much water as possible. Place the kale on a board and slice, then leave to cool. Remove the skins from the beetroot and cut into wedges.

Just before barbecuing, season the quail on either side with salt and pepper and barbecue first the flesh-side and then the boned-side, about 15–20 minutes in total, starting well away from the coals to allow them time to cook through without burning. Transfer to a plate and leave to rest for 5–10 minutes.

Arrange the beetroot and kale together on a plate. Pour over the lemon juice and 4 tablespoons of olive oil and season. Toss to coat the vegetables. Gently mix in the feta and drizzle over a little more oil. Serve the quail accompanied by the salad.

Indoors

Heat the oven to 190°C fan oven/200°C electric oven/Gas 6. Arrange the quail in a roasting pan. Pour over the lemon juice and 3 tablespoons of oil. Drizzle over the honey, scatter over the thyme and season. Roast for 35–40 minutes, basting halfway through. Leave to rest for 10 minutes, loosely covered with foil to keep them warm. Serve the quail with any juices in the pan spooned over, accompanied by the salad.

Arthur's Barbecued Sausages

Arthur Higgo, a neighbour in Normandy of South African origin, taught me this great way of cooking sausages in a sticky tomato sauce, a brae favourite in Cape Town. Apart from producing the ultimate caramelised bangers, the grill is freed up for 30 minutes at the end, leaving you plenty of space to grill whatever else is lined up. And if you are cooking for any number, this is a serious plus.

Serves 6

3 tbsp extra virgin olive oil

2 onions, peeled, halved and finely sliced

5 garlic cloves, peeled and finely chopped

1½ tsp light muscovado sugar

100 ml white wine

2 x 400 g tins chopped plum tomatoes

sea salt, black pepper

1.3 kg chunky bangers

Heat the olive oil in a medium-sized saucepan over a medium-low heat and sauté the onions for 10–12 minutes, stirring frequently, until lightly caramelised. Add the garlic and cook for a minute or two longer, again stirring frequently as the onions will caramelise quite quickly at this point.

Add the sugar and stir, then add the wine and simmer to reduce by half. Add the tomatoes and some seasoning, bring to a simmer and cook over a medium-low heat for 25–30 minutes, until well reduced and thick, stirring now and again, especially towards the end. Spoon the sauce into a large cast-iron roasting tray (approx. 25 cm x 38 cm) that will hold the sausages in a single layer.

Heat the oven to 180°C fan oven/190°C electric oven/Gas 6. Barbecue the sausages for 15–25 minutes until nicely caramelised without being fully cooked, turning them every so often to ensure they colour evenly. Arrrange them on top of the tomato sauce, spooning some of it over. Roast for 25–30 minutes, basting them halfway through. The sauce by the end should be caramelised at the edges, and the sausages deep gold and sticky.

Indoors

Heat a little olive oil oil in a large frying pan over a medium heat and slowly colour the sausages on all sides, for 20–25 minutes. Try to do this as evenly as possible, turning them frequently; they should by the end be a nice golden colour. You will need to fry them in two batches. Proceed to cook them in the oven in the tomato sauce as above.

Sesame-seared Sirloin

Here a thick slab of sirloin is grilled as one large piece, then thinly sliced. You'll need the help of your butcher to get the right thickness, and if you're especially partial to fat you may like to leave it on the sirloin. If so a water spray will come in handy to tame any flames that flare up from the coals.

Serves 6

2 tbsp sesame oil

2 tbsp light soy sauce

2 tbsp rice or white wine vinegar

2 x 500 g sirloin steaks, cut 5 cm thick, fat removed

2 cucumbers, peeled, halved and thinly sliced

sea salt

2 medium-hot red chillies, seeds and membranes removed and cut into thin 2 cm strips

6 spring onions, trimmed and cut into thin 5 cm strips

1 tbsp sesame seeds

Combine the sesame oil, soy sauce and vinegar in a shallow container that will hold the two sirloins snugly. Place the steaks in the dish and spoon the marinade over. Cover and marinate in a cool place for 1 hour, spooning the marinade over every so often.

Place the cucumber in a bowl, sprinkle with salt and set aside for 30 minutes. Rinse the cucumber thoroughly in a sieve and pat dry with a tea towel. Combine the cucumber with the chilli and spring onions in a salad bowl. Heat a small dry frying pan and toast the sesame seeds, stirring constantly, until a light gold, then transfer them to a small bowl.

Barbecue the steak over hot coals for 3 minutes on all four sides, 12 minutes in total. Remove and leave it to rest for about 10 minutes. Toss the salad with 4 tablespoons of the marinade and scatter over the sesame seeds. Slice the steaks thinly, and serve with the salad to the side.

Indoors
Heat a ridged griddle over a medium-low heat, and grill the steaks for 3 minutes on all four sides, 12 minutes in total.

Spiced Lamb Cutlets

Lamb cutlets grill particularly well, their fat turning crisp and golden and the meat along the bone nicely roasted. The potatoes are delicious eaten hot or warm, and I'm quite happy to tuck into them cold as well.

Serves 4

2 garlic cloves, peeled

1 tsp ground cumin

1 tsp ground coriander

1 tsp turmeric

½ tsp crushed chillies

3 bay leaves, torn into pieces

extra virgin olive oil

12 lamb cutlets

CRUSHED POTATOES

1 kg waxy potatoes, peeled

4 tbsp finely chopped flat-leaf or curly parsley

a squeeze of lemon juice

sea salt, black pepper

Place the garlic in a pestle and mortar and crush to a rough paste. Add the spices, chilli and bay leaves and 6 tablespoons of olive oil and blend together. Place the lamb cutlets in a large bowl, pour over the marinade and coat them, turning them with your hands. Cover and chill for a couple of hours.

About 40 minutes before serving, bring a large pan of salted water to the boil, add the potatoes and simmer for about 15 minutes until tender. Drain into a colander and leave for a few minutes for the surface moisture to evaporate. Return the potatoes to the pan, and, using a potato masher or the back of a spoon, gently crush them into pieces. Pour over 8 tablespoons of olive oil, scatter over the parsley, a squeeze of lemon juice and some seasoning and toss. The potatoes can be served straightaway or warm.

Just before grilling the chops, smooth any marinade that has run to the bottom of the bowl over the meat, season both sides with salt and barbecue for 7–8 minutes each side. Serve the chops with the crushed potatoes.

Indoors
Heat a double-ridged griddle for several minutes over a medium heat, and cook the chops for 5 minutes each side, then grill the fat for a moment until it colours.

Bread and Tomato Brochettes

Bread, tomatoes, olive oil, thyme and sea salt are ingredients that should be thrown together as often as possible and in as many different ways. Here the bread emerges crisply toasted and smokey from the grill. I make a point of threading up some of these every time I barbecue, and frequently grill them over our open fire indoors. Vegetarians can enjoy them with slivers of Parmesan or olives, or else they can serve as a starter with some Parma ham, or salami and gherkins.

Makes 6

24 cherry tomatoes (approx. 250 g)
8 x 2 cm slices of baguette, cut
  into 4 cubes
extra virgin olive oil
1 tsp thyme leaves, fresh or dried,
  or 1 tbsp fresh marjoram
sea salt

Thread the cherry tomatoes and bread cubes on to six 25 cm skewers, beginning and ending with bread. Just before grilling, drizzle a little olive oil down the length of each side of the brochettes, scatter over the thyme and season with salt. Barbecue for 4–8 minutes in total, 1–2 minutes on each side.

Indoors
Heat a double-ridged griddle for several minutes over a medium heat, and cook for about 4 minutes, a minute each side.

* Bamboo skewers are prettier than metal ones, which can look a little fierce on the plate. They can be found in most Oriental delis and come in different lengths. To prevent them from scorching, soak them in water before assembling the kebabs.
* If you are using metal skewers, flat rather than round ones prevent the food from slipping when you turn them.

Saffron Sardines

The scent of sardines on the barbecue grid is one of the most appetising I can think of. Call for a big basket of bread and a tomato salad, and an icy-cold rough Greek wine to wash it all down.

Serves 4

8 good-sized sardines (approx. 1 kg), cleaned and scaled
5 cm piece of root ginger, skin cut off and sliced
½ tsp saffron filaments
1 tsp fennel seeds
6 tbsp extra virgin olive oil
juice of ½ lemon
sea salt, black pepper

You can ask your fishmonger to scale the sardines for you, though they'll probably still need a good wash under the cold tap to completely remove them. Pat them dry.

Place the ginger, saffron and fennel seeds in a pestle and mortar and pound to a coarse paste. (Otherwise if you dice the ginger quite small you can whizz the ingredients in an electric coffee grinder.) Add 4 tablespoons of the olive oil and the lemon juice and stir to blend. Pour the marinade over the sardines in a large bowl and turn them, using your hands to coat them. Cover and chill for a couple of hours.

Just before grilling the sardines, baste the fish with any marinade that has run into the bottom of the bowl, and season on both sides with salt and pepper. Barbecue for about 5 minutes each side until golden and the fish comes away from the backbone of the fish.

Indoors

Try to use a non-stick griddle, and if it's single then you'll need to cook the sardines in two batches. Heat the griddle for several minutes over a medium heat, and grill the sardines for 4–6 minutes each side.

Green Peppercorn Tuna

Any cold leftover tuna makes a fine Niçoise salad, with salted anchovies, plum tomatoes, quarters of egg, black olives and some rocket. Alternatively, you could grill the tuna at the very beginning of the barbecue and throw the salad together as a starter. A 110–150 g steak is a good size if you are planning on having a mixed barbecue and want a little of everything. Otherwise you could grill 180–225 g steaks.

Serves 6

2 garlic cloves, peeled and coarsely chopped
1 tbsp green peppercorns
1 tbsp brandy
4 tbsp extra virgin olive oil
6 x 110–150 g tuna steaks, 2 cm thick (weight excluding skin and bones)
sea salt
25 g unsalted butter
600 g young spinach leaves
slim lemon wedges to serve

Place the garlic in a pestle and mortar and crush to a paste. Add the peppercorns and pound to break them up. Add the brandy and 2 tablespoons of the olive oil and blend. Use this paste to coat the tuna steaks in a large bowl, cover and chill for a couple of hours.

Reaquaint the tuna with any marinade that's run to the bottom of the bowl by turning it, and season on either side with salt. Barbecue for 5–6 minutes each side until golden and the fish feels firm when pressed. You should be able to see side-on when it is cooked, with just the faintest trace of pink in the centre, if you have a peek with a knife.

While the tuna is grilling, sauté the spinach; you will need to do this in two batches. Heat a tablespoon of olive oil and half the butter in a large frying pan over a high heat, add half the spinach, season with salt and sauté until it wilts. Transfer it to a bowl with any liquid given out and cook the remainder in the same fashion. Drain the spinach into a sieve, pressing out the excess water. The spinach can also be cooked in advance and reheated in a frying or saucepan. Serve the tuna steaks with the spinach and a lemon wedge or two.

Indoors

Heat a double-ridged griddle for several minutes over a medium heat, and cook for 5–7 minutes each side.

7.00pm

Crab Mayonnaise

Sitting round a table as the assembled company goes to work with a hammer, a pair of nutcrackers and a pick has a delicious sense of ritual. The anticipation of every sweet and hard-won morsel, the same pleasure as working your way from the outside of an artichoke to its heart, or prizing open mussels to extract the meat within, or scooping the flesh of an oyster clean of its shell with a piece of bread. Eating with our fingers is profoundly satisfying.

A freshly cooked crab eaten with homemade mayonnaise and crusty white bread in my book surpasses any other way of enjoying it, and in Normandy we're spoilt for choice. They come alive, thrashing and nipping, or freshly cooked that morning, common brown crabs as well as hairy-baked reddish spiders, which for many are the crème de la crème, and however tedious the task of extracting the meat, it is a worthwhile reward.

I always buy my crabs ready-cooked, and am too lily-livered to take on the task of dispatching them to the next world before plunging them into the pot. The season for both common brown and spider crabs is broadly March to September, peaking in June, while the cold water of the winter renders them sluggish. A cock if you can acquire one will be that much meatier than a hen, though the latter make good eating towards the autumn when they are rich with roe. It is perhaps inevitable that the claws of this ferocious warring crustacean should be that much more developed in the male than the female. The two are easily identified by their tail flaps, which are thin on the former and wide on the latter, where they are known as the apron. And a crab should be heavy, the weightier in the hand the more meat it will contain.

This may give you more crabmeat than you will need per person, but I don't see much point in going at anything smaller. And it's unlikely to go to waste, aside from a fresh crab sandwich, potted crab takes all of 10 minutes to prepare and is a rare treat (see page 26).

Serves 4

4 x 1 kg cooked crabs
crusty white bread to serve

White crabmeat is to be found in three places, the claws which give most generously, the spindly legs and cavities within the body. The brown meat, which is sometimes almost wet and at other times quite dry, mainly lines the upper shell.

First arm yourself with the necessary arsenal of equipment – a large bowl for the debris, a bread board, a rolling pin, a mallet or hammer, and a nutcracker (nothing too fancy here like a squirrel whose jaws pose as the tool, but rather a straightfor-ward pair shaped like pliers).

Remove the claw and three legs beside it on either side by breaking them off where they are attached to the body. Smash all three joints of the claws using the end of the rolling pin on a board. As crabs get larger the shells of their claws can get really quite tough, so you may need to be forceful. Picking off the broken shell, extract the crabmeat. Now crack the joints of the legs using the nutcracker and carefully pick out the meat inside. You will need to employ a crabpick or skewer here to extract every last bit. To my taste this is that much sweeter and finer in texture than the clawmeat.

And now for the messy bit. Insert a sharp knife between the upper shell and the body at the opposite end to the tail and lever the body section loose. Lift it free of the shell and pull it off. There will be a little brown meat clinging to the underside, spoon this out, then cut the body in half. You may find some more brown meat inside. Using a skewer pick out the white meat from the row of cavities in each half.

Now scrape out the brown meat lining the upper shell with a teaspoon. Pick the crabmeat over for any stray splinters, et voilà. You may have savoured the crabmeat along the way, otherwise you will by now have a lovely big pile of succulent white and creamy brown meat to settle to.

Mayonnaise

A spoonful of mustard in with the egg yolk not only stabilises mayonnaise but adds a welcome savour. Groundnut oil ensures the emulsion is creamy and light in texture, extra virgin olive oil would overwhelm the crab, and garlic would be a heresy.

1 medium organic egg yolk
1 tsp Dijon mustard
a pinch of fine sea salt
approx. 220 ml groundnut oil
a squeeze of lemon juice

Your egg yolk should be at room temperature. Place it in a bowl with the mustard and salt and whisk to blend them. Now add just a dribble of oil and whisk it in, then another and another until you can see the sauce thickening and you are confident the mayonnaise is taking.

You can now start to add the oil in bolder streams, whisking with each addition. By the end the mayonnaise should be so thick that it clings to the whisk and sits in mounds in the bowl. Season it with a squeeze of lemon juice. Cover and chill until required.

Crab Pick

This is a knitting needle-like device with a slim fork at one end and a shovel at the other, thin enough to enter the remotest cavities that are otherwise impossible to navigate. Failing these, an ordinary skewer will do.

Salad of Rump Steak with Carpaccio Dressing

Many of us fall shy of eating raw meat or carpaccio, and this plays it that much safer, without dispensing with the suave Harry's Bar dressing and Parmesan shavings. This is a little more dressing than you will need, but it's a good general salad dressing and will keep well for several days in the fridge.

Serves 4

750 g rump steak, cut 2 cm thick
   and trimmed of fat
extra virgin olive oil
sea salt, black pepper
75 g Parmesan shavings
1 tbsp capers, rinsed
rocket or other green leaves
   to serve
DRESSING
160 g mayonnaise, or 1 x quantity
   below*
3 tbsp milk
1 tsp Worcestershire sauce
1 tsp lemon juice

Heat a large frying pan over a high heat for several minutes. Brush the steak with olive oil on both sides and season. Fry 1 minute each side, then remove it to a plate and leave to cool. Place the cooled steak on a sheet of clingfilm and drizzle the meat juices over. Wrap it up and chill for at least 1 hour.

To make the dressing, whisk the mayonnaise with the milk, Worcestershire sauce and lemon juice in a bowl.

To serve the steak, thinly slice it at an angle across the grain and discard any fatty bits. Arrange the slices on four large plates. Drizzle a tablespoon of dressing over each serving, then place a pile of leaves in the centre and scatter over the Parmesan and the capers. Drizzle with another tablespoon of dressing. The salad can also be presented separately on a large platter or in a bowl, drizzled with the dressing.

* Homemade mayonnaise will of course be that much yummier than shopbought. Whisk 1 medium organic egg yolk with 1 teaspoon Dijon mustard and a pinch of fine sea salt. Now whisk in 100 ml groundnut oil and 120 ml extra virgin olive oil, a few drops at a time to begin with.

Grilled Chicken, Lentil and Lemon Salad

The pickled lemon provides a piquancy as only lemon can, with chilli and pine nuts in supporting roles. It's an all-in-one salad, just the ticket on a picnic. And it's smart enough for most occasions without being over-dressed.

Serves 4

75 g Puy lentils
50 g pine nuts
2 chicken breasts, skinned
extra virgin olive oil
sea salt, black pepper
200 g sugar snaps, topped and
   tailed
1 tbsp lemon juice
1 tbsp finely chopped Moroccan
   preserved lemon
1 heaped tsp finely chopped
   medium-hot red chilli
50 g baby spinach leaves

Bring a small pan of water to the boil, add the Puy lentils and simmer for 25–30 minutes until they are tender. Drain them into a sieve, and run cold water through them. At the same time, heat the oven to 180°C fan oven/190°C electric oven/Gas 5, arrange the pine nuts in a single layer in a small roasting dish or baking tray and toast in the oven for 7–9 minutes until lightly golden. Leave to cool.

Heat a ridged griddle over a medium heat for about 5 minutes. Cut out the tendon on the underside of each chicken breast, brush them with oil and season on both sides. Grill for about 4–6 minutes each side until the chicken feels firm when pressed and is golden and crusty at the edges. Leave it to cool, then slice it crosswise.

Bring a small pan of water to the boil, add the sugar snaps and cook for 1 minute, then drain into a sieve and run cold water through them.

Transfer the lentils to a large deep salad bowl. Add the lemon juice, 6 tablespoons of olive oil, the preserved lemon, chilli and a little salt, and mix. Arrange these in the bottom of a large deep salad bowl. Lay the sugar snaps on top of the lentils, then the chicken, the spinach and finally scatter over the pine nuts. Cover with clingfilm and set aside in a cool place.

Just before serving, gently toss the ingredients to coat them in the dressing.

Cold Lemon Chicken

A good eventer, as apt at a special occasion picnic as it is when friends are coming round to lunch with their children and you want to have everything done beforehand. You could slip a little double cream into the sauce if you want to enrich it, but I'm happy with its healthy profile, especially during the summer months.

Serves 4–6

POACHING LIQUOR

300 ml white wine

1 carrot, sliced

2 celery sticks, sliced

4 unpeeled garlic cloves, smashed

1 bay leaf

3 thyme sprigs

2 strips of lemon peel

CHICKEN

sea salt, black pepper

1 x 1.5 kg free-range chicken

300 g Greek yoghurt

juice of ½ lemon

2 tbsp coarsely chopped coriander

2 tbsp coarsely chopped flat-leaf parsley

2 spring onions, trimmed and sliced

Place all the ingredients for the poaching liquor with a teaspoon of salt in a casserole or saucepan that will hold the chicken snugly. Add 2–2.5 l of water, so that it will almost cover the bird when it is added. Bring to the boil then simmer over a medium-low heat for 10 minutes. Season the chicken all over, add it to the pot breast down, bring the liquor back to the boil, cover and cook over a low heat for 40 minutes. Don't worry if the tip of the chicken sticks out above the water, it will steam in the process. Remove the chicken and leave it to cool for 1 hour.

Discarding the skin, carve the chicken in the usual fashion and lay the meat out on a large platter or a shallow white gratin dish. Cover and reserve in a cool place. Add the carcass to the poaching liquor, bring to the boil and simmer over a low heat for 1 hour. Strain the liquor into a clean saucepan and reduce at a rapid boil to 300 ml of liquid. Transfer the stock to a measuring jug and leave to cool. Skim off the fat on the surface, then measure 150 ml into a bowl. The rest will turn into a delicious jellied stock, so chill or freeze it for later use.

Add the Greek yoghurt and lemon juice to the stock and whisk until smooth. Taste to check the seasoning, then pour over the reserved chicken. Cover and chill in the fridge for at least 1 hour; the sauce will thicken up as the stock jellies. Bring the chicken back up to room temperature for 30 minutes before eating. Scatter with the chopped coriander, parsley and spring onions and serve.

Chicken Tonnato

Classically prepared using veal, chicken makes a commendable understudy. It's a rich dish for when you feel like indulging, but all within a day's dieting if you're on the Atkins. In which case forgo the bread alongside and the tomato salad, which otherwise nestle naturally into the scheme of things. If you are reluctant to whisk up a homemade mayo, then substitute 250 ml of prepared mayonnaise.

Serves 4

4 chicken breasts, skinned and sliced into two thin escalopes
extra virgin olive oil
sea salt, black pepper
2 garlic cloves, peeled and finely sliced
4 x 5 cm rosemary sprigs
3 tbsp white wine
TO SERVE
small whole black olives, flat parsley leaves (coarsely chopped), anchovy fillets in oil (halved lengthwise)
SAUCE
1 medium organic egg yolk
1 tsp Dijon mustard
150 ml extra virgin olive oil
100 ml groundnut oil
1 x 180 g tin tuna in brine, drained and mashed with a fork
2 tbsp capers, chopped, plus 1 tsp, whole
6 anchovy fillets in oil, chopped

Heat the oven to 180°C fan oven/190°C electric oven/Gas 5. Lightly paint the chicken escalopes on both sides with olive oil and season them. Lay them in a tightly fitting single layer in a shallow casserole with the garlic, tucking in the rosemary. Pour over the wine, cover with foil and cook for 30 minutes.

Remove the foil, arrange the chicken on a large platter, discarding the rosemary, and decant the juices into a small saucepan. Simmer to reduce these to a couple of tablespoons of rich liquor. Pour over the chicken and leave to cool completely.

To make the sauce, prepare a mayonnaise by whisking the egg yolk with the Dijon mustard in a bowl, then very gradually whisk in the oils, a few drops at a time to begin with until the mayonnaise takes. By the end it should be too thick to whisk any further. Stir in the reserved liquor, then fold in the tuna, the chopped and whole capers, and anchovies.

When you are ready to eat, smooth the sauce over the chicken and decorate with a few olives, chopped parsley and slivers of anchovy.

Roasted Pepper, Rocket and Parmesan Salad

The pepper juices provide the basis of the dressing for the salad, with the weensiest drop of balsamic vinegar to offset their sweetness. The idea is to layer all the ingredients in a bowl, robust at the bottom and delicate at the top, which you can do hours in advance, then cover and forget about it.

Serves 4

4 red peppers, core, seeds and
    membranes removed
4–5 thyme sprigs
2 bay leaves
3 garlic cloves, peeled and sliced
6 tbsp extra virgin olive oil
sea salt, black pepper
1 tbsp balsamic vinegar
groundnut oil for shallow frying
2 large slices white bread, 1 cm
    thick, crusts removed and diced
100 g thinly shaved Parmesan
100 g rocket (preferably wild)

Heat the oven to 180°C fan oven/190°C electric oven/Gas 5. Cut each pepper into eight long strips and arrange in a crowded single layer in a baking dish or roasting pan. Tuck in the herbs and scatter over the garlic. Drizzle with 2 tablespoons of the olive oil and season with salt and pepper.

Roast for 45–50 minutes, stirring and basting at least twice to ensure the peppers emerge succulent and evenly singed at the edges. When they come out of the oven, drip over the vinegar and vaguely stir to mix it into the juices, and pour over the remaining 4 tablespoons of olive oil. Leave to cool.

In the meantime, heat about 7 mm of groundnut oil in a large frying pan over a medium heat until hot enough to immerse a cube of bread in bubbles. Add the bread cubes and fry, turning frequently, until evenly gold and crisp. Remove them using a slotted spoon and drain on a double thickness of kitchen paper. Leave to cool.

Transfer the peppers and juices to a large, deep salad bowl. Arrange the Parmesan on top, then the rocket and finally scatter over the croûtons. Cover with clingfilm and set aside in a cool place.

Just before serving, gently toss the salad ingredients together using two servers to coat them.

Tabbouleh with Green Mango

I love tart fruits tossed into tabbouleh, crisp strips of unripe mango and in the winter months the seeds from half a pomegranate too. Your parsley needs to be young and tender, so avoid any overgrown bunches.

Serves 4

1½ tbsp bulgar wheat
100g bunch of flat-leaf parsley,
    tough stalks removed, rinsed
    and shaken dry
1 handful of mint leaves, chopped
2 spring onions, trimmed, finely
    sliced and then chopped
½ tsp sea salt
½ tsp freshly ground black
    pepper
3 tbsp extra virgin olive oil
2 tbsp lemon juice
1 green or unripe mango

Rinse the bulgar wheat in a fine-mesh sieve and leave it on the side to absorb the remaining moisture. Chop the parsley by holding the bunch and slicing from leaf to stalk. Combine the parsley, mint and spring onions in a bowl, add the seasoning, the oil and lemon juice and combine. Mix in the bulgar.

Slice the skin off the mango, and cut off the two flat sides of flesh. Thinly slice these into long strips and toss into the tabbouleh. Transfer the salad to a clean bowl or plate, and serve as soon as possible.

Should you have any tabbouleh left over, seal the surface with a lettuce leaf and cover with clingfilm.

Chicory Salad with Parma Ham

In Normandy the supermarkets sell big bags of Belgian endive, and they keep so well I always have a supply in the bottom of the fridge. They relish a sweet mustardy dressing with some chopped flat-leaf parsley thrown in. At this time of year when we are flush for green leaves, you can bulk them out with whatever's on offer. And should red trevisse prove elusive, then I would up the Belgian endive quotient and throw in a few radicchio slivers for good measure. But only a few, it is less predictable in its bitterness.

Serves 4

DRESSING
1 tbsp cider vinegar
7 tbsp groundnut oil
2 tbsp Dijon mustard
1½ tbsp golden caster sugar
sea salt, black pepper
SALAD
400 g Belgian endive
400 g red trevisse
6 tbsp coarsely chopped flat-leaf parsley
12 slices Parma or other air-dried ham

Whisk all the ingredients for the dressing in a bowl to a thick creamy emulsion. If making this dressing in advance, you may need to give it a quick whisk just before serving, but it should hold for several hours at least.

To serve the salad, slice the root end off the bulbs of endive and red trevisse, discarding any damaged outer leaves. Separate the remaining leaves – given how tightly closed the heads are, I tend not to wash them. Place the leaves in a large bowl, drizzling over the dressing as evenly as possible, then toss to coat the leaves. You may find it easier to dive in there with your hands given how voluptuously thick it is. Toss in the parsley, then pile the leaves on six plates, draping the slices of ham by the side.

Mushroom, Parmesan and Chive Salad

I can't be alone in dipping into a punnet of button mushrooms as a favourite crudité, we get through many more raw than cooked in this house.

Serves 4

350 g button mushrooms, trimmed and finely sliced
3 tbsp extra virgin olive oil, plus a little extra to serve
3 tbsp groundnut oil
a squeeze of lemon juice
sea salt, black pepper
2 tbsp finely chopped chives, plus a few extra to serve
75 g finely shaved Parmesan or pecorino

Toss the mushrooms in a large bowl with the oils to coat them. Squeeze over a little lemon juice, season and toss again, then mix in the chives. Divide the mushrooms among four plates and pile the Parmesan or pecorino on top. Drizzle over a little more olive oil, scatter over a few more chives and serve straightaway.

Spinach and Redcurrant Salad

The sharpness of redcurrants enlivens salad leaves in the same way as lemon juice, with a little sweetness thrown in. And in winter redcurrants give way to pomegranate seeds.

Serves 4

young spinach leaves to feed 4
extra virgin olive oil
lemon juice
sea salt
4 spring onions, trimmed and
   finely sliced diagonally
50 g redcurrants

Pick over and wash the spinach leaves in a sink of cold water, then remove and either spin them in a salad spinner, or failing that place them in a clean tea towel, gather up the corners and give it a jolly good shake outside until the showers die out. Place the spinach in a bowl.

To serve the salad, drizzle over a little olive oil, and gently toss using your hands to coat the leaves. Now squeeze over a little lemon juice, scrunch over a few crystals of sea salt, scatter over half the spring onion slices and toss again. Taste a leaf to make sure the leaves are correctly dressed, then scatter over the remaining spring onions and the redcurrants and serve.

Lamb's Lettuce with Walnut Cream and Lardons

Oh that we had the same respect for salad leaves as the French. Big blowsy escaroles, frisée and large punnets of lamb's lettuce are the norm, never more delicious than when offset by crisp, salty lardons.

**Serves 2 as a main course,
4 as a starter**

150 g lamb's lettuce
75 g crème fraîche
1 tbsp walnut oil
½ tsp Dijon mustard
a few drops of cider vinegar
sea salt, black pepper
200 g unsmoked lardons*
30 g shelled walnuts, broken into
   nibs

Providing there are no roots attached to the lamb's lettuce, there is no need to separate the leaves out from every small plant. As they become bigger, however, it is a good idea to twist off the base where the leaves are attached. Give the leaves a good wash in a sink of cold water. A salad spinner comes in handy for drying it, otherwise gently pat it dry between two clean tea towels and place it in a large salad bowl.

To make the dressing, whisk the crème fraîche with the walnut oil, mustard, cider vinegar and a little seasoning in a small bowl.

Heat a large frying pan over a low heat, add the lardons and once they begin to render their fat, turn the heat up and sauté, stirring frequently until evenly golden and crisp. Remove with a slotted spoon to a small bowl, and add the walnuts to the pan. Sauté these for a couple of minutes, stirring constantly until lightly golden, then toss with the bacon. The salad can be prepared to this point in advance. There again, the bacon and walnuts can also be served warm.

Spoon the dressing over the salad leaves and scatter the bacon and walnuts over the top. Serve straightaway, either tossing the salad first or leaving everyone to do their own.

* Lardons are cut more thickly than bacon, a squared strip just under a centimetre wide. Failing these, streaky bacon will do.

Salmon Niçoise

Given the scarcity of fresh tuna, and that tinned doesn't quite make the grade, there are occasions when we need to look elsewhere for the wherewithal for a Niçoise salad. Grilled salmon still produces a winning combination. The ingredients are layered and tossed at the last minute, which means you can pack 'n go whenever the moment takes you.

Serves 4

4 medium eggs

2 x 200 g salmon fillets, skinned

extra virgin olive oil

sea salt, black pepper

1½ tbsp lemon juice

2 tbsp capers, rinsed

4 tbsp coarsely chopped flat-leaf parsley

1 fennel bulb, outer sheaves and shoots removed, halved and thinly sliced

4 salted anchovy fillets, rinsed and halved lengthwise

3 Little Gem lettuces, outer leaves removed

100 g radishes, ends removed and thinly sliced

Bring a medium-size pan of water to the boil, add the eggs and boil for 7–8 minutes to leave them slightly wet in the centre, then drain and cool in cold water. Shell and quarter the eggs, and arrange them on a plate. Cover them with clingfilm and set aside in a cool place.

Heat a ridged griddle over a medium heat for about 5 minutes. Brush the salmon fillets on both sides with oil and season them. Grill for about 3 minutes each side until golden and the flesh feels firm when pressed. Remove to a plate and leave to cool.

Whisk 6 tablespoons of olive oil, the lemon juice, some seasoning and the capers in a large deep salad bowl. Coarsely flake the salmon and drop it into the dressing, scatter over the parsley and turn to coat everything. Scatter the fennel over, and lay the anchovy fillets on top. Slice the Little Gems across about 1 cm thick, discarding the end slices, and arrange in a layer. Finally, scatter over the radishes. Cover with clingfilm and set aside in a cool place.

To serve, gently toss the salad ingredients to coat them, divide among plates and tuck the egg quarters in here and there.

Panzanella

One to ponder when the thermometer tops thirty degrees and even food has to present itself as being cooling before you can muster the energy to eat it. Vegetarians can simply omit the anchovies.

Serves 4

3 yellow peppers, core and seeds removed and cut into thin strips

extra virgin olive oil

sea salt, black pepper

500 g cherry or baby plum tomatoes, halved

½ tsp caster sugar

1 tbsp red wine vinegar

½ round loaf of coarse-textured white bread, crusts removed and torn into 1–2 cm chunks

8 anchovies in oil, slit in half lengthwise

2 tbsp capers, rinsed

100 g green and black olives, pitted and halved

a handful of basil leaves, torn in half

Heat the oven to 180°C fan oven/190°C electric oven/Gas 5. Arrange the peppers in a roasting dish in a crowded layer, drizzle over 2 tablespoons of olive oil and season them. Roast for 40–45 minutes until caramelised at the edges, stirring halfway through. Remove and leave to cool in the dish.

At the same time, place the tomatoes in a bowl, toss with a level teaspoon of salt and the sugar and set aside for 30 minutes. Drain the tomatoes into a sieve, collecting the juice in a bowl below. Add 6 tablespoons of oil and the vinegar. Place the bread in a bowl, sprinkle over the dressing and set aside until it has been absorbed.

Toss the tomatoes, peppers and bread with the anchovies, capers, olives and basil in a large bowl. Cover with clingfilm and set aside for about 1 hour for the bread to soften further, then give the salad a stir. The salad will be good for some hours. Drizzle over another 2 tablespoons of oil just before serving.

Pomegranate, Feta and Herb Salad

Come late summer the Middle Eastern delis local to us in London have the most alluring huge dark red pomegranates. And colour is everything with these fruits: the outside is the promise of the colour within, the size some indication of how juicy the seeds will be. Here cubes of feta sit marinading in olive oil and lemon juice, before being acquainted with a leafy mass of herbs, some pomegranate seeds scattered over.

Serves 4

1 pomegranate, halved

400 g feta, cut into 1 cm dice

6 tbsp extra virgin olive oil

1½ tbsp lemon juice

1 red onion, peeled, halved and finely sliced

50 g mixture of mint, coriander and flat-leaf parsley leaves

Working over a bowl, extract the pomegranate seeds by pressing down on the skin, effectively inverting each half until you can pop the seeds out. Remove any white pith from the bowl.

Place the feta in the bottom of a large deep salad bowl, pour over the olive oil and lemon juice, there is no need for additional salt and pepper. Scatter the onion on top, separating out the strands. Next arrange the herb leaves in a layer, and then finally scatter over the pomegranate seeds. Cover with clingfilm and set aside in a cool place until ready to eat.

Just before serving, plunge a couple of spoons into the bottom of the bowl and gently toss the salad, turning it just a few times to avoid breaking the feta up.

Warm Potato Salad

A good one to plump for when you can't make up your mind whether to enjoy your new potatoes boiled or in a salad, it's halfway between the two, potato slices dressed with a warm vinaigrette.

Serves 6

SALAD
extra virgin olive oil
½ head of garlic
2 x 7 cm rosemary sprigs
3 thyme sprigs
sea salt
750 g small new potatoes,
    scrubbed or peeled as necessary
3 shallots, peeled and finely
    chopped
2 tbsp finely chopped chives
SHERRY VINAIGRETTE
½ tsp Dijon mustard
black pepper
1 tbsp sherry
½ tbsp sherry vinegar
3 tbsp grapeseed oil

Place a litre of water in a medium-size saucepan with 3 tablespoons of olive oil, garlic, rosemary, thyme and some sea salt. Bring to the boil, then add the potatoes, bring back to the boil and simmer over a medium-low heat for approximately 15 minutes until just tender when pierced with a knife. Remove from the heat and leave to cool. Drain the potatoes, discarding the garlic and herbs, and slice them. Place in a bowl, cover and set aside.

Whisk the mustard and some salt and pepper with the sherry and sherry vinegar in a bowl, then whisk in the grapeseed oil and 2 tablespoons of olive oil until the dressing emulsifies. If preparing the dressing in advance, rewhisk it before serving.

Just before serving, place the vinaigrette and the shallots in a large saucepan, and arrange the potatoes on top. Gently warm the potatoes through, using a spatula to carefully turn them once or twice. Remove from the heat and stir in the chives.

New Potatoes with Garlic and Yoghurt

Unless your new potatoes are genuine earlies and can be scrubbed clean of most of their papery skins, they will need peeling. For an alternative thrill you could use blue potatoes, whose mealiness goes well with a creamy dressing.

Serves 6

1 head of garlic, cloves separated
    and peeled
2 bay leaves
3 tbsp extra virgin olive oil
sea salt
750 g new potatoes, scrubbed and
    halved if large
250 g Greek yoghurt
squeeze of lemon juice
hot paprika*

Place the garlic, bay leaves, olive oil, 500 ml of water and a little salt in a large saucepan. Bring to the boil, then add the potatoes, bring back to the boil, cover and simmer for 15 minutes or until the potatoes are tender when pierced with a knife. Transfer the potatoes to a bowl to cool using a slotted spoon, leaving the garlic and bay leaves in the liquor. Turn the heat up, bring back to the boil and cook to reduce to several tablespoons of liquid. Add the bay leaves to the potatoes, and using a potato masher, mash the garlic into the juices. Transfer to a bowl and leave to cool, then whisk this into the yoghurt with a squeeze of lemon juice. Taste for seasoning and add a little more salt if necessary.

Once the potatoes are cool, arrange them on a plate or dish, with the bay leaves. Spoon the sauce over and scatter with paprika.

* Spanish delis sell both hot and sweet paprika, but any will do.

THE BIG EVENT

The two biggest annual events on the culinary calendar that few of us escape are Christmas and Easter, both of which we spend as a family at our farmhouse in Normandy. But old habits die hard, and I tend to transport most of our British traditions with us (the French do many things better than we do but it doesn't run to Christmas dinner). Plumping that out with local ingredients, I reckon we get the best of both worlds.

I've always loved Christmas dinner in all its traditional glory, somehow the 'alternatives', which on occasions I've tried, don't quite do it. Ringing the changes with a different bird or stuffing is one thing, a Galician fish stew is another. And to eat a particular line-up of foods or menu once a year is hardly overdoing it. That said, we could afford to make a few choices of 'either or' instead of having both, whether it's sausagemeat stuffing, chipolatas AND bacon rolls, bread AND cranberry sauce, parsnips AND roast potatoes, all of which double up, we could with serious self-control agree to just the one. But then granny comes along and says she wants the other, so it's back to square one. Still, no harm in starting out with good intentions.

Equally, if you number four or less, rather than risk a freezerful of leftover turkey, there are a number of smaller birds that can be every bit as much of a treat, and there's no reason why they shouldn't come with a host of trimmings, which for most of us are as important as the bird itself. It's the tradition of dressing the bird so popular across the Atlantic, a roast duck served with fried black pudding and apple, or quail with wild mushrooms and sausages. A grouse is famously dressed with bread sauce, game crumbs and a bunch of watercress, a great way of dishing up any roast bird including a turkey.

Christmas pud I prefer to save for later in the day if we've eaten lunch, or have it on Boxing Day, and push out a boozey trifle instead. And for anyone too full for that, I'd suggest a sliver of Roquefort with some walnuts and a small glass of sticky sweet wine, or a big bowl of lychees.

A ham for me is as essential to the celebrations as the tree and the turkey. Plan it right and it can span several days, first eaten hot with a parsley or Cumberland sauce, and thereafter cold with a myriad of pickles, mustardy sauces and spiced fruits. The third delight is the stock left over from boiling the ham or made with the proceeds of the bone on which it was cooked. With a few modest vegetables, some pearl barley and strips of ham you have day three of the ham feast.

Like Clockwork

Most of us fret about Christmas dinner, unsurprisingly if we've been counting down since September. It all stems from that first fateful conversation with family members about 'what are you doing for Christmas?' Last year I made it through to October but that was exceptional. This year as I write it's July and I've already had it. And on from there it's only a matter of time before you start discussing what you're going to eat, or who's going to do what. Any event with that kind of anticipation can't afford to simply be good, it has to be fantastic.

But if you think of it as a lavish Sunday lunch it isn't quite so daunting. And there are all manner of little jobs that can be done in advance. I like to have a list to hand, so that I don't feel as though I'm perpetually in a state of dress rehearsal trying to remember what to do when.

The more that can be done on Christmas Eve, the less time you have to spend in the kitchen on Christmas Day. A trifle can be prepared the day before so all you have to do is apply any last-minute touches. Little eats like roasted nuts, too, can be assembled in advance, as can the stuffing, the cranberry sauce, and to an extent the bread sauce. And the sprouts can be peeled.

Christmas Day

The classic line-up is roast turkey, stuffing, bread sauce, sprouts with chestnuts, chipolatas and roast tatties. Assuming you are planning on eating at lunchtime and will start grazing with a glass of bubbly around 1 pm, the morning can be arranged as follows. If you're planning on eating in the evening then obviously the preparation can be spread out over the day.

Early Morning – **7 or 8 am**

1. Remove the turkey from the fridge, and leave it covered to come up to room temperature. If you have a particularly large turkey, you can always leave it in the garage or in an unheated room overnight, providing it is well protected and there are no cats or other animals that can get to it.

Mid Morning – **10 am**

1. If your turkey is an average size of about 6 kg then you need to allow a total cooking and resting time of 3 hours. Stuff and prepare it for the oven.
2. Peel the potatoes and reserve in water.
3. Boil and drain the sprouts. Fry the bacon and chestnuts.

Late Morning – **11 am**

1. Put the turkey in to roast, or according to the cooking times set out in the chart below.
2. Finish preparing the bread sauce, cover the surface with clingfilm and leave on top of the stove.

Midday – **12 pm**

1. Parboil the potatoes and pop them into the oven at 12.45 am.
2. Turn the turkey breast up to brown at 12.50 pm.

Forty minutes before lunch – **1.20 pm**

1. Pop the chipolatas into the oven; they will take 30–40 minutes to cook.

Twenty minutes before lunch – **1.40 pm**

1. Take the turkey out of the oven, transfer it to a warm carving plate and leave to rest for 20 minutes, loosely covered with foil.
2. Make the gravy and finish cooking the brussel sprouts.
3. A few minutes before carving, heat a large plate for the carved turkey. Once the sausages and potatoes come out of the oven, pop the dinner plates in for a few minutes. If you are serving the vegetables separately at the table, providing your serving dishes are heatproof, these too can be included.
4. Rewarm the bread sauce.

Roast Turkey

Serves 8–10

1 x 6 kg turkey
groundnut oil
approx. 1.2 kg stuffing
sea salt, black pepper

Heat the oven to 200°C fan oven/220°C electric oven/Gas 7. Fill the main cavity of the turkey with the stuffing, packing it loosely, and leaving half the cavity empty but plugging the opening. You can also stuff the neck end, using a different stuffing if you like or half an onion with a couple of sprigs of thyme or rosemary and a piece of lemon zest. Brush the turkey all over with groundnut oil, then rub salt and pepper into the skin.

Set the turkey breast down in a large oiled roasting tray. Protect the wings and legs with foil to prevent them from drying out. Place the turkey in the oven and roast for 30 minutes, then turn down to 180°C fan oven/190°C electric oven/Gas 5 and continue roasting for the times suggested below. Baste periodically with the juices in the roasting tray. About 30–45 minutes before the bird is cooked, turn it breast uppermost so that it can brown. To check if the bird is cooked through, insert a skewer into the thickest part of the thigh – the juices should run out clear. If not, give the bird another 10 minutes, then check again. Remove the turkey to a carving plate and leave it to rest for around 20 minutes while you make the gravy.

Recommended Roasting Times
Allow extra time if using aluminium foil
For a bird up to 5 kg allow 15 minutes per 500 g
For a bird over 5 kg allow 13 minutes per 500 g

Sage and Onion Stuffing

Makes 600 ml stuffing,
serves approx. 4

50 g unsalted butter
2 large onions, peeled, quartered
   and thinly sliced
1 tbsp finely sliced sage
finely grated zest of 1 lemon, plus
   a squeeze of lemon juice
100 g fresh white breadcrumbs
sea salt, black pepper

No other stuffing has been quite as abused as sage and onion. 'Just add water' to a mixture of dried breadcrumbs, onion and sage out of a packet and your stuffing will dominate the entire meal. This is gently sweet and fragrant and perfumes the kitchen as the bird roasts. You can add the turkey liver (see Black Pudding and Apple Stuffing, opposite) if you have it.

Melt half the butter in a large frying pan over a medium heat, add the onions and sweat for 10–15 minutes until lightly golden and caramelised, stirring frequently. Stir in the sage just before the end, then remove from the heat and add the lemon zest, a generous squeeze of lemon juice and the remaining butter. Once this has melted, stir in the breadcrumbs and season with salt and pepper.

Black Pudding and Apple Stuffing

Over the years this has emerged as a favourite way of stuffing a turkey, goose or guinea fowl. As well as black pudding and apple being a perfect match for each other, it does away with the need for additional sausages, unless of course you fancy both.

Makes 600 ml stuffing, serves approx. 4

50 g unsalted butter

6 shallots, peeled and finely chopped

3 eating apples, peeled, cored and cut into 1 cm dice

250 g black pudding, skin removed and cut into 1 cm dice

turkey liver, membranes removed and sliced (optional)

3 tbsp Madeira, brandy or Calvados

sea salt, black pepper

1 tsp thyme leaves (optional)

1 bay leaf

Heat half the butter in a large frying pan over a medium heat, add the shallots and sweat for a couple of minutes until softened. Add the apples and continue to sauté for 5–6 minutes, stirring occasionally, until softened and starting to colour. Transfer the apple and shallots to a bowl. Add the remaining butter to the pan, and the black pudding and turkey liver if you have it, and sauté for a couple of minutes until they change colour, again stirring occasionally. Add this to the apple and shallots. Pour the Madeira or brandy into the pan and simmer to reduce by half, scraping up any sticky bits, then mix this in with the stuffing. Season with salt and pepper, and stir in the thyme, if using. Add the bay leaf and leave to cool. Cover and chill until required. It can be prepared a day in advance.

Squash Purée

This will banish any notion of stuffing being dry or heavy, it's sweet, buttery and succulent, and doubles up as a vegetable to boot.

Makes 600 ml stuffing, serves approx. 4

1 x 1 kg butternut squash

50 g unsalted butter

1 large onion, peeled and finely chopped

3 garlic cloves, peeled and finely chopped

finely grated zest of 1 lemon, plus a squeeze of juice

sea salt, black pepper

Cut the skin off the butternut squash, remove the seeds and slice it or cut into wedges.

Place in a steamer set over boiling water in the base of the pan, cover and cook for 20–25 minutes until tender. You may have a dedicated steamer, I use a petal steamer inside a large saucepan.

In the meantime, heat the butter in a large frying pan over a medium heat, add the onion and sweat for 8–10 minutes until nicely golden, stirring frequently. Add the garlic a minute or two before the end.

Drain the liquid from the squash pan, remove the steamer insert and reduce the squash to a coarse purée using a potato masher. Mix in the contents of the frying pan, the lemon zest and some salt and pepper, and enliven with a few drops of lemon juice. Set aside to cool, then cover and chill until required. The stuffing can be made a day in advance.

Sausage, Prune and Chestnut Stuffing

Sausagemeat stuffing works better out of the bird than in, the top of the balls turning deliciously golden and caramelised. I find the best bet for sausagemeat is to buy a really good pork banger and remove the skins.

Serves 4

75 g prunes, stoned and
    presoaked, finely chopped
1 scant tbsp brandy
50 g unsalted butter
75 g chestnuts, cooked, peeled
    and finely chopped
sea salt, black pepper
450 g sausagemeat
2 medium egg yolks
2 tbsp coarsely chopped flat-leaf
    parsley
180 ml rich chicken stock

Place the prunes in a large bowl, pour over the brandy and leave for at least 30 minutes for the fruit to absorb it. Melt half the butter in a small frying pan over a medium heat, add the chestnuts, season and fry for several minutes, stirring frequently until lightly golden. Add these to the bowl with the prunes.

Break up and add the sausagemeat and work the ingredients together – you can use your hands for this. Add the egg yolks and mix in, and then add the parsley.

Shape heaped tablespoons of the mixture into balls the size of a plum and arrange in a shallow ovenproof dish, spaced about 1 cm apart. The stuffing can be prepared to this point several hours in advance, in which case cover and set it aside in a cool place.

Heat the oven to 190°C fan oven/200°C electric oven/Gas 6 if not already hot. If you are roasting a turkey, turn the oven up after you take it out to rest; this will allow you 20 minutes of resting and about 10 of carving in which to cook the stuffing. Otherwise gauge the cooking time according to what you are roasting. Pour the stock into the base of the baking dish to a depth of a few millimetres, dot the stuffing balls with the remaining butter and roast for 30–35 minutes until lightly golden.

Minimal Stuffing

Although we traditionally stuff turkeys, there are no rules that you have to. Simply place a halved onion, some strips of lemon zest pared with a potato peeler, and a few sprigs of thyme and rosemary into the bird's cavity.

Leftover Stuffing

La Trompette in Chiswick, West London, dishes up a Scotch egg that would have us all moving north of the border if it was more ubiquitous. A soft runny yolk within its sausagemeat casing, that spills as you cut into it, and a leafy pile of salad. This is the deconstructed version.

Serves 4

400 g leftover stuffing
mixture of rocket leaves,
    coriander,dill and parsley sprigs
white wine vinegar
4 large eggs
groundnut oil
lemon juice
sea salt

Fill your largest saucepan with water and bring it to the boil. Slice the stuffing and arrange it on four large plates. Place the salad leaves in a large bowl. Add a good slug of white wine vinegar to the boiling water. Now turn the heat down and keep the water at a trembling simmer while the eggs are poaching.

Break the eggs one at a time into a teacup (or use 4 teacups). Gently stir the water into a whirlpool using a large spoon and drop the eggs into it. They will immediately sink to the bottom of the pan leaving strands of white floating. After about 4 minutes remove them using a slotted spoon, trimming off the tendrils of white against the side of the saucepan.

Place the poached eggs on top of the stuffing. Toss the leaves with just enough oil to coat them, a few drops of lemon juice and a pinch of sea salt and divide between the plates. Serve straightaway.

Roast Goose with Prune and Apple Stuffing

Whenever I choose goose over turkey for Christmas dinner, I stand around thinking that I must have forgotten something. The sheer opulence of its crackly parchment-crisp skin and succulent dark flesh does away with the need for a host of trimmings. I enjoy it best stuffed with prunes and apples, some crispy potatoes and a pile of watercress or other green leaves to the side. And maybe a little bread sauce (page 143) thrown in.

Although goose has a reputation for being meaner than a turkey, I find a 4.4 kg bird does nicely for six, and the average oven will accommodate up to 5.3 kg. One of the great joys in roasting a goose is the copious golden fat given off, which makes for the best ever roast and sauté potatoes, not to mention fried eggs. Any fat that comes separately with the giblets, or that you remove from the bird's cavity, can also be put to use. Gently heat it in a small frying pan or saucepan, strain and bottle it in a wide-necked pot such as a jam or kilner jar. It keeps almost indefinitely in the fridge.

Order of Work
The only difference in the timetable if you are having goose instead of turkey is to prepare the gravy in advance of cooking the bird (see page 140).

Serves 6

PRUNE AND APPLE STUFFING
250 g stoned prunes (no need to soak)
225 ml port
25 g unsalted butter, clarified
450 g Bramley apples, peeled, cored and diced
1 tbsp caster sugar
GOOSE
1 x 4.4 kg goose, with giblets
sea salt, black pepper
watercress to serve 6

Place the prunes in a small saucepan with the port. Bring to the boil, then simmer over a low heat for 15–20 minutes until all but a tablespoon of syrupy liquid remains, stirring towards the end. At the same time, heat the butter in a large frying pan over a high heat, add the apples and sauté for about 5 minutes, stirring frequently, until lightly coloured and just beginning to lose their shape. Sprinkle over the sugar and cook for a minute or so longer until you have the beginnings of an apple sauce, with whole pieces still evident. Combine the prunes and residual syrup with the apples in a bowl, cover with a plate or clingfilm and leave to cool. Chill if preparing more than a few hours in advance of using.

Heat the oven to 200°C fan oven/220°C electric oven/Gas 7. Place a rack in a baking tray that contains a few millimetres of water in the bottom. Place two large sheets of foil on top of the rack, overlapping widthwise, and pierce so that the fat can drain through. Remove any surplus fat at the entrance to the body cavity of the goose. Leaving the bird trussed, spoon the stuffing into the cavity, pushing it well back.

Prick the skin and fat gland under each wing, and season it all over. Cover the legs with some of the surplus fat and then wrap them in foil. Place the goose breast-side up on the foil and wrap it into a parcel.

Cook the goose for 17 minutes per 500 g, so allow 2½ hours for a 4.4 kg goose. Roast for 30 minutes, then turn the oven down to 180°C fan oven/190°C electric oven/Gas 5. A third of the way into cooking, unwrap and remove the foil, leaving the legs covered. Drain off any excess fat, reserving it for later use, turn the goose breast-down and roast for another third of the time. Turn the goose breast-up again, draining off any more excess fat and removing the foil from the legs, and roast for the remainder of the cooking time. Transfer the goose to a warm serving plate, loosely cover with foil and leave to rest for 30 minutes. Carve and serve with a spoonful of the stuffing, and a pile of watercress to the side. Serve the gravy and any bread sauce separately at the table.

Gravy for the Goose

Whereas we usually base gravy on the roasting juices in the bottom of the pan, with goose it is better to play safe and prepare it using the giblets. You can include the goose liver in this line-up, though in Normandy my French countryman friend Georges Corniguel, who rears stunningly good geese does things the Gallic way and saves the liver for the next day to have in a warm salad.

**goose gizzard, neck bone and
    heart**
1 tbsp goose fat or groundnut oil
sea salt, black pepper
400 ml chicken stock
100 ml port
1 tsp plain flour, sifted

To prepare the giblet stock, heat the oven to 200°C fan oven/220°C electric oven/Gas 7. If buying your goose from a friendly butcher, ask him to chop up the gizzard and neck bone for you. Otherwise, chop the heart and place it together with the whole gizzard and neck bone in a medium roasting dish. Drizzle over a tablespoon of goose fat or groundnut oil, season with salt and pepper and roast for 20 minutes until lightly coloured. Place the giblets in a small saucepan with the chicken stock. Bring to a simmer, skim the surface if necessary, cover and simmer over a very low heat for 30 minutes, then strain.

At the same time, skim any excess fat from the giblet roasting dish, add the port and simmer on the hob until well reduced.

To finish making the gravy, reheat the giblet pan juices, stir in the flour, dispersing any lumps with the back of the spoon, and once this is seething, gradually stir in the stock. Simmer the gravy long and hard enough for it to amalgamate into a smooth sauce. Taste and season if necessary. Pass through a sieve into a clean saucepan, cover and set aside. Reheat just before eating, and pour into a jug to serve.

Roast Duck with Black Pudding and Apple

The surest way of ensuring a crisp golden skin to offset against the creamy black pudding and fried apple is a long slow roasting. I usually serve baked potatoes with this which cook better at a lower temperature than roast ones. And farmed duck is preferable to wild here.

Serves 4

ROAST DUCK

1 x 2.5 kg duck, oven-ready
sea salt
**a handful each of sage leaves,
    oregano and thyme sprigs**
DRESSING
3 tbsp rendered duck fat
**2 eating apples, peeled, cored and
    sliced**
8 x 1 cm slices black pudding
watercress to serve 4

Heat the oven to 180°C fan oven/190°C electric oven/Gas 5. Prick the duck skin all over with a skewer and generously rub with salt. Stuff the cavity of the duck with the herbs. Place the duck breast-side up on a rack within a roasting tin and roast for 1 hour. Drain the fat into a bowl, turn the oven down to 150°C fan oven/160°C electric oven/Gas 3 and roast for a further 1½ hours, draining it a second time halfway through. Remove the duck to a warm plate, loosely cover it with foil and leave to rest for 20 minutes while you make the gravy.

While the duck is resting, heat 2 tablespoons of the duck fat in a large frying pan over a highish heat and sauté the apples for about 6 minutes, turning them now and again until golden on both sides. Transfer these to a warm plate, add another tablespoon of duck fat to the pan and colour the black pudding slices for about 1 minute on either side. Serve the roast duck and gravy with the black pudding and apple, and a pile of watercress.

Roast Turkey Breast Stuffed with Leeks and Porcini

This is more like a Sunday joint, a quieter affair than a whole roast turkey, but just as worthy of a celebration. Turkey breasts come off the bone and on, when they are known as a crown roast. I like to buy mine boned and rolled and to stuff it myself.

Serves 6

STUFFING

115 g unsalted butter

5 leeks (600 g trimmed weight), sliced

sea salt, black pepper

40 g dried porcini, soaked in 300 ml boiling water for 30 minutes

2 tbsp chopped flat-leaf parsley

finely grated zest of 1 lemon, plus a squeeze of juice

80 g unsweetened brioche

2 medium egg yolks

300 ml rich chicken stock

TURKEY AND GRAVY

1.5 kg turkey breast, boned and rolled

5 rashers unsmoked streaky bacon, rind removed

6 tbsp port

1 tbsp cranberry sauce

To make the stuffing melt 50 g of the butter in a large frying pan over a medium heat, add the leeks, season them and sweat for 12–15 minutes until soft and lightly coloured, stirring occasionally. Transfer them to a bowl. Drain and finely chop the porcini, reserving the liquor. Stir the mushrooms into the leeks together with the parsley, lemon zest and juice. Leaving the crusts on the brioche, reduce to fine crumbs in a food processor then stir these into the stuffing, and then add the egg yolks and blend using a wooden spoon. The stuffing can be prepared to this point several hours in advance, in which case cover and set it aside in a cool place.

Heat the oven to 190°C fan oven/200°C electric oven/Gas 6. Snip the string binding the turkey breast and slip the ties off. Lay the bacon rashers in a row on the chopping board about 2 cm apart, and lay the turkey breast skin-side down on top. Open out the pocket of the breast and stuff with about a third of the stuffing. Bring the bacon slices up around the sides then tie it up again, wrapping a piece of string around each rasher of bacon to secure it. Season it on both sides with salt and pepper and place skin-side up in a roasting dish that holds it snugly. Dot with 50 g of the butter, pour over the reserved mushroom soaking liquor and roast for 18 minutes per 500 g (including the weight of the stuffing). Baste the joint a couple of times in the course of roasting, adding a drop more water or chicken stock to the roasting pan towards the end if the juices get too syrupy.

Shape the remaining stuffing into balls the size of a plum and arrange in a shallow ovenproof dish, spaced about 1 cm apart. Pour half the chicken stock into the base of the baking dish to a depth of a few millimetres, dot the stuffing balls with the remaining 15 g of butter and roast for 30–35 minutes until lightly golden (i.e. put it in the oven about 10 minutes before the turkey is ready to allow for resting time).

Once the turkey is cooked, transfer the joint and any stuffing on the bottom of the pan to a warm carving dish, loosely cover with foil and leave to rest for 20 minutes. Skim any excess fat from the roasting pan, add the port and simmer to reduce by half, scraping up all the sticky bits. Stir in the cranberry sauce and once the jelly has melted blend in the stock. Simmer for a few minutes until it tastes nice and rich. Taste and add a little more seasoning if necessary. Carve the turkey, adding any juices given out to the gravy.

If you prefer you could make all the stuffing into balls, in which case dot with 25 g of butter and pour over 200 ml of stock.

Roast Quail with Wild Mushrooms, Puréed Beetroot and Sausages

The crimson beetroot purée, delectable with the wild mushrooms, guarantees a festive edge. This is another good one for when you're two, three or four and feel like spoiling yourself.

Serves 4

DRESSING
350 g cooked and peeled beetroot
40 g unsalted butter
sea salt, black pepper
3 tbsp crème fraîche
a few drops of lemon juice
groundnut oil
350 g cocktail sausages
2 shallots, peeled and finely
   chopped
250 g girolles, trimmed and halved
   or sliced if large
1 tbsp coarsely chopped flat-leaf
   parsley
ROAST QUAIL
8 quail, oven-ready
50 g unsalted butter
juice of 1 lemon
1 tbsp thyme leaves

Finely chop the beetroot in a food processor. Melt 25 g of the butter in a medium-sized saucepan over a medium heat, add the beetroot and sweat for about 3 minutes, stirring occasionally and seasoning it. Stir in the crème fraîche, then return the beetroot to the food processor and whizz to a smooth but textured purée. Spoon back into the saucepan. Season to taste with a few drops of lemon juice, and a little more salt if needed.

Heat the oven to 220°C fan oven/230°C electric oven/Gas 8. Arrange the quail in a roasting dish, spaced slightly apart. Dot with the butter, pour over the lemon juice, season and scatter over the thyme.

Select a small roasting dish that will hold the sausages snugly and brush it with oil. Arrange them in a single layer without pricking them.

Put the quail and sausages in the oven. Roast the quail for 20–25 minutes, basting halfway through, and the sausages for 25–30 minutes, stirring them halfway through, until evenly gold all over. When you remove the quail from the oven, leave them to cool in the roasting tray for 10 minutes.

While the sausages finish cooking and the quail is resting, gently rewarm the beetroot purée. Heat a tablespoon of oil and the remaining butter in a large frying pan over a highish heat, add the shallots and sauté for 1 minute until they soften, then add the girolles and sauté for a couple of minutes longer, seasoning them at the end. Sharpen with a couple of drops of lemon juice and stir in the parsley. Serve the quail with the pan juices spooned over and accompanied by the girolles, beetroot purée and cocktail sausages.

Partridge with Game Crumbs and Bacon

The traditional line-up for grouse of bread sauce, buttery crumbs and watercress is just as good with other game birds. A grey partridge for me steals the show, its tender gaminess goes unsurpassed. It does one for one, which makes it ideal for small odd numbers. I prefer to buy birds untrussed and without bacon, and to dress them myself.

Serves 4

4 grey-leg partridge, oven-ready
50 g unsalted butter, softened
sea salt, black pepper
8 rashers unsmoked streaky bacon,
   rind removed
bread sauce (see below)
redcurrant jelly or other game
   sauce and watercress to serve
GAME CRUMBS
150 g unsalted butter
150 g fresh white breadcrumbs

Heat the oven to 200°C fan oven/220°C electric oven/Gas 7. Smear the birds with the butter, season with pepper and the tiniest pinch of salt, then wrap two rashers of bacon around each bird, one securing the legs. Place in a roasting dish about 1 cm apart and roast for 30 minutes, basting halfway through. Transfer the birds to a warm serving plate to rest for 10 minutes. Unwrap the bacon rashers and lay these out in another small baking dish and return to the oven to crisp for a few minutes while the bird is resting and you make the gravy.

While the bird is roasting, make the game crumbs, melt the butter in a large frying pan over a medium heat and once it is sizzling nicely add the breadcrumbs and fry, stirring frequently until they are evenly gold; this may take up to 15 minutes depending on how fresh they are. Spread these in a thin layer on a double thickness of kitchen paper to drain for a few minutes, then transfer to a bowl. They can be made up to about an hour in advance, but keep them somewhere warm in the kitchen so they remain feathery light and the butter doesn't set.

Serve the partridge at the table with the game crumbs, some bread sauce (see below) and redcurrant jelly. Accompany each bird with a small bunch of watercress.

Bread Sauce

Serves 4

30 g unsalted butter
1 large onion (ideally white),
   peeled, halved and sliced
½ tsp sea salt
100 ml double cream
1 bay leaf
5 cloves
75 g fresh white breadcrumbs
300 ml full cream milk
freshly grated nutmeg

Melt the butter in a small non-stick saucepan over a medium heat, add the onion, sprinkle over the salt and sweat for 6–8 minutes, stirring frequently until soft and silky but not coloured. Add the cream, bay leaf and cloves, cover and cook over the very lowest heat for about 5 minutes, stirring at least once to make sure it's not catching. Remove from the heat and leave to infuse for 20 minutes. Discard the bay leaf and cloves and whizz to a smooth purée in a food processor.

Combine the breadcrumbs and the milk in the same non-stick saucepan, and bring to the boil, stirring until smooth. Simmer for 5–10 minutes over a low heat, stirring occasionally until you have a thick sauce. Add the onion purée and heat through, and season with freshly grated nutmeg and a little more salt if needed. Unlike a normal bread sauce, this can be made in advance, anything up to a couple of hours. Cover the surface with clingfilm and leave in the pan on the hob. Gently reheat without boiling to serve.

Making breadcrumbs

Remove the crusts from some day-old coarse-textured white bread, break it up into chunks and whizz in a food processor until reduced to fine crumbs. Should you have forgotten to buy the bread a day ahead, you can use fresh bread, providing it is a good quality pain de campagne or other such rustic bread that has a sturdy dry crumb.

Parmesan-glazed Parsnips

Christmas is spent in our French farmhouse, but since the French don't share our love of parsnips or brussel sprouts, come Christmas Eve there is a mad scramble for them in our vicinity. Guests arriving from England are welcomed with open arms should they have been kind enough to stash a few bags between the presents. Maris Piper and King Edward potatoes, too, could be auctioned for a fortune. Divine as La Ratte potatoes are, they're hopeless roasters, and mash doesn't quite do it with the turkey. I first tasted Parmesan-glazed Parsnips one Christmas at a friend's down the road – Jo Higgo, the other half of Arthur's Barbecued Sausages (see page 108).

Serves 4

600 g parsnips, peeled, halved or
    quartered lengthwise and cut
    into 2 shorter lengths
50 g unsalted butter, melted
30 g freshly grated Parmesan
sea salt, black pepper

Heat the oven to 180°C fan oven/190°C electric oven/Gas 5 and bring a large pan of salted water to the boil. Add the parsnips and parboil for 10 minutes, then drain them into a colander and leave for a few minutes for the surface water to evaporate. Place them in a roasting dish, drizzle over the butter and shake a little from side to side to coat them, then sprinkle over the Parmesan and season with pepper. Roast for 40–45 minutes until the cheese is golden and crisp, baste and loosen them with a spatula halfway through. Serve straightaway.

Brussel Sprouts with Bacon and Chestnuts

Given a spell in a frying pan brussel sprouts are scarcely recognisable from their boiled counterpart. And the smaller the better, look out for button brussels. I also like to toss in nibs of bacon and do away with the rolls that are only ever crisp on the outside.

Serves 6

700 g button brussel sprouts
8 rashers rindless unsmoked
    streaky bacon, diced
100 g chestnuts, cooked, peeled
    and sliced
50 g unsalted butter, clarified
sea salt, black pepper

Trim the base of the sprouts and remove the outer leaves. Bring a large pan of salted water to the boil. Add the sprouts and cook for about 8 minutes until just tender, larger sprouts will take longer accordingly. Drain into a colander.

Heat a large dry frying pan over a medium heat, add the bacon and cook for 7–8 minutes, stirring frequently, until crisp and golden. Remove it with a slotted spoon and drain on kitchen paper. Add the chestnuts to the pan and sauté in the bacon fat for several minutes, stirring frequently until lightly golden. Transfer to a bowl and add the bacon.

Ten minutes before eating, heat the butter in a large frying pan over a medium-high heat, add the sprouts, season and sauté for 7–8 minutes until lightly golden. Add the bacon and chestnuts just before the end, to heat through.

All-in-one Roast Vegetables

This is for those who curse having to juggle three different vegetables, an all-in-one of crisp potatoes, parsnips and silken strips of sage-scented onion.

Serves 6

3 parsnips, trimmed and peeled
3 carrots, trimmed and peeled
800 g maincrop potatoes, peeled
3 tbsp groundnut oil
40 g unsalted butter
2 red onions, peeled, halved and
    cut into wedges
2 handfuls of sage leaves
sea salt, black pepper

Cut the vegetables roughly the same size. Cut the parsnips and carrots into two pieces, then either quarter or halve these depending on their thickness. The thin end of the parsnips can be left whole. Cut the potatoes into quarters or chunks of a similar size.

Bring a medium-sized pan of salted water to the boil, add the potatoes and simmer for 8 minutes, then drain into a sieve and leave for a few minutes for the surface moisture to evaporate. Return them to the pan and give them a shake to fluff up the surface.

Heat a tablespoon of the oil and half the butter in a large frying pan over a highish heat, add half the carrot, parsnip and potato and sauté for 6–7 minutes, turning occasionally until evenly gold. Transfer the vegetables to a large roasting dish (about 38 x 25 cm), add another tablespoon of the oil and the remaining butter to the pan and cook the remaining carrot, parsnip and potato in the same fashion. Turn the heat down a little if the vegetables start to colour too quickly. Add these to the other vegetables, then add the onion and sage leaves to the frying pan and sauté for 1–2 minutes, turning them, until glossy. Mix these into the vegetables. The vegetables can be prepared to this point an hour or two in advance. Cover with clingfilm and set aside.

Drizzle the remaining tablespoon of oil over the vegetables, season and roast them beneath the turkey for 50–55 minutes, stirring halfway through, until evenly gold and crisp at the edges.

Roast Potatoes

Should you happen to have a jar of goose fat in the fridge or be roasting a goose (in which case you can use some of the rendered fat), you're quids in. Otherwise, clarified butter gives luxuriously crisp roast potatoes.

Serves 6–8

1.5 kg maincrop potatoes
150 g unsalted butter, clarified
sea salt

Heat the oven to 180°C fan oven/190°C electric oven/Gas 5 if it's not already on. Peel and cut up your potatoes and reserve in a bowl of cold water. Bring a large pan of salted water to the boil. Add them to the pan and cook for 8 minutes. Drain the potatoes into a sieve and leave for a minute or two for the surface water to evaporate. Return them to the pan and roughly shake it from side to side, tossing them in the air until they appear textured and floury on the surface.

Tip them into a roasting tray, trickle over the butter and scatter over some sea salt. Roast the potatoes for 1¼ hours, turning them at least once during cooking. They should be evenly gold all over, the colour of a crisp.

Making clarified butter
Melt some unsalted butter, skim off the surface foam and reserve the clear yellow butter discarding the milky residue below.

Port Gravy

I don't normally add flour to gravy, but at Christmas when you need a large jug to go round it benefits from a little thickening.

Serves 6–8

100 ml port
1 level tbsp plain flour, sifted
either 300 ml giblet stock
  (page 140), or 300 ml chicken
  stock
sea salt, black pepper

Skim off any excess fat from the roasting tray, leaving just one or two tablespoons. Place the roasting pan on a lowish heat, add the port and cook for several minutes until reduced by half, scraping up all the sticky roasting juices in the bottom of the pan. Stir in the flour and once this is seething, gradually stir in the stock. Simmer the gravy long and hard enough for it to amalgamate into a smooth sauce. Taste and season if necessary. Add any juices given out on carving the turkey and pour into a jug to serve. If there are a lot of bits, you may like to strain it first.

Gravy Tip

Gravy to go with game birds relishes a teaspoon of redcurrant jelly stirred into the juices along with the wine when you deglaze the pan.

For bread sauce see page 143

Cranberry Sauce

Turkey is unthinkable without this sweet and sour condiment. Just the one tip – cooking the cranberries before adding the sugar avoids tough skins. That aside, I don't think it's improved by the addition of spices or more alcohol, there's enough of that going on elsewhere.

Serves 6–8

450 g cranberries
juice of 2 oranges
125 g caster sugar

Place the cranberries and orange juice in a small saucepan, bring to the boil, cover and simmer over a low heat for 5 minutes. Stir in the sugar, turn the heat up to medium and simmer uncovered for 10–15 minutes longer until the juices are reduced and syrupy. Transfer the sauce to a bowl, cover with clingfilm and leave to cool. This sauce can be prepared several days in advance. In this case chill and bring it back up to room temperature before serving.

Homemade Mincemeat

Nothing strikes nostalgia into the heart quite like that first crumbly morsel of mince pie that releases a host of sugared memories when all the Christmases were white and Santa could be relied upon to bring you what you asked for. And it was no coincidence that he never passed up on the pie and glass of brandy you left out for him.

I am the first to take advantage of ready-made Christmas puddings, but shop-bought mince pies are that little bit too ersatz, overly sweet and cakey. If you can be bothered to rustle up a batch, it's a one-off task before Christmas, they'll keep for a good week or longer, and can be rewarmed at whim.

Mincemeat is one of those eccentric British masterpieces, a blend of dried fruit and nuts, spices, brown sugar and brandy. My own concoction employs stem ginger in lieu of crystallised fruit, lots of currants, grated apple and lemon, create it to suit your own taste. You may be partial to glacé cherries and candied peel, or prefer rum in lieu of brandy, and orange instead of lemon.

The mix is drier than commercial mincemeat, which is almost jammy by comparison, but once baked the suet, grated apple and dark brown sugar meld to coat everything in a lovely spicy slick. Jars of mincemeat are not to be sniffed at though, and can be titivated with a little help. Spoon a 400 g jar of mincemeat into a bowl and stir in a tablespoon of brandy or Cognac, the finely grated zest of a lemon and a knifetip of ground cinnamon.

Makes 500 g

150 g currants

125 g raisins

25 g blanched almonds, finely
   chopped

1 knob of stem ginger, finely
   chopped

1 dessert apple, peeled and grated

50 g shredded suet (beef or
   vegetarian)

¼ tsp ground cinnamon

¼ tsp ground nutmeg

knife tip of ground cloves

finely grated zest and juice of
   1 lemon

2 tbsp brandy

1 tbsp dark muscovado sugar

Combine all the ingredients for the mincemeat in a bowl, cover and set aside for at least 12 hours.

Mince Pies

Apart from the sheer prettiness of these mince pies, with a star posing as a lid, I prefer the ratio of pastry to mincemeat than with a closed one.

Makes 2–3 dozen

1 quantity of mincemeat (see left)
icing sugar for dusting
PASTRY
450 g plain flour
250 g unsalted butter, chilled and
** diced**
finely grated zest of 1 lemon
150 g icing sugar, sifted
2 small egg yolks
milk

To make the pastry place the flour and butter in a food processor, give it a quick burst at high speed to reduce it to a crumb-like consistency, then add the lemon zest and icing sugar and give it another quick burst. Add the egg yolks and enough milk to bring the dough together, wrap it in clingfilm and chill for several hours or overnight.

Heat the oven to 170°C fan oven/180°C electric oven/Gas 4. You may find it easiest to work half the pastry at a time. Roll it out on a lightly floured worksurface, and using a fluted pastry cutter, cut out circles to fit a fairy cake baking tray (ideally non-stick). Place these in the tray and fill each with a heaped teaspoon of mince-meat. Roll the pastry again and this time cut out stars or Christmas trees, or some other shape, slightly smaller than the diameter of the pies. Lay one of these in the centre of each pie and bake for 15–25 minutes until the pastry is a pale gold. Leave to cool, then dust with icing sugar and slip out of the tins. They can be served warm, about 20 minutes out of the oven, or reheated for 5 minutes in an oven heated to 150°C fan oven/160°C electric oven/Gas 2½. A spoonful of rum butter, or Calvados cream is ever a treat if you're serving them for pudding.

And On Top
In my over-indulged childhood you didn't have either rum butter or brandy cream, you had both. A bowl of these in the fridge over Christmas will see you through any number of puddings, not least with the Christmas pudding itself.

Rum Butter

Serves 6–8

175 g unsalted butter, softened
175 g icing sugar, sifted
6 tbsp dark rum

Beat the butter and icing sugar together until light and fluffy (I use a food processor for this). Gradually beat in the rum, until you have a smooth creamy butter. Transfer to a bowl, cover and chill until required. Remove the butter from the fridge about 20 minutes before serving.

Calvados Cream
A thick, sweet pouring cream laced with Calvados, divine with warm mince pies as well as apple pies and the like. Don't go out and buy a bottle of Calvados specially – you can use any fruit eau-de-vie, Armagnac or brandy here.

Serves 6–8

225 g crème fraîche
1–2 tbsp Calvados
50 g icing sugar, sifted

Whisk the ingredients together in a bowl, cover and chill until required.

Christmas Pudding Gratin

I frequently make this in lieu of the usual flaming spectacular, often on Boxing Day when we all have room to enjoy it. It's something like a bread and butter pudding, but richer and boozier, and fills the whole house with a wonderfully evocative smell that mingles with the pine needles and candle smoke. Always go for the most luxurious pudding available, with the maximum amount of dried fruit, nuts and alcohol.

Serves 6

1 x 900 g Christmas pudding
  (chilled)
350 ml full cream milk
300 ml crème fraîche
100 g caster sugar
3 tbsp dark rum or whisky
3 medium eggs
icing sugar for dusting

Heat the oven to 150°C fan oven/160°C electric oven/Gas 3. Cut the pudding into slices 1 cm thick. Now halve these vertically. Lay them in two or three overlapping rows in a 30 x 20 cm gratin dish, or equivalent that holds them snugly.

Whisk the milk, crème fraîche, sugar, rum or whisky and eggs in a jug. You can prepare the pudding to this point in advance, in which case heat the oven later. Strain the milk mixture over the Christmas pudding, making sure you coat the whole of the surface. There should be small crags peeking out, but not too much, otherwise it will burn. Place the pudding in the oven and bake for 45–50 minutes until the custard is set and lightly golden on the surface. Leave it to cool for 15 minutes. Dust it with icing sugar and serve.

Cranberry-mincemeat Shortcake

My mother used to make something along these lines with the unlikely title of Sahara mincemeat. It became a great family favourite and disappeared with even greater speed than her mince pies.

Makes 12 squares

BASE

175 g unsalted butter, diced
75 g golden caster sugar
150 g plain flour
1 tsp baking powder, sifted
100 g ground almonds
4 medium eggs, separated
MINCEMEAT TOP
400 g mincemeat
150 g cranberries
icing sugar for dusting

Heat the oven to 160°C fan oven/170°C electric oven/Gas 3 and butter a 30 x 23 x 4 cm baking tin. Reduce the butter, sugar, flour, baking powder and ground almonds to a crumb-like consistency in a food processor. Once these start to cling together, add the egg yolks and continue to process to a sticky dough. Press this into the cake tin base, laying a sheet of clingfilm over the top and smoothing it with your fingers. Remove the clingfilm. Bake for 25–30 minutes until light golden and slightly risen.

Whisk the egg whites until stiff, you can use an electric hand-held whisk for this. Spoon the mincemeat into a bowl and fold in the whisked whites in two goes. Fold in 100 g of the cranberries and smooth the mixture over the shortcake base. Scatter over the remaining cranberries, pressing them down into the mixture, and bake for 20–25 minutes until lightly coloured on the surface. Remove and run a knife around the edge of the shortcake, then leave it to cool. Cut it into 7 cm squares, dust with icing sugar and transfer to a plate. The shortcake will keep well in a covered container for several days. In this case dust it with icing sugar before serving.

Christmas Ice Cream

Try this with a small glass of something fiery like brandy, Armagnac or Calvados before testing your inner warmth with the cold of the outside, and a nice long walk. The night before making the ice cream, make up a half quantity of the mincemeat recipe (see page 148), omitting the suet.

Serves 6

300 ml full cream milk
6 medium organic egg yolks
150 g caster sugar
350 ml double cream
½ recipe for mincemeat (see p 148)

Pour the milk into a small saucepan and bring to the boil. Whisk the egg yolks and sugar in a bowl, then whisk in the milk. Return this to the pan and heat gently until you have a thin pouring custard that coats the back of the spoon, taking care not to overheat it. Pour it through a sieve into a bowl. Cover the surface with clingfilm and leave to cool, then chill it.

Whip the cream until it forms soft peaks (you can use an electric whisk for this), and whisk it into the custard. Freeze the ice cream according to the instructions for your ice cream maker, adding the mincemeat towards the end. I like ice cream best eaten straight from the machine, when it is thick and sticky rather than scoopable. But if you want it a tad firmer, simply chill it for an hour or two in the freezer. And if it has been frozen for longer than this then give it 30 minutes out of the freezer to soften.

Big Apple Pie

A is a big no-nonsense apple pie, the stuff of falling leaves, conkers and smokey fires, pure Thanksgiving. It carries few pretences of being refined, a biscuity pastry and cinnamon-scented apples in a thin sea of caramel.

Serves 4

SWEET SHORTCRUST
150 g unsalted butter, softened
150 g caster sugar
2 medium eggs
400 g plain flour, sifted, plus
   1 tbsp
50 g ground almonds
APPLES
900 g Bramley apples (3 good
   sized), peeled, cored and sliced
125 g light brown sugar
½ tsp ground cinnamon
finely grated zest of 1 lemon, plus
   juice of ½ lemon
25 g unsalted butter
caster sugar for dusting

Cream the butter and sugar for the pastry together in a bowl using a wooden spoon until soft and fluffy. A food processor or mixer will make light work of this. Beat in the eggs until well combined, then gradually add the 400 g of flour and the ground almonds and bring the dough together. Wrap it in clingfilm and chill for at least 2 hours – it will keep for several days.

Heat the oven to 170°C fan oven/180°C electric oven/Gas 4. Allow the dough to come to room temperature for a few minutes, then knead it until pliable. On a lightly floured surface, thinly roll out two thirds of the dough. Use this to line the base of a shallow 1.6 l/30 cm gratin dish, letting the extra hang over the sides, then trim off the excess. Don't worry if the dough tears and you end up partly pressing it into the dish. Sprinkle the tablespoon of flour over the apples in a bowl and toss, then mix in the brown sugar, spice, lemon zest and juice. Tip the apples into the pie dish, arranging them evenly, and dot with the butter. Roll out the remaining third of pastry with the trimmings, and lay it over the top. I find it easiest to wrap it around the rolling pin and lift it up, as it's quite short. Press the pastry together at the rim and trim it leaving 1 cm for shrinkage, then crimp the edge using the tip of your finger or else the tip of a knife. Cut several diagonal slits in the surface and dust with caster sugar. Bake the pie for 40 minutes until golden.

Baked Apples Stuffed with Mincemeat

Mincemeat contains everything that apples love – currants, raisins, lots of spices and citrus zest. You can serve these as they are, or with the rum butter or Calvados cream.

Serves 4

4 x 225 g Bramley cooking apples
4 heaped tbsp mincemeat
4 tbsp maple syrup
2 tbsp light muscovado sugar

Heat the oven to 160°C fan oven/170°C electric oven/Gas 3. Using the tip of a sharp knife, incise a circle around the middle of each apple. This ensures the apple has room to expand as it cooks without the skin splitting. Cut out a central core from each one about 4 cm in diameter. Place the apples in a baking dish that holds them snugly side by side, and loosely stuff with the mincemeat. Drizzle over the syrup, and scatter the sugar over the top. Bake for 40–45 minutes, basting them halfway through. Serve the apples 10–15 minutes out of the oven with the syrupy juices spooned over.

Apple Butterscotch Pie

One of those unlikely puddings that begins life drowned in a thin sea of caramel, which soaks into the sponge on top as it bakes and thickens into a delectable sauce surrounding the apples below. It's half pie, half cake.

Serves 6

600 g Bramley apples, peeled, quartered and sliced
SPONGE
150 g self-raising flour
50 g caster sugar
80 g unsalted butter, chilled and diced
1 medium egg
100 ml milk
finely grated zest of 1 lemon
50 g currants
SAUCE
80 g light muscovado sugar
25 g unsalted butter
100 ml water
¼ tsp sea salt
juice of ½ lemon

Preheat the oven to 180°C fan oven/190°C electric oven/Gas 5. Place the flour and sugar for the sponge in a bowl, and rub in the butter (this can also be done in a food processor or mixer). Now incorporate the egg and the milk, then fold in the lemon zest and the currants. Arrange the apples in the base of a shallow 1.5 l ovenproof dish (I use a 30 cm white oval gratin dish), and smooth the sponge mixture on top.

Place the sugar, butter, water and salt for the sauce in a small saucepan and bring to the boil. Stir in the lemon juice, then pour this mixture over the pudding. The sauce will seem very liquid at this point, but once baked will be transformed to a rich butterscotch. Bake the pudding for 30–35 minutes until golden on the surface and bubbling around the edges. Serve 5–10 minutes out of the oven.

Vanilla Cream

Altogether more luxurious than whipped cream, one for serving with a bowl of berries, fruit tarts and pies, or with cakes for pud. You can also make it using crème fraîche, at which point it is more like a thick pouring cream.

Serves 6

250 g mascarpone
1 vanilla pod, slit
40 g icing sugar, sifted

Place the mascarpone in a bowl. Open out the vanilla pod and run a knife along the inside to remove the tiny black seeds. Blend these and the icing sugar with the mascarpone. Transfer to an attractive serving bowl, cover and chill until required. You can make this a day in advance, in which case stir it before serving.

Christmas Trifle

Brandy, oranges, pomegranates and cinnamon, this is tailormade to suit the Christmas mood. There are several stages here, and I suppose it is a fair bit of work, but it can at least be made a day or two in advance, and the results are well worth it.

Serves 8

CUSTARD

425 ml whole milk
1 x 8 cm cinnamon stick
3 medium organic egg yolks
50 g icing sugar
50 g plain flour

TRIFLE

4 oranges (medium-sized rather than navel)
40 g caster sugar
50 ml Cointreau
25 ml brandy
5–6 trifle sponges
60 g amaretti or ratafias
180 g seedless raspberry jam
1 tbsp lemon juice
1 tbsp pomegranate seeds

SYLLABUB

zest of 1 orange, plus 2 tbsp juice
squeeze of lemon juice
125 ml sweet wine
2 tbsp Cointreau
50 g icing sugar
300 ml double cream

Place the milk for the custard and the cinnamon stick in a small saucepan, bring to the boil and leave to infuse while you prepare the syrup.

Halve and juice 2 of the oranges, and reduce with the 40 g caster sugar in a small saucepan over a medium heat to 50 ml of syrup. Add this to the 50 ml Cointreau and the brandy in a jug. Arrange the trifle sponges on the base of a 20 cm trifle dish about 8 cm deep and splash all but a few tablespoons of the syrup over them.

To make the custard, whisk the egg yolks and icing sugar in a bowl until pale in colour. Now whisk in the flour in three lots. Bring the milk back to the boil, discard the cinnamon stick, and gradually whisk it onto the egg and sugar mixture, which should thicken instantly. Return the custard to the pan and cook over the very lowest heat, stirring constantly for 1–2 minutes until it is very thick, without allowing it to boil. Pass the custard through a sieve over the trifle sponges, cover the surface with clingfilm and leave to cool and set.

Slice the skin and outer pith off the remaining 2 oranges and run a knife between the segments to remove them from the pith that separates them. Drain the segments in a sieve set over a bowl. Crumble the amaretti into a bowl and sprinkle over the remaining orange syrup, which may by this time have thickened. Place two thirds of the jam in a bowl and work it with a spoon until it is smooth, then spread it over the custard. Scatter over the amaretti and then the orange segments.

To make the syllabub, whisk the orange zest and juice with the squeeze of lemon juice, sweet wine, Cointreau and icing sugar in a bowl. Slowly whisk in the cream, and continue to whisk until you have a light and fluffy syllabub. While it needs to be the consistency of whipped cream, care should be taken not to overwhisk otherwise it can separate. I use a hand-held electric whisk for this. Pour the syllabub over the trifle and smooth the surface, cover with clingfilm and chill overnight. During this time the syllabub will firm up, and the syrup and juices will continue to soak into the trifle sponges, which should be very moist by the time you serve it. You can, in fact, make it up to 2 days beforehand if preferred.

Shortly before serving the trifle blend the remaining jam with the lemon juice in a bowl. Drizzle this over the top of the trifle and scatter over the pomegranate seeds just before eating.

* If you like you can decorate the trifle further with a few physalis, their petals pulled back, arranged in the centre of the trifle and dusted with icing sugar.

Pan-fried Stollen with Zabaglione

Stollen is even better fried than eaten at room temperature, the marzipan toasts on the outside and the edges turn soft and chewy. With zabaglione it is nothing short of sumptuous. Zabaglione will stand around for a few minutes without sinking, but if there's an idle pair of hands around, you could enlist someone to whisk the zabaglione while you cook the stollen.

Serves 6

4 medium organic egg yolks
50 g golden caster sugar
100 ml marsala
50 g unsalted butter
6 x 1 cm slices stollen

Set a bowl over a pan with 2 cm of simmering water in the base. Choose a largish bowl that will allow for the zabaglione to swell into a foamy mass and whisk the egg yolks and sugar together. Set the bowl over the simmering water, add the marsala and using an electric hand-held whisk (you can of course do this with an ordinary whisk), start whisking the mixture on a medium speed. It will rise and become frothy relatively quickly. Continue to whisk until it is the consistency of whipped cream. This will take about 5–8 minutes. Remove the bowl from the heat.

Melt the butter in a large frying pan over a medium heat and fry the stollen until golden, about 2 minutes the first side and 1 minute the second. Serve on warm plates with the zabaglione spooned over.

Sweet Chestnut Trifle

Marrons glacé, crystallised ginger and Armagnac are all good Christmas staples. And being virtually fat-free this trifle is something of a first, which isn't to stop you pouring some cream over it.

Serves 6–8

PEARS
300 ml water
125 g caster sugar
1 vanilla pod, slit, or 1 tsp vanilla extract
2 Comice pears
4 tbsp Armagnac
TRIFLE
100 g amaretti
1 x 435 g tin chestnut purée
3 medium organic eggs, separated
50 g caster sugar
150 g trifle sponges
cocoa for dusting
marrons glacé or crystallised ginger to decorate

To poach the pears, place the water, sugar and vanilla pod or extract in a small saucepan and bring to the boil, stirring until the sugar dissolves. Peel and halve the pears, add them to the syrup cut-side up so that as far as possible they are submerged, cover with a circle of baking parchment and poach over a low heat until they are tender when pierced with a skewer; this can take anywhere between 4 and 15 minutes depending on their ripeness. Allow them to cool in the syrup, then remove and drain thoroughly on a double layer of kitchen paper. Now quarter, core and finely slice them. Mix 5 tablespoons of the syrup with the Armagnac. Break the amaretti into a shallow bowl and pour half this solution over them.

To prepare the chestnut cream, whizz the chestnut purée in a food processor until smooth and creamy, then incorporate the egg yolks. Transfer the mixture to a large bowl. In another bowl whisk the egg whites until they hold their shape, then gradually sprinkle over the sugar, whisking well with each addition until you have a glossy meringue. Fold this into the chestnut purée in three goes.

To assemble the trifle, smear a spoon of the chestnut cream over the base of a deep 20 cm bowl. Lay the trifle sponges on the base, cutting them to fit and sprinkle over the remaining brandied syrup, then smooth over half the chestnut purée. Scatter over the amaretti, leaving behind any syrup they haven't absorbed, then the pears, and spread over the remaining chestnut purée. Cover and chill the trifle for at least 2 hours, though it is best eaten the day it is made. Just before serving dust with cocoa and decorate with the marrons glacé or crystallised stem ginger, sliced or whole as you wish.

Cure-all Butty

A toasted bacon sandwich puts most excess to rights, and there's a fair chance on this of all mornings that there might be a call. This has the full complement of relishes that I would hope to find inside mine, but if you're rushed start with the chilli sauce and build up from there.

Makes 2 rounds

1 tbsp vegetable oil

1 red onion, peeled, halved and thinly sliced

sea salt, black pepper

4 slices smoked back bacon, rind removed

4 slices malted granary bread

unsalted butter

sweet chilli sauce

mustard and cress

Heat the oil in a medium-sized saucepan, add the onion and sweat over a gentle heat for about 10 minutes. Season, turn the heat up a little and cook for another few minutes, stirring constantly until caramelised.

Heat the grill, lay the bacon rashers out on the grid of a grill pan and lightly grill each side until the fat begins to colour. Toast the bread and butter it. Make a sandwich by layering first the bacon, then spread over the onions, daub with some sweet chilli sauce, and add a good bunch of mustard and cress. Close the sandwich and cut either into two triangles or four.

Sweetcorn Pancakes with Smoked Salmon

If you're looking for a way of using up some of that side of smoked salmon, this is a good lunch or supper, and light enough to indulge in some mince pies or Christmas pudding afterwards. The pancakes have that chunky drop scone charm. If you're in the mood for something green then pile some rocket or watercress salad on top.

Serves 4

PANCAKES

1 potato (approx. 180 g), peeled

1 medium egg, separated

100 ml milk

75 g plain flour, sifted

sea salt, black pepper

150 g tinned sweetcorn (drained weight)

1–2 tsp groundnut oil

TO SERVE

4 tsp crème fraîche

300 g smoked salmon

snipped chives

Bring a small pan of water to the boil, add the potato and cook until it is tender. Drain and pass the flesh through a mouli-légumes or a sieve into a bowl. Add the egg yolk and the milk, then gradually fold in the sifted flour and some seasoning and leave to stand for 30 minutes.

Just before cooking the pancakes, stir in the sweetcorn. Stiffly whip the egg white and fold this into the mixture. Heat a teaspoon of oil in a non-stick frying pan over a medium heat, and drop enough pancake mixture into the pan to form a thick pancake about 8 cm in diameter; you should be able to fit about three in the pan at a go. After 45–60 seconds when they are golden on the bottom, turn them using a spatula and cook the other side. Store on a plate, covered with foil to keep them warm while you cook the remainder. Add a little more oil to the pan if necessary. Serve the pancakes with a spoon of crème fraîche on top. Drape the salmon partly over the pancakes and scatter over some chives.

Ham

What Ham?

Those who have never cooked a gammon (an uncooked ham) before might well feel daunted by the various types which go by any number of different names, as I was when I first approached the subject. The most popular cut around Christmas is the leg that comes on the bone, or the corner cut boned and rolled. The latter can be obtained in almost any size, though a 2 kg joint will do nicely for eight people and just fit your biggest saucepan. While a knuckle-end gammon joint (half leg on the bone) is good for ten plus. From there it comes smoked or unsmoked, and that's about as complicated as it need get.

On Or Off The Bone

Many people insist that ham on the bone is superior in flavour. There again, only a boned gammon will be compact enough to braise, and this in my experience renders the most succulent results, especially if you are eating it hot.

The Cure And Soaking

The type of cure, which can vary considerably, will determine whether or not you need to soak your gammon in advance of cooking it. Good butchers, some of whom cure their own gammons, will be able to advise on this. If, however, buying from a supermarket where such information is less readily available, just to be on the safe side I would recommend soaking the gammon overnight as a matter of course. As to unsmoked or smoked, it's a question of taste. The latter will keep the staunch of palate happy, while the former is that much milder. Whatever your taste in bacon should help you decide.

Storing Ham

A larder makes the ideal environment for storing a cooked ham, basically somewhere cool and slightly damp, a garage is an alternative. Your ham will keep well for about a week, or if it has been sliced then three days.

The Stock

If you braised a boned and rolled gammon, bring the stock to the boil and cook over a medium-high heat until reduced by half. Strain it into a bowl, leave to cool, then cover and chill until required, skimming the surface of fat before using.

If you baked a gammon on the bone, you are in for an even greater treat, a rich golden stock that jellifies as it cools. Simply cover with water, bring to the boil and simmer over a low heat for 1½ hours. Strain the stock into a bowl, leave to cool, then cover and chill until required, skimming the surface of fat before using.

Honey-glazed Ham on the Bone

The sight of a glazed ham studded with cloves sitting on the sideboard is fit for a Dickensian feast, but unless you are feeding the proverbial five thousand there is no need to cook a whole leg. Ask your butcher for the knuckle end, which is just as pretty and should do for at least ten people. Weighing in the region of 3.5 kg, should you need to soak it overnight, a preserving pan or bucket should do the trick.

Serves 10

1 x 3.5 kg knuckle-end gammon joint on the bone
2 tbsp runny honey
2 tbsp Dijon mustard
approx. 40 cloves
cider (optional)

Heat the oven to 170°C fan oven/180°C electric oven/Gas 4. Try to use the broadest width of foil. Tear off a long sheet, large enough to envelop the gammon, allowing plenty of air within the package to circulate. Place the gammon on top, bring the long sides together, and fold to seal them, then do the same with the sides. Place the gammon within a roasting or grill pan. The gammon needs to bake for 60 minutes per kilo, so calculate it accordingly, subtracting 30 minutes for the final glazing. A 3.5 kg gammon will need to bake for 3 hours prior to glazing.

Just before the end, blend the honey and mustard together in a bowl. Remove the ham from the oven and turn the temperature up to 180°C fan oven/190°C electric oven/Gas 5. Unwrap the ham and slip out the foil, slice off the rind underneath the ham which will have softened in the cooking juices, leaving behind as much fat as possible. Next carefully incise a long slit into the rind across the top without cutting into the fat, and partly pull and partly cut the skin off. You can use oven gloves or a tea towel to protect your hands from getting burnt. Glaze the top and sides of the ham as evenly as possible with the honey-mustard mixture. Slice the fat at 2 cm intervals with a crisscross pattern and insert cloves into the crosses on the fat.

Return the ham to the roasting or grill pan and pour a few millimetres of water or cider into the base to prevent any sugar that trickles down from burning. Roast for 25–30 minutes until the glaze is golden and dry. Transfer the ham to a warm serving plate, loosely cover with foil and rest for 30 minutes if serving it hot. If serving it cold then place it somewhere cool or unheated and leave to cool completely.

Hazelnut-crumbed Ham

Coating a ham to be eaten cold with breadcrumbs is one of the plainest ways of presenting it. I like to include crushed hazelnuts that give the crust more in the way of flavour. This goes beautifully with the sweet and sharp mustard and Cumberland sauce, in fact it wouldn't be overdoing it to serve both.

Serves 6–8

1 x 2 kg unsmoked gammon, boned and rolled

3 outer ribs of celery, trimmed and sliced

2 carrots, trimmed and sliced

1 leek, trimmed and sliced

2 bay leaves

50 g fresh white breadcrumbs

50 g hazelnuts, skinned

¼ tsp cayenne pepper

Soak the gammon in cold water overnight, then drain. Place the gammon in a large saucepan, cover with cold water and bring to the boil. Discard the water and start again with fresh water to cover, this time adding the sliced vegetables and bay leaves. Bring to the boil, then maintain at a gentle simmer over a low heat for 2 hours.

In the meantime, heat the oven to 170°C fan oven/180°C electric oven/Gas 4. Spread the breadcrumbs in a thin layer on the base of a roasting or baking dish and toast in the oven for 8–9 minutes until lightly golden. Remove and leave to cool. Place the hazelnuts in a single layer in a small baking dish and again toast for 8–9 minutes until golden. Remove and leave to cool. Place the hazelnuts in a food processor and whizz until very finely chopped, stopping short of a powder. Combine the breadcrumbs, hazelnuts and cayenne pepper on a large plate.

Transfer the ham to a plate using two forks, and leave to cool for 30 minutes. Pull the rind off the ham using your fingers. Roll the ham on all sides in the breadcrumbs, pressing it down firmly to coat it as generously as possible. Place on a clean plate and leave to cool completely, then carve and serve.

Ham and Root Vegetable Hash

As Boxing Day dawns so, too, does a desire for a hearty fry-up. Hash can favour potatoes, squashes and here some wintery root vegetables. Throw in some ham, and pepper with a fiery chilli sauce. I find my largest frying pan can only accommodate enough hash for two to three people. If you are more than this, you'll need to double-up and use two frying pans.

Serves 2–3

200 g carrots, trimmed, peeled and diced

200 g swede, peeled and diced

200 g parsnips, trimmed, peeled and diced

3 tbsp extra virgin olive oil

1 red onion, peeled, halved and sliced

2 sprigs of rosemary

3 red chillies

4 garlic cloves, peeled

sea salt

3 slices ham, cut into broad strips

Place the carrots, swede and parsnips in the top half of a steamer set over about 2 cm simmering water in the lower half and steam for 15 minutes. At the same time, heat the olive oil in a large frying pan over a medium-low heat and sweat the onion for 12–15 minutes, stirring frequently until nicely golden and slightly crisp. Remove to a bowl and reserve.

Add the steamed vegetables to the frying pan with the rosemary, chillies and garlic cloves and sauté, again over a medium-low heat for about 25 minutes, turning them frequently. Season with salt halfway through. At the end of cooking, add the onions and ham to heat through. Discard the rosemary and garlic cloves and serve. The flesh of the chillies can be eaten, scraped off the skin.

Muscovado Roast Ham with Parsley Sauce

Juicy pink slabs of ham smothered in green parsley sauce are so good together there is little call for anything alongside, though buttery boiled potatoes or swede mash naturally fit into the equation.

Serves 6–8

1 x 2 kg unsmoked gammon, boned and rolled

3 outer ribs of celery, trimmed and sliced

2 carrots, trimmed and sliced

1 leek, trimmed and sliced

2 bay leaves

25 g dark muscovado sugar

1 tbsp Dijon mustard

approx. 20 cloves

SAUCE

75 g flat-leaf parsley, leaves and thin stalks

50 g unsalted butter

40 g plain flour

200 g crème fraîche

1 tsp Dijon mustard

sea salt, black pepper

Soak the gammon in cold water overnight, then drain. Place the gammon in a large saucepan, cover with cold water and bring to the boil. Discard the water and start again with fresh water to cover, this time adding the sliced vegetables and bay leaves. Bring to the boil, then maintain at a gentle simmer over a low heat for 1½ hours. Towards the end of this time, finely chop the parsley, a food processor will make light work of this.

Heat the oven to 180°C fan oven/190°C electric oven/Gas 5. Reserving the stock, transfer the ham from the saucepan on to a board using two forks. Pull off the rind from the ham. Slice the fat at 2 cm intervals with a crisscross pattern. Blend the sugar and mustard in a bowl, using the back of a spoon to disperse any lumps, and use this to coat the ham evenly all over. Now insert cloves into the crosses on the fat. Place the ham in a roasting tray and pour a few millimetres of the ham stock into the base to prevent any sugar that trickles down from burning. Roast for 20–30 minutes until the glaze is mahogany-coloured and dry. Transfer the ham to a warm serving plate, and rest for 20 minutes while you prepare the sauce.

Melt the butter in a small non-stick saucepan. Stir in the flour and allow the roux to seethe for about a minute. Working off the heat, gradually incorporate 300 ml of the ham stock. Bring the sauce to the boil stirring constantly, then stir in the crème fraîche and mustard, and simmer over a low heat for 10 minutes, stirring occasionally. Stir in the parsley, then season with pepper and salt if needed. Carve the ham and serve on warm plates with the sauce spooned over.

Vegetable and Barley Soup with Mustard Cream

Another meal eked out from the proceeds of the ham, the starting point being the stock, and a variety of vegetables that you may already have in the basket.

Serves 6

50 g unsalted butter
1 celery heart, trimmed and sliced
2 large carrots (approx. 250 g),
    trimmed, peeled and thinly
    sliced diagonally
2 leeks, trimmed and thinly sliced
75 g pearl barley
2 l reduced ham stock (see p 160)
6 thin slices of ham, fat removed,
    cut into 1 x 5 cm strips
150 g crème fraîche
1 tbsp Dijon mustard
sea salt, black pepper
chopped flat-leaf parsley

Melt the butter in a large saucepan over a medium heat, add the celery, carrots and leeks and sweat for 5 minutes, stirring occasionally, until glossy but not coloured. Stir in the pearl barley and sweat for a minute or two longer. Add 2 litres of the reduced ham stock, bring to the boil and simmer over a low heat for 30 minutes, adding the ham just before the end. In the meantime, blend the crème fraîche and mustard in a bowl.

Season the soup with black pepper and more salt if necessary. Serve in warm bowls with the mustard cream spooned in the centre, scattered with parsley.

Turkey in Herb Cream Sauce

This is the kind of dish that is everyone's best friend at this time of year, lively and fresh after a fashion that is pure relief in the midst of so much feasting. It can also be made up to a couple of days in advance, and removed from the fridge some 30 minutes before eating.

Serves 4–6

1.2 l turkey stock
700 g cold turkey, sliced white
    meat and brown
300 g Greek yoghurt or crème
    fraîche
1 tbsp lemon juice
50 g watercress, tough stalks
    removed and coarsely chopped
25 g dill fronds, coarsely chopped
3 spring onions, trimmed and
    sliced
1 tbsp capers, rinsed
sea salt
cayenne pepper

Place the turkey stock in a medium-sized saucepan and reduce at a rapid boil to 150 ml of liquid. This will take 30–50 minutes, and you will need to watch it carefully at the very end to make sure it doesn't completely evaporate. Transfer the stock to a bowl and leave it to cool.

Arrange the turkey in a shallow dish, I use a 35 cm oval china gratin dish. Skim off the fat on the surface of the stock, then add the Greek yoghurt or crème fraîche and lemon juice and whisk until smooth. Reserving a third of the watercress, dill and spring onions, fold the remainder into the sauce along with the capers. Season with salt to taste, then pour this over the turkey. Cover and chill in the fridge for at least 1 hour; the sauce may thicken up as the stock jellies. Bring the turkey back up to room temperature for 30 minutes before eating. Dust with a little cayenne pepper, scatter with the reserved chopped herbs and spring onions and serve. If you are chilling the turkey for longer, chop the garnish just before serving.

Coronation Turkey

Banish all memory of the last sandwich you ate filled with Coronation chicken, and ponder instead a liberally spiced homemade mayonnaise with apricots in it. You may like to scatter over some toasted flaked almonds or pine nuts, and some chopped coriander. Don't be put off by the long list of ingredients – it's all said and done in 30 minutes.

Serves 4

2 tomatoes
⅓ tsp ground cumin
⅓ tsp ground coriander
¼ tsp turmeric
⅛ tsp cayenne pepper
¼ tsp ground cinnamon
¼ tsp ground ginger
225 ml groundnut oil, plus 2 tbsp
1 onion, peeled, halved and thinly
   sliced
75 g dried apricots (no need to
   soak) boiled for 10 minutes,
   sliced
sea salt
1 medium organic egg yolk
1 tsp Dijon mustard
a squeeze of lemon juice
black pepper
450 g cooked turkey (or chicken)
   meat, cut into strips

Bring a small pan of water to the boil, cut out a cone from the top of each tomato, dunk them into the boiling water for 20 seconds and then into cold water. Remove them, slip off the skins and coarsely chop them. Combine all the spices in a bowl.

Heat the 2 tablespoons of oil in a large frying pan over a medium-low heat, add the onion and sauté for several minutes until soft and translucent. Add the spices and give them a stir, then add the tomatoes and apricots and season with salt. Turn the heat down low and cook for 8–12 minutes until the sauce is thick and reduced and the oil separates out from the tomatoes, stirring frequently. Transfer the mixture to a bowl or plate and leave to cool.

Whisk the egg yolk with the mustard in a bowl, then slowly whisk in the groundnut oil, to begin with just a few drops at a time. Combine the mayonnaise with the cooled tomato and onion mixture, then add a squeeze of lemon juice and a grinding of black pepper. Stir in the turkey and taste for salt.

Balsamic Caramelised Onions

A jammy compote of onions that makes the perfect foil to ham, and also goes beautifully with all those Christmas cheeses. Try a late night snack of Stilton toasted on granary bread with some of this dolloped on top.

Serves 6

1 tsp groundnut oil

700 g large onions, peeled, quartered and finely sliced

1 tbsp caster sugar

1 tsp sea salt

black pepper

2 tbsp balsamic vinegar

Heat the oil in a medium-sized saucepan, add the onions, sprinkle over the sugar, salt and a grinding of pepper and stir. Cover and sweat for 35 minutes over a low heat, stirring occasionally, until the onions are soft and translucent. Remove the lid and cook for another 30–35 minutes, until dried out and lightly caramelised, stirring frequently. Add the balsamic vinegar and cook for a few minutes longer to drive off the sharpness of the vinegar and render the onions syrupy. Transfer them to a bowl, cover and leave to cool. Chill until required, the relish will keep well for several days. Bring back up to room temperature for 30 minutes before eating.

Cumberland Sauce

Quintessentially English, this sauce can be made days in advance of eating, and it's as good with the leftover turkey as the ham.

Serves 6

1 orange, scrubbed

1 lemon, scrubbed

1 shallot, peeled, halved and finely sliced

100 ml port

250 g redcurrant jelly

1 tsp English mustard

Pare the rind off the orange and lemon using a potato peeler, leaving behind the white pith. Stack the strips and finely slice diagonally into long thin slivers about 2 cm long. Bring a small pan of water to the boil and blanch the zest and the shallot for 2 minutes. Drain into a sieve.

Halve and juice the fruits, and pour into a small saucepan, adding the remaining ingredients and the blanched zest and shallot. Bring to the boil, stirring well to blend in the mustard, then simmer over a low heat for 10 minutes until viscous and syrupy. Transfer to a bowl, cover and leave to cool completely. The sauce will thicken as it cools without setting, it should be pourable.

Sweet and Sharp Mustard

There is a small gem of a farm shop just off the A1 north of Dunbar, where Hilary Cochran produces a wide range of preserves and sauces. This is one of her best-sellers, a recipe handed down by her mother.

Serves 6–8

100 ml cider vinegar

40 g Colman's mustard powder

2 medium organic egg yolks

75 g caster sugar

Blend the vinegar and mustard powder in a bowl and leave to slake for 2 hours, during which time it will thicken up. Whisk in the egg yolks and sugar. Transfer the mixture to a bowl set over a pan of simmering water, and heat for 5–10 minutes, stirring frequently, until the mustard thickens into a custard. Pass through a sieve into a bowl, cover and leave to cool. Chill until required when it should thicken up enough to make a trail if trickled back on itself. The mustard will keep for a week. Bring back up to room temperature for 30 minutes before serving.

Gigot on a Bed of Thyme and Garlic with Flageolet Beans

The place a gigot holds in the heart of the average Frenchman cannot be overestimated. It is their equivalent of our roast chicken, something to which they turn at the very suggestion of a celebration. And very fine our local lamb in France is too, slightly farther north than Mont Saint Michel, it is reared like pre salé on salt marshes, and is dark and rich to show for it.

Serves 6

LAMB

1 x 2.2 kg leg of lamb, knuckle removed

extra virgin olive oil

sea salt, black pepper

2 handfuls of thyme sprigs

1 head of garlic, separated into cloves (unpeeled)

90 ml port

180 ml chicken, beef stock or water*

BEANS

450 g flageolet beans, soaked overnight in cold water

2 sprigs of thyme

2 bay leaves

600 g beefsteak tomatoes

5 shallots, peeled, halved and finely sliced

6 tbsp coarsely chopped flat-leaf parsley

Calculate the total cooking time of your joint at 35 minutes per kilo for medium-rare, and 15 minutes over, and 45 minutes per kilo for medium, with 20 minutes over (my own preference). A 2.2 kg leg of lamb cooked to medium will take 2 hours.

Heat the oven to 190°C fan oven/200°C electric oven/Gas 6. Pour some olive oil into the palm of your hand and lightly coat the lamb. Season it all over and place fat-side up in a roasting tray that holds it snugly, on top of the thyme. You can also tuck any knuckle bones under the edges of the joint. Roast according to the above times, basting it occasionally. Forty minutes before the lamb has finshed cooking, surround the joint with the garlic cloves, basting them and the joint with the juices.

Once the lamb is in the oven, begin to prepare the beans. Drain them, then place them in a large saucepan and cover with water by a fingertip. Bring to the boil and then drain the beans. Repeat, this time plentifully covering the beans with water and adding the herbs. Simmer the beans for 1½ hours until very tender, topping up the pan with boiling water if necessary. Check them after about 1¼ hours, they should ideally be very creamy, bearing in mind that beans can differ in the time they take to cook, usually depending on how fresh they are.

In the meantime, bring a medium-sized pan of water to the boil. Cut out a cone from the top of each tomato, plunge them into boiling water for 20 seconds and then into cold. Slip off the skins, quarter, deseed and dice the flesh.

When the beans are cooked, measure 300 ml of the cooking liquid into a jug and pour into a food processor or liquidiser. Add 225 g of the beans and purée until smooth. Drain the beans, discard the herbs, return them to the pan and stir in the purée. Season with salt and pepper.

Once the meat is cooked, transfer the lamb and garlic cloves to a warm carving plate, cover with foil and leave to rest in a warm place for 15–20 minutes. Discard any bones, leaving in the thyme, and spoon any excess fat from the roasting tray. Add the port and simmer over a fairly low heat for several minutes, scraping up the sticky residue on the bottom of the pan. Add the stock, discard the thyme and simmer for several minutes until you have a smooth amalgamated gravy.

Just before serving, finish preparing the beans. Heat 2 tablespoons of olive oil in a large frying pan over a medium heat, add the shallots and sauté for a few minutes until lightly golden. Add the tomatoes and stir to heat through. If necessary reheat the beans, then stir in the tomatoes and onions, and the parsley.

Carve the lamb across the grain, adding any juices given out to the gravy. Serve on warm plates with the garlic cloves, accompanied by the beans and the gravy.

Grilled Oysters with Wild Garlic

At Eastertime there are banks and banks of wild garlic around our house in France, and that's not to mention the primroses, wild orchids, violets and fields of dandelions. The floral harvest is there for the reaping, and wild garlic is a magical touch for the local oysters from Blainville-sur-mer. If you are unsure of where to find wild garlic, then look for bluebells and follow your nose, it announces itself on the breeze for many yards around, and where there are one you will usually find the other.

The oysters are Pacific as opposed to native, and admitting a little in the way of local bias I actually prefer them. Certainly they are better for grilling.

Serves 6

8 leaves of wild garlic
2 medium egg yolks
½ tsp Dijon mustard
120 ml crème fraîche
3 dozen oysters, opened
sliced baguette or sourdough
    bread to serve

Finely slice and chop the leaves of wild garlic. Whisk the egg yolks, mustard and crème fraîche in a bowl and stir in the wild garlic. The cream can be made in advance, in which case cover and chill it.

Drain the oysters of their juices and arrange in a single layer in ovenproof gratin or roasting dishes. Heat the grill on high and place the rack as close to the heat as possible. Spoon a teaspoon of the garlic cream over each oyster and grill them for about 5 minutes until sizzling and patched with gold. You may need to do this in batches depending on the size of your grill. Whisk the gratin dishes to the table as they are ready and serve straightaway with bread for scooping the oysters out.

Oyster Cracker

In the interests of preserving the palm of your hand (and however great those chain-mail gloves may look, they're more a fashion statement than something you want hanging around the tea-towel drawer), I cannot recommend an oyster cracker highly enough. A nifty gadget that punches a hole in the side of the oyster, allowing you to slip the thin blade attached inside and wriggle it open. Ironically, even though it was designed by a French enthusiast, I now import them to Normandy via Rossmore Oysters in Ireland who distribute them there and in the UK (see page 220).

To go, hold the oyster cupside down in your hand. Punch a hole at the very edge of the oyster at the frilly end where the muscle is weakest. Slip the knife into the hole and work it round to cut through the muscle, then lift off and discard the upper shell, pick out any stray splinters and place the oyster with its juices on a plate.

CHILDREN'S HIGH DAYS

By way of feasting, most adults will settle for Christmas and Easter with a little seasonal entertaining in between. But children have their own agenda, with high expectations of what they hope to be served at any particular occasion. And they're conservative at heart: birthdays aren't birthdays without jelly, cake and ice cream. They all abide by an international list of approved foods, bring on the pancakes, sausages and pizzas. Arguably none of it is especially good for you, but equally it's not particularly bad for you, and in the name of fun, good intentions can wait. If you can't have what you want at your own party then when can you?

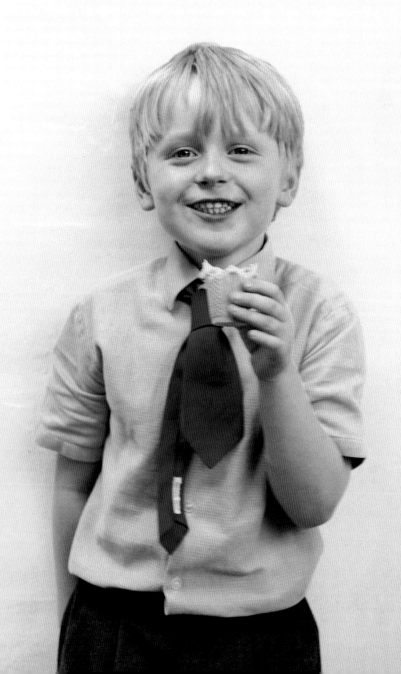

3.30pm

Angel Smartie Cake

For any toddler besotted by Bob the Builder, Thomas the Tank Engine, Barbie or Buzz Lightyear, there seems little point in exhausting yourself with coloured marzipan and the like when you can buy a themed cake off the shelf. The real fun begins later on around six, when as though to test your prowess in the kitchen the request is for 'a cake shaped like a beehive with Darth Vader and Luke Skywalker fighting a duel with clashing light sabres'. I think Louis has mapped out every single birthday in between now and twenty-one and the cake he will set me as a task at each.

And when all else fails, Smarties seem to be an acceptable compromise for most children providing there are enough. When we photographed our cake, within minutes of the click of the camera it was totally denuded of every single one by a mad flurry of highly skilled little fingers.

Use Smarties to design whatever pattern or creature you think will most appeal, a spiral, the child's age, a dinosaur or rose traced with pink and mauve. You can either cut out a paper template and then trace around the edge with a fine knife on to the icing to give a shape. Or, you may already have shaped biscuit cutters that can be used to mark an outline.

Makes one 23 cm cake

ANGEL SPONGE
8 medium egg whites
¼ tsp sea salt
1 tsp cream of tartar
250 g icing sugar, sifted
140 g plain flour, sifted
RASPBERRY CREAM FILLING
250 g mascarpone
100 g raspberry jam (such as St Dalfour 'no added sugar')
FROSTING
120 g unsalted butter, softened
100 g icing sugar, sifted
300 g cream cheese
1 tsp vanilla extract
several tubes of Smarties and candles for decoration

Heat the oven to 150°C fan oven/160°C electric oven/Gas 2½. Whisk the egg whites in a large bowl with the salt and cream of tartar until risen – I use a hand-held electric whisk. Now whisk in the icing sugar a couple of tablespoons at a time, sprinkling it over the egg whites and whisking for about 20 seconds with each addition. Fold the sifted flour into the meringue in three goes, then divide the mixture between two unbuttered 23 cm cake tins with removable bases. Bake the two sponges for 35–40 minutes until light golden on the surface, springy to the touch, and shrinking from the sides. Run a knife around the edges of the tins and leave them to cool.

Blend the mascarpone with the jam in a bowl. To make the frosting, place the butter and icing sugar in the bowl of a food processor and blend until smooth and creamy. Transfer the buttercream to a large bowl and work in the cream cheese and vanilla extract.

Using a serrated bread knife, slit one of the sponges in half. Slice the top off the other one, then cut the sponge off its base to make up the middle layer of cake. Spread half the raspberry cream over the base of the sponge, lay the middle section in place, spread with the remaining raspberry cream, then lay the top over. Smooth the cream cheese frosting over the top and sides of the cake using a palette knife. Transfer the cake to a 25cm cake board; there is no need to remove it from the base of the tin. Chill the cake and remove it from the fridge 30–60 minutes before serving. Decorate with Smarties and candles close to the time of eating, otherwise the colour of the Smarties can bleed.

Jelly on a Plate

Wobbly plate jellies are the foundation of any children's party, no other food elicits quite as much giggling and delight. Little point in making your own here, they'll never be as crystal clear as what comes out of a packet. I simply buy a selection of flavours and colours – pineapple, orange, strawberry, blackcurrant and the like. And the plates need to be those shiny plasticised paper ones, as plain card absorbs the jelly and collapses. Because of the logistics of setting the jelly in the fridge, you'll need to start making these the morning of the day before the party. You can stack them jelly to jelly once they are set, and store the pairs on top of each other in the fridge.

Makes 16

4 packets of different coloured jelly

16 x 22 cm plates

Lay out as many plates as will fit on the racks of your fridge. Make up the jelly accordingly (allowing 1 packet for 4 plates) and fill them in the fridge about 5 mm deep. This is easier than filling and transferring them to the fridge. Once set they can be sandwiched in pairs and stacked on top of each other, while you prepare more.

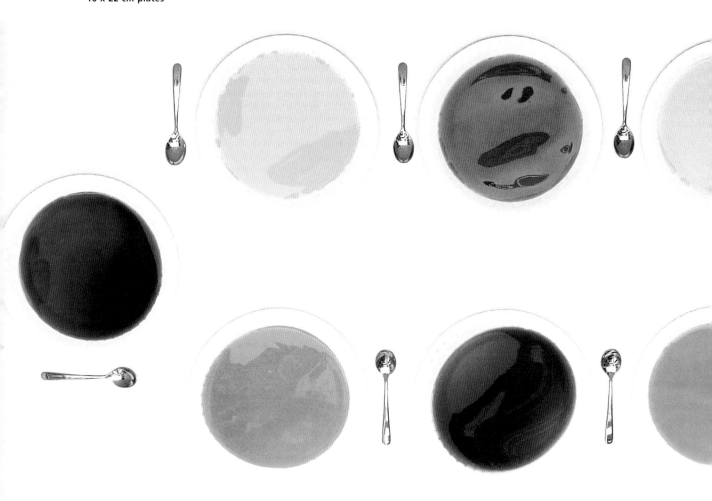

Marmite Stacks

Variation on the theme of Marmite soldiers are miniature tiered squares, a club sandwich for tots. If ready-sliced bread is unavailable, thinly slice a large sandwich loaf.

Serves 10

unsalted butter
**9 thin slices white or wholemeal
   bread**
Marmite

Butter and spread a slice of bread with Marmite, place another slice on top and repeat, then sandwich with a third slice. Using a bread knife, remove the crusts and cut into strips 2 cm wide. Then using a sharp knife so as not to tear the crumb, cut these into 2 cm cubes. Pile on to a large plate and repeat with the remaining bread. Cover with clingfilm if not serving straightaway.

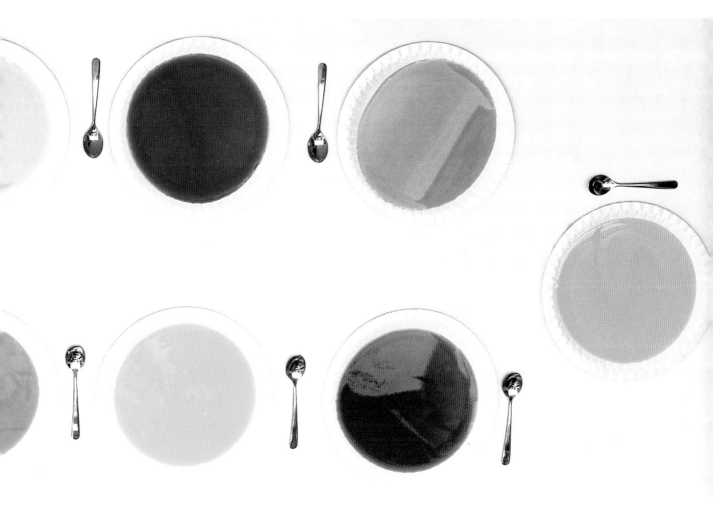

Cupcake Mountain

As well as needing a good recipe for cupcakes up your sleeve, piled high and stuck with candles cupcakes make an alternative birthday cake that allows every child their very own cake, and they can be eaten on the hoof should the excitement of the occasion prove too much for good table manners. While boys are invariably married to chocolate cupcakes, girls are more likely to be thrilled by pink icing and silver balls, a choice depending on whose birthday it is.

Girl Mountain

Makes 24

CAKE
225 g unsalted butter, diced
225 g golden caster sugar
finely grated zest of 1 orange
3 medium eggs, separated
150 ml milk
275 g plain flour
2 tsp baking powder
½ tsp sea salt
DECORATION
300 g icing sugar, sifted
4 tbsp orange flower water
pink or red food colouring
silver balls
pink and white candles

Heat the oven to 170°C fan oven/180°C electric oven/Gas 4. Cream the butter and sugar in a food processor until almost white. Incorporate the orange zest and egg yolks, then the milk, and continue beating until homogenised. Transfer the mixture to a large bowl. Sift the dry ingredients twice, then fold them a third at a time into the butter mixture. Whisk the egg whites in a bowl until stiff, then fold in two goes into the cake mixture, as lightly as possible. Fill 24 paper cases set in two fairy cake baking trays two-thirds full with the cake mixture and bake for 15–20 minutes. The lower tray may take a few minutes longer. Remove and leave them to cool in the trays.

Blend the icing sugar with the flower water in a bowl and dye it pink with a few drops of colouring. Smooth a heaped teaspoon of icing over the surface of each cake – don't worry about completely covering the edges – and scatter over a few silver balls. Leave to set for 1 hour, then stack into a mountain on a plate. Stick with pink and white candles.

Boy Mountain

Makes 24

CAKE
replace 50 g of the flour with
   cocoa and omit the orange zest
DECORATION
200 g dark chocolate, broken up
50 g unsalted butter
80 g dark and white chocolate
   chips, mixed
blue and white candles

Place the chocolate and butter in a bowl set over a pan of simmering water, or in the top half of a double boiler, and melt gently. Smooth a heaped teaspoon of chocolate icing over the surface of each cake, don't worry about completely covering the edges. Scatter over some dark and white chocolate chips and leave to set for about 1 hour. Stack into a mountain on a plate and stick with blue and white candles.

Jammy Dodgers

The cut-out in the centre could be any shape, heart, star, moon or diamond. The added bonus are the miniature cut-outs themselves, which I sandwich together with chocolate spread.

Makes approx. 30

225 g unsalted butter, diced
100 g caster sugar
200 g plain flour
115 g ground almonds
150 g raspberry jam (such as St Dalfour's no added sugar)
icing sugar for dusting

Place the butter, sugar, flour and ground almonds in the bowl of a food processor and process to a dough. Wrap the dough in clingfilm and rest in the fridge overnight.

Heat the oven to 140°C fan oven/150°C electric oven/Gas 2. Knead the dough until it's pliable, then, working with half at a time, thinly roll it out on a lightly floured worksurface and cut out 5 cm biscuits. The dough can be rolled twice. Using a palette knife, transfer the biscuits to baking sheets, then cut out hearts or some other shape from the centre of just over half of them (to allow for breakages once they are cooked) using a miniature cutter about 2 cm diameter. Bake the biscuits (including the cut outs) for 30 minutes until a pale gold, then remove them and leave to cool. Depending on the size of your oven and how many baking trays you have, you may need to cook the biscuits in two batches, in which case store the second batch on a plate in the fridge while the first one is baking.

Work the jam in a bowl with a spoon until it's smooth. Dust the cut-out biscuits and shapes you removed with icing sugar. Using the palette knife, spread a little jam into the centre of each plain biscuit and sandwich with one of the cut-out biscuits so the jam shows through the hole. Arrange these on plates as you go.

Chocolate Marshmallows

Older children will delight in cocktail sticks, otherwise just arrange the marshmallows on a plate.

Makes 30

60 g dark chocolate, broken up
1 x 200 g packet pink and white marshmallows
cocktail sticks

Put the chocolate in a bowl set over a pan of simmering water, or in the top half of a double boiler, and gently melt. Dip the top of each marshmallow into the chocolate, then place chocolate-end up on a plate to set for 1 hour. Skewer the marshmallows with cocktail sticks through the uncoated base, and arrange on a plate.

Mango Cornets

These cornets can be eaten while charging around, and if you make them in the cups that stand on their base they can be lined up on a tray. There are plenty of excellent ready-made sorbets to be had, but should you feel like dusting off the ice cream maker then this mango sorbet would be my first choice of flavour. Try to remember to chill your sorbet mixture before churning to save overworking your ice cream machine, as some of them are more efficient than others.

Makes 12

12 cornets
hundreds and thousands
MANGO SORBET
1.8 kg mangoes (to yield 600 ml
    mango purée)
425 ml sugar syrup (recipe below)
2 tbsp lemon juice

The number of mangoes you will need depends on how heavy the stones are and how thick the skin is, the importance being to end up with 600 ml of sieved purée, so use as many as are necessary. Incise the skin into quarters and peel it off, or else slice it off with a sharp knife. Cut the flesh off the stone and place it in a liquidiser. Reduce to a purée and press through a sieve into a bowl to remove any fibrous threads. Add the sugar syrup to the purée and the lemon juice and stir well to combine. Freeze the mixture in your ice cream maker according to the manufacturer's instructions. If not serving it straightaway, scoop it into a plastic container, seal and freeze for 2 hours. If freezing for longer than this, leave it out of the freezer for up to 40 minutes depending on how hard it has frozen.

Place a scoop of sorbet in each cornet and sprinkle with hundreds and thousands.

Sugar Syrup

Makes 425 ml

300 g caster sugar
300 ml boiling water

Place the sugar in a bowl, pour the boiling water over and stir until the sugar dissolves. Leave the syrup to cool to room temperature then cover and chill it until required.

Strawberry Bowl

At my son's school they seem to have cracked the fresh fruit and veg dilemma by offering the children crudités or a piece of fruit at the very start of the meal, thereby getting them when they're hungry. Sadly, this has never worked for me at home and mothers with children who munch on batons of carrot can only be envied. But a bowl of hulled strawberries usually tempts.

Crisps and Things

Organic crisps are now widely available and there is a new trend for named varieties of potato, some of which are very good. Other relatively child-friendly options are:

* Twiglets
* Cornchips (unflavoured)
* Prawn crackers
* Vegetable crisps
* Banana chips

Drop Scones

As a child I knew these as Scotch pancakes. Pudgey and slightly sweet we would eat them hot from the pan for tea, a tradition I revisit with Louis who perches precariously on the worksurface, and has a capacity for eating them that defies the size of his tummy.

Makes approx. 25 Serves 6

225 g plain flour
½ tsp sea salt
2 tsp baking powder
1 medium egg
2 tbsp golden syrup
300 ml full cream milk
lard or beef dripping for grilling
softened salted butter to serve

Sift the dry ingredients into a large bowl. Whisk the egg, golden syrup and milk in another bowl until blended, without being too particular if there's a little bit of syrup in the bottom of the bowl or clinging to the whisk. Pour this mixture on to the sifted dry ingredients and whisk until smooth. Leave to stand for 10 minutes.

In the meantime, heat a griddle or castiron frying pan on a low heat for 10 minutes until it reaches an even snug warmth. Drop a few fine slivers of lard or beef dripping on to the hot iron and smooth with the back of a spoon to oil the surface, then drop tablespoons of the mixture into the pan, spaced slightly apart. I can fit 4 scones into a 26 cm frying pan, or 6 on a double griddle.

Cook for 1–2 minutes until the surface pits with bubbles, then carefully turn the drop scones using a palette knife and cook for about 1 minute more until golden on the underside. You should find the first side is completely smooth, while the underside looks more like a crumpet. Remove them to a plate, smear with a little softened salted butter, and eat while you put some more on to cook, reoiling the griddle now and again between batches as it needs it. Or, if you are making them in advance of tea, then keep them covered with foil on a plate for up to half an hour. They can also be reheated in an oven heated to 160°C fan oven/170°C electric oven/Gas 3. Stack them about 6 high, wrap in foil and heat for 20 minutes.

Pancakes

Cooking pancakes instils the same kind of fear into many as making a soufflé, which can only have to do with tossing them. The last time I tried this, and only for Louis's satisfaction, it ended up in the bowl of mixture itself. This method is for the non-sporting type, where the pancakes are flipped over with a palette knife. The melted butter in the batter prevents them sticking, that and a non-stick pan should see you through.

Makes approx 16 Serves 4–6

250 g plain flour, sifted
caster sugar
pinch of sea salt
3 large eggs and 2 egg yolks
600 ml milk
40 g unsalted butter, melted

Whizz all the ingredients except the butter in a blender until smooth, adding a tablespoon of sugar for sweet pancakes and just a pinch for savoury. Give the blender a stir to make sure there's no flour clinging to the sides, and whizz again. Transfer to a bowl, leave to stand for 30 minutes, then stir in the melted butter.

I swear by a non-stick frying pan for cooking pancakes, but otherwise a well-seasoned one, and if you want to speed things up then have two on the go. Heat a frying pan with an 18 cm base over a medium heat and ladle in just enough batter to coat the base, tipping it to allow it to run evenly over the surface. Cook for 30 seconds until the top side appears dry and lacy at the edges and it is golden underneath, then loosen the edges using a palette knife or spatula (non-stick for a non-stick pan), slip the knife underneath and flip it over. Give it another 30 seconds and then slip it on to a plate. I always discard the first one, for no explicable reason it never seems to work properly, it's only once you've done three or four you really get into the swing of it. Cook the remainder likewise. You can either dish the pancakes out as they are cooked, or pile them up on a plate and cover with foil to keep warm.

I also quite often make them in advance, cover and chill them, and reheat them briefly on each side in a dry frying pan. In this case they keep well for several days.

To Serve
Whether you serve them rolled or folded is largely a cultural consideration. With increasing experience of the galette van at the end of a morning's shop in Normandy, I come down in favour of the latter, cradled in a napkin to save burnt fingers.

Sweet
* At their simplest dab them with unsalted butter
* Sprinkle with golden caster sugar and squeeze over a little lemon
* Drizzle with maple or golden syrup
* Spread with some warmed raspberry jam
* Smear with a scoop of ice cream
* Sprinkle with grated dark chocolate (and a drop of Kahlua for mums and dads)

Savoury
Having turned the pancake, sprinkle the cooked surface with the filling, and once the underside is ready fold it into quarters.

* Dot with salted butter and scatter over some grated Parmesan
* Scatter over strips of Parma ham and nibs of feta
* Scatter with skinned and diced tomato and chopped mozzarella
* Scatter with fried wild mushrooms

Sausage Party

Firework Night is an occasion when you have to keep a huge span of ages happy. My solution is trays piled high with golden caramelised sausages.

The starting point is lots of cocktail sausages and chipolatas. There are few children who don't adore cocktail sausages and ketchup, but try to vary the sauce and they will turn their nose up, it simply has to be tomato. On from that sausages tend to fall either side of a broad divide – free-range pork flavoured with herbs, venison, wild boar or duck. Or hot and spicy like merguez and chorizo. For vegetarians you can always include some Glamorgan sausages made with Caerphilly or Lancashire cheese.

Pile a selection of breads in the middle of the table for everyone to help themselves. Favourites include thin buttered French sticks, warm crusty garlic and herb bread, pitta breads, soft torpedo-shaped rolls, cheese or onion bread, and olive or sun-dried tomato bread.

Serves 6–8

SAUSAGES

1.5 kg sausages (Cumberland, Toulouse, chorizo, merguez, free-range pork, venison, wild boar, chipolatas, cocktail)
1 tsp finely chopped mint
150 ml natural yoghurt

Heat the oven to 170°C fan oven/180°C electric oven/Gas 4. Without pricking the sausages lay them on two baking trays spaced about 1 cm apart to ensure they caramelise evenly. The exact time it will take for each type of sausage to cook will vary. Cocktail sausages may take 35–45 minutes, whereas fat Cumberland rings can take an hour. A classic banger takes about 50 minutes. Cook chorizos separately, they tend to give off a dark red paprika oil as they cook, and can take as little as 30 minutes. Either remove the sausages as they are cooked and keep them warm covered with foil, or else put smaller sausages in to cook later than large ones. Turn the sausages halfway through. You can also switch the trays around if they are cooking unevenly.

Cucumber, Spring Onion and Mint Relish

1 cucumber, peeled
1 tsp caster sugar
1 tsp sea salt
2 spring onions, trimmed, finely sliced and chopped

Quarter the cucumber lengthwise, remove the seeds, and finely dice the flesh by first slicing the quarters into thin strips. Place the cucumber in a bowl, toss with the sugar and salt and set aside for 30 minutes.

Drain the cucumber into a sieve, rinse under the cold tap, then shake dry and return to the bowl. Add the spring onions, yoghurt and mint and toss. Transfer to a clean serving bowl and drizzle over a little olive oil.

Roasted Red Onions

900 g red onions, peeled, halved and sliced
extra virgin olive oil
1 tsp red wine vinegar
sea salt, black pepper

Heat the oven to 170°C fan oven/180°C electric oven/Gas 4. Lay the onions in a thin layer on two baking sheets, breaking the slices into rings as far as possible. Drizzle over a little olive oil and roast for 35 minutes, stirring halfway through to ensure they caramelise evenly. Place them in a bowl, and toss with the vinegar and some seasoning. Serve warm or at room temperature.

Crispy Bacon

250 g smoked streaky bacon, rind removed

Heat the grill and cook the bacon until golden and crispy on both sides. Remove the grill pan and leave the bacon to cool. Break the pieces in half and pile them in a bowl.

BAKING DAYS

Whatever may have happened to teatime, something we aspire to more than practice, our love of cake remains undimmed. If anything, cakes have become that much more indulgent over the years, in our house they frequently replace pudding with some ice cream or a sorbet, or a few fruits. All of which makes perfect sense given that they can be made in advance, something we demand of most puddings.

In addition to standard round cakes, I am particularly fond of traybakes, which can be just about anything cooked in a shallow rectangular tin – an almond sponge scattered with raspberries, or a lemon cake with a crystalline glaze of lemon juice and granulated sugar. Ultimately child friendly, you can ration their intake by cutting them whatever size of square you want. Being shallow, they also take less time to cook than larger cakes, and you get lots of crusty surface. Loaf cakes, too, are particularly satisfying to make in the way they rise in the tin, break open on top, and offer lots of moist cake and crisp edges.

Most tins these days are non-stick, which, as well as doing what they say, don't rust. The recipes here revolve around a couple of sizes of round cake and traybake, and just one size of loaf, which avoids cluttering up the cupboard with endless tins that only get an occasional outing (see page 220).

Without the space for one of those whirring retro mixers, which I well remember from childhood are a delight to cook with, all my cake mixtures have to withstand the rigours of a food processor blade. But a cake that is basically foolproof is no bad thing. You can do pretty much what you like with the mixtures that follow; there is no secret code of whipping in enough air and keeping it there, or knack in adding the eggs. They are all straightforward friendly cakes to make and bake.

If experience has taught me anything, it is that a drop of milk in a cake mixture works wonders to lighten it, and replacing either all or some of the flour with ground almonds makes for a supremely moist and tender crumb. Beyond this I like to use organic eggs and unrefined sugar, which might be golden caster or light muscovado. The exception being icing sugar – nothing quite does it like the final flourish of a snowy white shower.

Raspberry and Almond Traybake

This one does as pudding with a spoonful of crème fraîche or scoop of vanilla ice cream.

Makes 30 x 23 cm traybake

225 g ground almonds
30 g flaked almonds
270 g golden caster sugar
2 tsp baking powder, sifted
60 g fresh white breadcrumbs
6 large organic eggs
300 ml sunflower or groundnut oil
finely grated zest of 2 oranges
125 g raspberries

Heat the oven to 190°C fan oven/200°C electric oven/Gas 6. Mix the ground and flaked almonds, 180 g of the caster sugar, the baking powder and breadcrumbs together in a large bowl. Thoroughly beat in the eggs using a wooden spoon, then the oil, then stir in the orange zest. Transfer the mixture to a greased 30 x 23 x 4 cm baking tin and smooth the surface. Scatter over the raspberries, then the remaining sugar, and bake for 25–30 minutes until the cake is golden and a skewer inserted into the centre comes out clean. Run a knife around the edge of the cake and leave it to cool before cutting into squares or slices.

Sugared Lemon Traybake

As if you needed proof that the simplest is so often the best, this relies on a minimum of fuss, just the proven equation of lemon, butter and the crunch of sugar. The sponge itself is meltingly tender and fluffy, which I put down to the milk in the mixture.

Makes 30 x 23 cm traybake

225 g unsalted butter, diced
225 g golden caster sugar
3 medium eggs
150 ml milk
225 g self-raising flour, sifted
1½ tsp baking powder, sifted
finely grated zest and juice of
    2 lemons
100 g golden granulated sugar

Heat the oven to 170°C fan oven/180°C electric oven/Gas 4 and butter a 30 x 23 x 4 cm baking tin. Place the butter and caster sugar in the bowl of a food processor and beat together until pale and fluffy. Incorporate the eggs one at a time, scraping down the sides of the bowl if necessary, then add the milk and whizz until creamy. Gradually add the flour and baking powder through the funnel with the motor running, then incorporate the lemon zest.

Transfer the mixture to the baking tin, smoothing the surface and bake for 30 minutes until golden and shrinking slightly from the sides and a skewer comes out clean from the centre. Run a knife around the edge of the tin and prick the cake with a skewer at about 2 cm intervals. Combine the lemon juice and golden granulated sugar in a bowl, stirring to evenly distribute it, then spoon over the top of the cake. Leave it to cool, allowing the juice to sink into the sponge. The surface should have a lovely crystalline sheen. Cut into whatever size squares you fancy.

Angel Mint Cakes

Having coveted the idea of sitting around and sipping crème de menthe through crushed ice with minutely fine straws since the age of six, it came as a rude shock some thirty years later to discover it tastes like toothpaste in a glass. But it does have its uses, as a peppermint essence, just the tiniest drop in with some mascarpone and icing sugar creates a delectable mint cream for spreading over a lily-white angel sponge. I'm sure it makes a great mint choc-chip ice cream, too. Whatever happened to those blocks of it they used to sell in the Sixties?

Makes 30 x 23 cm traybake
Approx. 35 squares

SPONGE
8 medium egg whites, at room temperature
¼ tsp sea salt
1 tsp cream of tartar
250 g icing sugar, sifted
140 g plain white flour, sifted
ICING
500 g mascarpone
4 tbsp crème de menthe
40 g golden syrup
25 g mini white marshmallows

Heat the oven to 150°C fan oven/160°C electric oven/Gas 2½, and butter and line the base of a 30 x 23 x 4 cm baking tin with baking parchment. Whisk the egg whites in a large bowl with the salt and cream of tartar until risen, I use a hand-held electric whisk. Now whisk in the sugar a couple of tablespoons at a time, sprinkling it over the egg whites and whisking for about 20 seconds with each addition. Fold the sifted flour into the meringue in three goes, then transfer the mixture to the prepared cake tin and smooth the surface. Bake the sponge for 30 minutes until lightly golden on the surface and springy to the touch. Run a knife around the edge of the tin, turn the cake out on to a board and leave it paper-side down to cool.

To prepare the filling, spoon the mascarpone into a bowl and beat in the crème de menthe, and then the syrup. Remove the paper from the base of the cake, slit it in half using a bread knife, and spread the lower half with half the mascarpone using a palette knife. Sandwich with the top half and smooth over the remaining icing. Cut off the edges of the cake and slice into 3–4 cm squares, again a bread knife is best for this. Scatter the marshmallows over the squares, and gently press into the icing, then transfer to large plates.

Apple Flapjack

A halfway house between a flapjack and a crumble.

Makes 12–16 slices

SHORTBREAD

180 g unsalted butter

70 g golden caster sugar

150 g plain flour

100 g ground almonds

FRUIT

850 g Bramley cooking apples,
peeled, cored and sliced

100 g currants

75 g light muscovado sugar

finely grated zest of 1 lemon

FLAPJACK

200 g unsalted butter

200 g golden syrup

1 tsp sea salt

225 g rolled oats

icing sugar for dusting (optional)

Place all the ingredients for the shortbread in the bowl of a food processor and reduce to crumbs, then keep the motor running until the mixture comes together into a ball. It will be very soft and sticky at this point. Press it into the base of a 30 x 23 x 4 cm non-stick baking tin, laying a sheet of clingfilm over the top and smoothing it with your fingers. Cover the surface of the tin with clingfilm and chill for 1 hour. Then remove the clingfilm.

Heat the oven to 150°C fan oven/160 electric oven/Gas 3, prick the shortbread all over with a fork and bake for 25–30 minutes until just beginning to colour. Leave to cool.

Either turn the oven up to 170°C fan oven/180°C electric oven/Gas 4, or heat if you have turned it off. Toss the apples, currants, muscovado sugar and lemon zest together in a large bowl and distribute evenly over the shortbread.

Gently melt the butter for the flapjack mixture in a small saucepan with the syrup and the salt, then fold in the oats. Scatter the flapjack mixture over the apples, there should still be some fruit showing through. Bake for 25–30 minutes until the top is golden and crusty. Run a knife around the edge of the cake and leave it to cool. Cut it into two long halves, then across into 2–3 cm slices. If you like, dust with icing sugar, then transfer the slices to a plate. They will keep well covered with clingfilm for a day or two.

Paradise Slice

At least halfway up the staircase to heaven. It's the bakewell tart factor – cake and pastry narrowly separated by a smear of raspberry jam.

Makes 16 slices

SHORTBREAD

175 g unsalted butter

75 g golden caster sugar

150 g plain flour

100 g ground almonds

finely grated zest of 1 orange

SPONGE

120 g raspberry jam (such as
St Dalfour no added sugar)

110 g unsalted butter, diced

150 g golden caster sugar

4 medium eggs

150 g desiccated coconut

75 g ground almonds

1 tsp baking powder, sifted

110 g sultanas

icing sugar for dusting

Place all the ingredients for the shortbread in the bowl of a food processor and reduce to crumbs, then keep the motor running until the mixture comes together into a ball. It will be very soft and sticky at this point, but press it into the base of a 30 x 23 x 4 cm baking tin, laying a sheet of clingfilm over the top and smoothing it with your fingers. Cover the surface of the tin with clingfilm and chill for 1 hour. Then remove the clingfilm.

Heat the oven to 140°C fan oven/150°C electric oven/Gas 2, prick the shortbread with a fork and bake for 25–30 minutes until just beginning to colour. Leave to cool.

Heat the oven to 170°C fan oven/180°C electric oven/Gas 4. Work the jam with a spoon in a bowl until it's smooth, then spread it in a thin layer over the shortbread base using a palette knife. Place the butter and sugar in the bowl of a food processor and cream together, then incorporate the eggs. Pour the mixture into a bowl and fold in the coconut, ground almonds, baking powder and sultanas. Smooth the mixture on top of the jam and bake for 25–30 minutes until the sponge has set and the top is golden. Run a knife around the edge of the cake and leave it to cool. Cut it into two long halves, then across into 2 cm slices. Dust with icing sugar and transfer to a plate.

Cheesecake Brownies

Brownies are a particular genre of American sticky chocolate cake, whose success lies in whipping them out of the oven at the right moment, when they are just set. If you apply the usual rules of clean skewers and all that you end up with a tough old mat. This cheesecake version is given a twist with creamy young goat's cheese instead of the usual Philly. Brownies are an obvious one for serving barely cooled with a scoop of vanilla ice cream, and they are at their best eaten freshly made.

Makes 15

CHOCOLATE MIXTURE

200 g dark chocolate (min. 70% cocoa solids), broken up

120 g unsalted butter, diced

130 g golden caster sugar

75 g plain flour

75 g ground almonds

1 level tsp baking powder

½ tsp sea salt

3 medium eggs

2 tbsp espresso or strong black coffee

CHEESECAKE MIXTURE

250 g young goat's cheese

70 g golden caster sugar

½ tsp vanilla extract

1 medium egg

Preheat the oven to 170°C fan oven/180°C electric oven/Gas 4. You need a tin 30 x 19 cm x 4 cm, or the equivalent in size. Provided it is non-stick there is no need to butter and flour it. To make the chocolate mixture, melt the chocolate with the butter in a double boiler or a bowl set over a pan of simmering water. Remove from the heat, add the sugar and stir to combine, then leave to cool slightly. Sift the flour, ground almonds, baking powder and salt through a coarse-mesh sieve into a large bowl. Add the eggs to the chocolate mixture one by one, beating after each addition; the mixture by the end should be very glossy. Gently fold in the ground almonds and flour, without overmixing, then stir in the coffee and set aside.

To make the cheesecake mixture, beat the goat's cheese with the sugar in a bowl until smooth. Add the vanilla extract and egg, and mix until well combined.

Pour the chocolate mixture into the tin. Pour the cheese mixture on top and spread evenly using the back of a spoon. Using a knife, swirl the cheese mixture into the chocolate mixture lifting it to create a marbled effect on the surface. Bake for 15–20 minutes until just set in the middle. A skewer inserted into the centre should come out clean with just a few moist crumbs on it. Run a knife around the edge of the tin, then leave the cake to cool in the tin for 15–20 minutes before cutting into 5 cm squares. Leave to cool completely, then carefully remove the brownies to a plate using a palette knife.

11.00am

Red, White and Blue Buns

Granny would approve, honey-scented sponge and a nip of sherry in the icing. Though if I have kids in mind then it's orange juice in lieu of sherry. And you can make these in fairy cake baking trays, or as small scallop or boat-shaped cakes if you happen to possess the moulds.

Makes approx. 18

2 large eggs

25 g golden caster sugar

finely grated zest of 1 lemon

2 tbsp clear honey or golden syrup

50 g plain flour

1 heaped tsp baking powder

50 g ground almonds

125 g unsalted butter, melted and
   cooled

ICING

200 g icing sugar, sifted

2–3 tbsp dry sherry or orange juice

1–2 drops of blue food colouring

red and white rose petals* for
   decorating, or sugar flowers

Heat the oven to 180°C fan oven/190°C electric oven/Gas 5. Whisk the eggs and sugar together in a bowl until almost white, I use a hand-held electric whisk for this. Now whisk in the lemon zest and honey or syrup. Sift the flour and baking powder together and then lightly fold into the egg mixture with the ground almonds. Take care not to overwork. Gently fold the cooled melted butter into the egg and almond mixture. You can use the dregs of the butter in the pan to grease the cake tins.

Spoon the mixture into the prepared moulds, filling each one two-thirds full. Bake the cakes in the oven for 8–10 minutes until golden. Run a knife around the edge of the tins and turn them out on to a wire rack to cool, placing them baked-side up.

When the cakes are just cool blend the icing sugar with the sherry in a bowl and dye it a pale turquoise with a drop or two of colouring. Smooth a little icing over the surface of each cake using a tablespoon or small palette knife, and scatter over a few rose petals or sugar flowers. Leave to set for 1 hour and eat as soon as possible.

* If the roses come from your garden then you may be able to vouch for their purity, otherwise try to buy them from an organic outlet.

Italian Currant Cake

The idea of a fruit cake is sometimes more appealing than the product itself. In addition to being heavy they do have a habit of overstaying their welcome by sitting around half-eaten long after the popping of Champagne corks is a distant memory. This one I find cuts just the right balance, a few currants set within a sponge scented with rum. The recipe comes courtesy of Carol Field, a San Fransiscan who specialises in artisanal Italian breads and pastries. If you prefer, you can soak the currants in the rum overnight.

Makes 1 x 22 cm loaf cake

225 g unsalted butter, diced
225 g golden caster sugar
4 medium eggs, plus 1 egg yolk
90 ml rum, Madeira or vin santo
1 tsp vanilla extract
200 g currants
225 g plain flour, sifted
1 tsp baking powder, sifted
35 g flaked almonds
icing sugar for dusting

Heat the oven to 170°C fan oven/180°C electric oven/Gas 4 and butter and flour a 1.3 l/22 cm loaf tin. Place the butter and caster sugar in the bowl of a food processor and cream for several minutes until very pale and fluffy. Add the eggs and the yolk one at a time, scraping down the bowl if necessary. Incorporate the rum or whatever alcohol you are using, and the vanilla, and continue to process for a couple of minutes. Pour this mixture into a large bowl.

Toss the currants with a little flour to coat them. Sift the remaining flour and baking powder over the cake mixture and gently fold in, then add the currants.

Transfer the mixture to the prepared tin, mounding it a little in the centre. Sprinkle the flaked almonds over the top. This may seem like quite a lot but once the cake has risen they will spread out.

Bake the cake for 60–65 minutes until golden and risen and a skewer inserted into the centre comes out clean. Leave it to cool in the tin for several minutes, then run a knife around the edge and turn it out onto a rack. Place it the right way up and leave to cool.

Dust with icing sugar before serving.

Layered Espresso Walnut Loaf Cake

The two off-the-shelf cakes that never fail to tempt in our house are sticky ginger and layered walnut sponges sandwiched with buttercream, and this is a take on the latter. If you are after something plainer, however, simply ice the top and leave off the walnuts.

Makes 1 x 22 cm loaf cake

CAKE

225 g self-raising flour

225 g light muscovado sugar

½ tsp sea salt

225 ml groundnut oil

4 medium eggs, separated

50 ml espresso, or very strong filter coffee, cooled

50 ml milk

75 g nibbed or chopped walnuts

COFFEE CREAM

250 g mascarpone

1 tbsp espresso, or very strong filter coffee, cooled

25 g golden syrup

10 g icing sugar, sifted

ICING

100 g icing sugar, sifted, plus a little extra

1 tbsp espresso or very strong filter coffee

6–8 walnut halves to decorate

Heat the oven to 170°C fan oven/180°C electric oven/Gas 4 and butter a 1.3 l/ 22 cm loaf tin. Sift the flour, sugar and salt into a large bowl. Add the oil, the egg yolks, espresso and milk and beat with a wooden spoon until smooth. Whisk the egg whites until stiff in a large bowl (I use a hand-held electric whisk for this) and fold into the mixture in two goes. Stir in the nibbed walnuts and transfer the mixture to the cake tin, smoothing the surface. Give the tin several sharp taps on the worksurface to allow any bubbles to rise. Bake for 55–65 minutes until a skewer inserted into the centre comes out clean. Leave the cake to cool in the tin for 10 minutes, then run a knife around the edge and turn it on to a wire rack. Place it the right way up and leave to cool. If not icing it straightaway, wrap it in clingfilm.

To make the coffee cream, spoon the mascarpone into a bowl and beat in the coffee, then the syrup and icing sugar. Slit the cake into three layers, cutting the first just below the top line of the tin to take into account the risen surface. Spread the cream over the lower two layers and sandwich together. Blend the 100 g of icing sugar and coffee for the icing together in a bowl and drizzle down the centre of the cake, smoothing it towards the sides using a palette knife. Don't worry about completely covering the surface, or about it trickling down the sides. Decorate the surface with the walnut halves, then dust over a little icing sugar using a tea strainer. Leave to set for 1 hour.

White Chocolate Mousse Cake

Creamy, delicate and white, a summertime special for eating when berries are in season.

Makes 1 x 23 cm cake

MOUSSE AND FRUIT
400 ml whipping cream
250 g white chocolate, broken into pieces
125 g raspberries
125 g strawberries, hulled and halved or quartered
icing sugar for dusting
SPONGE
100 g plain flour
pinch of sea salt
6 large eggs
150 g caster sugar

Bring the cream to the boil in a small saucepan. Pour half of it over the chocolate in a bowl and stir until it is almost melted, then pour the rest over and stir until smooth. Leave this to cool, then cover and chill for at least 1 hour.

To make the sponge, heat the oven to 180°C fan oven/190°C electric oven/Gas 5. Butter two 23 cm sandwich tins with a removable base. Sift the flour into a bowl and add the salt. Place the eggs and sugar in a bowl and whisk for 8–10 minutes using an electric whisk, until the mixture is almost white and mousse-like. (You can also do this in a food processor using the whisking attachment, but reduce the time to about 5 minutes.) Lightly fold in the flour in two goes. Divide the mixture between the prepared tins, and give them a couple of sharp taps on the worksurface to eliminate any large bubbles. Bake for 12–14 minutes until the sponge is lightly golden, springy to the touch and shrinking from the sides. The cake on the lower shelf may need a few minutes longer than the top one. Remove from the oven, run a knife around the collar to loosen them, then leave to cool, when they will sink a little.

Given the delicacy of the sponge, the cake is most easily assembled on the plate you want to serve it from. Loosen the two sponges using a palette knife and place one on a plate. Using an electric whisk, beat the chocolate mixture until it forms soft but firm peaks, taking care not to overwhisk however otherwise the cream will split. Using a palette knife, spread a third of this over the surface of the sponge, sandwich with the second sponge and spread another third over the top. Use the remaining mousse to lightly coat the sides of the cake, you may need a smaller knife to do the bottom sponge. Tidy up around the edges of the plate with kitchen paper, and chill the cake for a couple of hours for the mousse to set. If keeping it any longer than this then cover with clingfilm at this point.

Just before serving, scatter the raspberries and strawberries over the top of the cake, mainly towards the centre, and dust with icing sugar. Like a trifle, the cake itself should be served lightly chilled, but the fruit is nicest at room temperature.

Towering Alaska

Shades of a baked Alaska here, a medley of sponge, jam, cream and meringues. I'm not quite sure why it should look as though it's been dragged out of the Fifties; I'm sure post-war parsimony didn't allow for anything quite as indulgent, but it does have definite retro appeal.

Serves 6–8

MERINGUES
3 medium egg whites
120 g caster sugar
pink and blue food colouring

CAKE
4 medium eggs, separated
175 g caster sugar
225 g ground almonds
1 tsp baking powder, sifted

FILLING
200 g black cherry jam (such as St Dalfour no added sugar), stirred until smooth
300 ml whipping cream, whipped

To make the meringues, heat the oven to 120°C fan oven/130°C electric oven/Gas 1. Place the egg whites in a bowl and whisk them until they rise into a froth the consistency of shaving foam. From here sprinkle over a heaped tablespoon of sugar at a time, whisking well with each addition until you have a smooth, glossy meringue. Divide the mixture into two, and colour each one a different pastel shade with a few drops of food colouring.

Line one or two baking trays with baking parchment. Drop teaspoons of the mixture on to the paper leaving plenty of space between each meringue. Place the meringues in the oven and turn it down to 100°C fan oven/110°C electric oven/ Gas ¼. Cook for 1 hour, if you are using two trays then switch them around halfway through. The meringues by the end should be crisp on the outside, and if you tap the base it should sound hollow within. Remove and leave them to cool.

To prepare the sponge, turn the oven up to 180°C fan oven/190°C electric oven/Gas 5 and butter a 23 cm tin with a removeable base. Whisk the egg yolks and sugar together in a bowl; the mixture should not be too pale and thick. Stiffly whisk the egg whites and gently fold them into the mixture in three goes. Fold in the ground almonds and the baking powder.

Pour the cake mixture into the tin and give it a couple of taps on the worksurface to bring up any air bubbles. Bake for 30–35 minutes until the top feels springy to the touch and the sides are shrinking away from the sides. A skewer inserted into the centre should come out clean. Remove the collar from the cake and leave it to cool.

Place the cake on a serving plate and using a palette knife spread the surface with the jam, taking it right to the edge. Smooth the whipped cream on top, then decorate with the meringues. Serve as soon as possible, though the cake will keep well in a cool place for a couple of hours.

Ricotta and Amaretti Cheesecake

A good cheesecake, like a quiche or savoury tart, has everything to do with set, and by design this is nothing like as firm as many. And relying on ricotta which has about half the calories of cream cheese, it is that much lighter than the norm. You could also use blueberries instead of blackcurrants, adding a couple of tablespoons of water to the pan when you heat them with the sugar.

Serves 6–8

PASTRY

40 g unsalted butter, softened

40 g caster sugar

1 large egg yolk

100 g plain flour, sifted

ALMOND CREAM

100 g amaretti

40 g unsalted butter, diced

1 large egg

FILLING

3 x 250 g tubs of ricotta

225 g caster sugar

40 g cornflour, sifted

4 medium organic eggs

2 tsp vanilla essence

150 g fromage frais

250 g blackcurrants

200 g raspberries

To make the pastry, cream the butter and sugar together until light and fluffy in a food processor or bowl. Beat in the egg yolk, and then add the flour. As soon as the dough begins to form a ball, wrap it in clingfilm and chill for at least an hour. You may need to add a couple of drops of water to bring the dough together.

Preheat the oven to 180°C fan oven/190°C electric oven/Gas 5. To make the almond cream, put the amaretti in a food processor and reduce to almost a powder. Add the butter, and cream together into the amaretti, then beat in the egg.

Butter the base of a 20 cm cake tin with a removable base. On a lightly floured surface roll out the dough to a round about 23 cm in diameter and cut a circle to fit the base of the tin. Spread the almond cream over the pastry in the tin and bake in the oven for 20 minutes until golden and firm. Allow to cool.

Reduce the oven temperature to 170°C fan oven/180°C electric oven/Gas 4. To make the filling, blend the ricotta with 175 g sugar and the cornflour in a food processor for a couple of minutes until very creamy. Now add the eggs one at a time, the vanilla essence and the fromage frais.

Wrap foil around the tin. Pour in the mixture and smooth the surface. Place it in a roasting tray with hot but not boiling water that comes 2 cm of the way up the sides of the tin and bake for 1½ hours until the centre has set and the top is golden. It may wobble a little if moved from side to side, but it shouldn't have the appearance of being sloppy beneath the surface. Once cooked, run a knife around the collar, remove it and allow to cool completely. Cover with clingfilm and chill for several hours or overnight, during which time it will set to the perfect consistency.

In the meantime, place the blackcurrants and remaining sugar in a small saucepan and heat gently for a few minutes, stirring occasionally, until the sugar has melted and the currants are almost submerged in juice. Transfer to a bowl and leave to cool, then stir in the raspberries. You can prepare the fruit in advance, and cover and chill it. Bring back up to room temperature before serving.

Remove the cheesecake from the fridge about 20 minutes before eating, and serve with the fruit spooned over.

Guilt-free Chocolate Cake

With no butter and cream, there are a host of occasions when this cake is actually preferable to a very rich one. It delights in the company of a large espresso or cup of strong black filter coffee, and keeps well for several days in the fridge, the moisture in the ricotta seeping down into the sponge and keeping it moist.

Makes 1 x 20 cm cake

SPONGE

4 medium eggs, separated
150 g golden caster sugar
3 tbsp cocoa, sifted
225 g ground almonds
1 tsp baking powder, sifted
RICOTTA CREAM
2 x 250 g tubs of ricotta, drained
   of any liquid
3 tbsp set honey
4 tbsp coarsely grated 85% cocoa
   solids dark chocolate (or other
   high percentage)

Heat the oven to 180°C fan oven/190°C electric oven/Gas 5 and butter a 20 cm springform cake tin, or one with a removable base. Stiffly whisk the egg whites in a medium bowl, I use a hand-held electric whisk for this. Also whisk together the egg yolks and sugar in a large bowl until pale and creamy. Fold the egg whites into the egg and sugar mixture in three goes, then fold in the cocoa, ground almonds and baking powder. Transfer the cake mixture to the prepared tin, smooth the surface and bake it for 35 minutes until the sponge has begun to shrink from the sides and a skewer inserted into the centre comes out clean. Run a knife around the edge of the cake and leave it to cool in the tin.

Place the ricotta and honey in a food processor and whizz until smooth – if you do this by hand it will remain grainy. Remove the collar from the cake, you can leave it on the base for ease of serving. Slit it in half, taking into account the height in the centre of the cake. Reserving a couple of tablespoons of the ricotta cream, spread the rest over the base and sandwich with the top half. Spread the reserved cream in a thin layer over the surface of the cake and scatter over the grated chocolate, which should conceal all but the very edge of the cream. Set aside in a cool place. If keeping the cake longer than a few hours, cover, chill and bring it back up to room temperature for 30–60 minutes before serving.

Old-fashioned Sponge Cake

Having grown up with them, nothing for me can beat a fluffy Victoria sponge, they are what afternoon tea on the lawn while podding beans and making daisy chains is all about. Small wonder it remains the nation's favourite cake.

Makes 1 x 20 cm cake

225 g unsalted butter, diced
225 g golden caster sugar
225 g self-raising flour
2 tsp baking powder
4 medium eggs
100 ml milk
finely grated zest of 1 lemon
   (optional)
icing sugar for dusting

Heat the oven to 170°C fan oven/180°C electric oven/Gas 4 and butter a 20 cm cake tin with a removable base. Place all the cake ingredients, except the icing sugar, in the bowl of a food processor and cream together. Transfer the mixture to the cake tin, smoothing the surface, and bake for 50–55 minutes until a skewer inserted into the centre comes out clean. Run a knife around the collar of the tin and leave it to cool. You can leave the cake on the base or remove it as you prefer. Slit with a bread knife and fill as desired, then dust with icing sugar.

* For a chocolate cake replace 25 g of the flour with sifted cocoa, and omit the zest. You can also replace the milk with coffee.
* For a coffee sponge, replace the milk with very strong black coffee, and omit the zest
* For a spiced sponge, add ½ teaspoon of ground cinnamon with the flour and use orange instead of lemon zest.

Thoroughly Modern Fillings

Espresso Cream
This is great for coffee, chocolate and nut cakes.

Makes enough to fill 1 x 20 cm cake

250 g mascarpone
1 tbsp espresso, or very strong instant coffee, cooled
25 g golden syrup
10 g icing sugar, sifted

Spoon the mascarpone into a bowl and beat in the coffee, then the syrup and icing sugar. Cover and chill until required.

Lemon Curd Cream
A good filling for orange and lemon sponges.

Makes enough to fill 1 x 20 cm cake

100 g lemon curd
250 g mascarpone

Blend the lemon curd and mascarpone in a bowl. Cover and chill until required.

Butterscotch Cream
This sits elegantly with a chocolate or coffee sponge, and with spice cakes.

Makes enough to fill 1 x 20 cm cake

250 g mascarpone
1 tsp treacle
20 g icing sugar, sifted
knife tip of ground cinnamon

Blend all the ingredients together in a bowl. Cover and chill until required.

Chocolate Cream
Any decent chocolate spread will do here, delicious in both chocolate and coffee cakes.

Makes enough to fill 1 x 20 cm cake

100 g chocolate spread
250 g mascarpone

Blend the chocolate spread and mascarpone together in a bowl. Cover and chill until required.

PUDDINGS

By the pudding stage of a meal I am feeling too pleasantly lulled by what has gone before to muster the energy for yet more cooking. I can just about manage to reach over to the worktop (and send someone else for the plates), anything more seems like untimely effort. With this in mind the vast majority of the puddings here are cold, and even the hot ones are very pleasant eaten at room temperature should you want to get everything out of the way before you sit down.

Broadly speaking they divide into light puds, the kind that round off the occasion on a sweet note without demanding too much in the way of stamina, and more substantial ones of a typically British pedigree. There is little, when you feel like sinking into the experience, that quite does it like a spiced peach crumble, a trifle, or bread and butter pudding. And if this is the mood it's not a bad idea to make it the starting point of planning a menu and to work backwards. Preceding such puddings with anything too substantial is to steal their thunder: they're the stars.

Sometimes summer is as apt a time to enjoy comfort puds as winter, especially crumbles that are so good made with peaches or apricots and plums, raspberries and blackberries. Given that menus tend to be that much lighter in the warmer months they readily adapt. And so often it's cold in any case, a chocolate macaroni pudding can come at just the moment when you're wondering whether to put the central heating back on again.

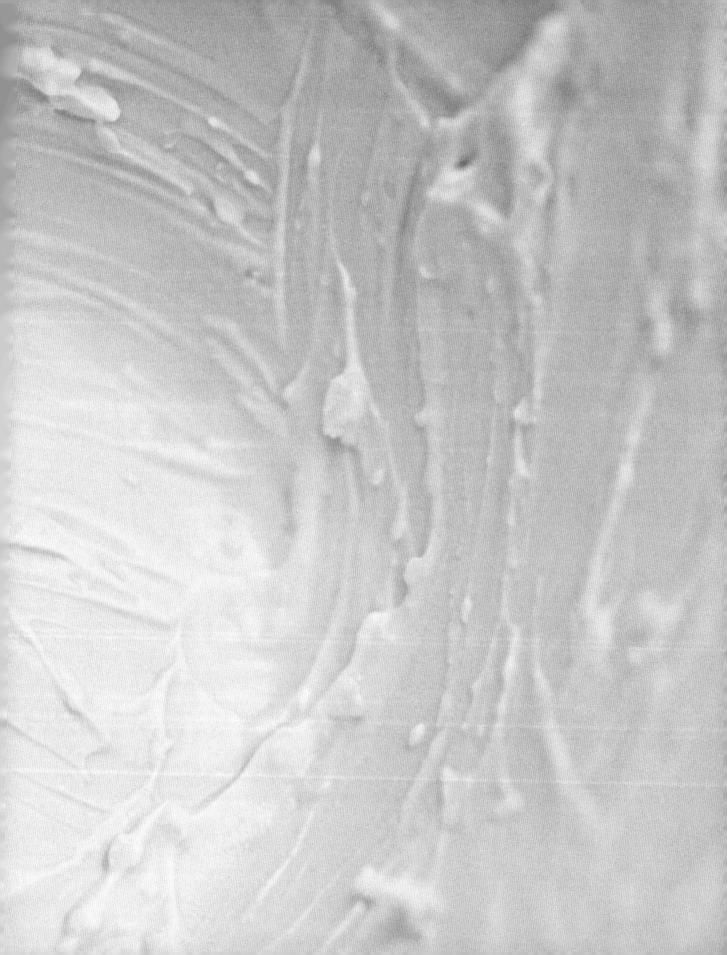

Figs Poached with Whole Spices

As a show of unparalleled hope we have two fig trees in pots in our tiny north-facing terrace that serves as a garden in London. And they are game enough to join in the pretence that we look on to a sun-drenched south-facing slope on a Greek island by putting on a show with the tiniest, Lilliputian green figs in the spring, which sadly never ripen. You can serve these on their own, or perhaps with some Greek yoghurt flavoured with rosewater and sweetened with icing sugar.

Serves 6

6 large or 12 small figs, stalks trimmed

SYRUP

1 bottle white wine

175 g caster sugar

1 star anise

1 cinnamon stick

6 green cardamom pods

Combine all the ingredients for the syrup in a medium-sized saucepan, bring to the boil and simmer for about 15 minutes until reduced by a third. Add the figs, cover with a circle of baking parchment and cook for 8 minutes, then remove the figs to a bowl. Continue to simmer the syrup for another 10–15 minutes until it is nice and syrupy. Pour this over the figs, leaving in the whole spices, and leave to cool.

Raspberry and Clotted Cream Ice

Raspberries, sugar and clotted cream crushed and frozen to an icy slush. Eat it freshly churned or at least within an hour of being frozen.

Serves 6

450 g raspberries

350 g clotted cream

150 g icing sugar, sifted

cantuccini to serve

Place the raspberries in the bowl of a food processor and briefly whizz to reduce to a textured purée. Beat the cream and sugar in a large bowl until smooth, then fold in the raspberries in two goes. You can make this in advance and freeze it shortly before serving, in which case cover and chill it.

Freeze the raspberries and cream mixture according to the instructions for your ice cream maker. Ideally serve the ice straightaway, but it will keep in the fridge for up to an hour. Accompany with cantuccini.

Turkish Delight Syllabub

The Middle Eastern delis at the bottom of Kensington High Street always have big trays of pastel-coloured cubes of Turkish delight concealed by a blanket of icing sugar, which make it as hard to eat without licking your lips as doughnuts.

Serves 4

juice of 1 orange
50 g caster sugar
6 tbsp sweet white wine
300 ml double cream
1 tbsp rosewater
a couple of drops of pink food
   colouring
2 squares of pink Turkish delight
icing sugar for dusting

Place the orange juice and sugar in a bowl and leave for 2 hours. Stir to dissolve the sugar, there will probably still be a small amount left on the bottom, but don't worry about this.

Add a little of the wine to the cream in a bowl and whip until it just starts to form a trail. Gradually whisk in the remaining wine and then the orange juice, whisking well with each addition until the mixture thickens. If the wine and orange juice are added too quickly, the mixture will curdle. Finally whisk in the rosewater and a couple of drops of pink food colouring.

If not serving straightaway, cover and chill. In this case give it a stir before serving. Spoon into glasses, bowls or one large bowl. Cut the Turkish delight into 1 cm nibs and toss these with a little icing sugar in a bowl to stop them sticking together. Scatter over each glass or the bowl and serve.

Jelly and Cream

Try serving the Turkish Delight Syllabub with Watermellon Jelly (see page 210), less the marshmallows.

Blackberry Fool

The countryside surrounding our farmhouse in Normandy is known as the bocage, *a medieval arrangement of fields traced by the lines of hedgerows, an impenetrable tangled mass of vegetation made up of an anarchic diversity of flowers, bushes, small trees and grasses. I start eyeing up the rich promise of elderberries and blackberries that drip down at every pace as early as August.*

We used to do a huge amount of blackberry picking as children, and my mother made bramble jelly every year. We always laid our booty out on big trays for a couple of hours in the kitchen to let any wormies and other residents make their way out before using them, which I still do.

Serves 4

500 g blackberries
110 g vanilla sugar*
300 ml whipping cream

Reserving 75 g of the blackberries, place the remainder with the sugar in a small saucepan and heat gently until the berries turn a pinker shade of purple and shed copious juices into the pan. Remove from the heat, whizz the fruit to a purée in a food processor and press through a sieve, then leave to cool.

Whip the cream in a large bowl as stiffly as possible without it curdling. Fold in two thirds of the blackberry purée a third at a time, and stir the reserved berries into the remainder. Cover both the fool and the sauce and chill if not serving straightaway. Serve it spooned into small bowls or glasses, trickling the reserved sauce on top.

* You can make vanilla sugar by whizzing a chopped vanilla pod in a food processor with 225 g caster sugar. Sieve and keep it in an airtight jar.

Lemon Jelly

Saffron dyes the jelly as yellow as the outside of a lemon, as well as scenting it. Its mouthpuckering sharpness makes this jelly a grown-up thing, but a rude shock to the average child used to the saccharine delights of packet jelly. All the more for you.

Serves 6

a small pinch of saffron filaments, (approx. 10)
1 x 11 g sachet gelatine
180 g caster sugar
juice of 3 lemons
150 g blueberries

Grind the saffron filaments in a pestle and mortar, cover with 1 tablespoon of boiling water and leave to infuse for 30 minutes.

Sprinkle the gelatine on to 4 tablespoons of just boiled water in a small bowl, leave for 3–4 minutes and then stir to dissolve. If the gelatine has not completely dissolved, stand the bowl in another bowl of just-boiled water for a few minutes, then stir again.

Place the sugar in a measuring jug and fill up to the 300 ml mark with boiling water. Stir to dissolve the sugar, then pour in the gelatine solution and stir well. Now add the lemon juice and the saffron liquor and make up to 600 ml of liquid with boiling water. Strain through a sieve into 6 rinsed 9 cm or 150 ml ramekins, or one large glass bowl. Cover with clingfilm (I place them in a roasting dish for this), leave to cool and then place in the fridge to set overnight.

You can either serve the jellies straight out of their little pots, scattered with the blueberries, or briefly dip the moulds into a bowl of boiling water, run a knife around the edge and turn out on to plates, and then scatter with a few blueberries.

Watermelon Jelly

Watermelon has never been my favourite fruit, the interruption of all those pips. But here it redeems itself, and this jelly just might take the fancy of any young offspring.

Makes 6

900 g watermelon flesh (trimmed weight), diced and deseeded
2 tbsp lemon juice
180 g caster sugar
1½ x 11 g sachets of gelatine
6 pink marshmallows

Place the watermelon in a liquidiser and reduce to a purée. Pass through a sieve into a measuring jug, and add the lemon juice. You should have about 900 ml of liquid. Transfer to a small saucepan and heat gently with the sugar until this dissolves; it should feel hot if you dip in your finger, without scalding.

Sprinkle the gelatine over several tablespoons of just-boiled water in a small bowl and leave for several minutes to dissolve, then stir. If necessary place it within a second bowl of just-boiled water and leave it a few minutes longer, then stir again. Stir a couple of tablespoons of the watermelon purée into the gelatine solution, then mix this back in with the rest of the purée. Transfer to a bowl or jug and leave to cool. Rinse six individual moulds or small dishes with water, stir the jelly solution and divide it between them. Cover with clingfilm and chill for 2 hours until the jelly has just started to set. Give it a stir, then cover and chill overnight.

To serve the jellies, run a knife around the outside to loosen them and turn out on to plates. Heat the grill, place the marshmallows on a sheet of foil on the rack of a grill pan, and toast until the tops lightly colour while retaining their shape. Using a palette knife, carefully slip one on to the top of each jelly. Serve straightaway.

Floating Islands with Apple Purée

While almond custard is the favourite pool on which to float these poached meringues, when I make them in France a purée of local apples embellished with a drop of Calvados and a spoonful of raw cream seems a better treatment. Given the last-minute kerfuffle of poaching meringues, you can make them in advance of lunch or dinner if preferred, they're still yummy at room temperature.

Serves 6

APPLE PURÉE
1.3 kg eating apples, quartered
100 g caster sugar
a squeeze of lemon juice
3 tbsp mature Calvados
FLOATING ISLANDS
2 large egg whites
a pinch of salt
50 g caster sugar
TO SERVE
6 tbsp crème fraîche
225 g raspberries or wild strawberries
6 almond tuiles or other dessert biscuits

To make the apple purée, place the quartered apples in a saucepan, add the sugar and 300 ml of water. Bring this to a simmer then cover with a lid and cook gently for 20 minutes, stirring occasionally until the apples are soft and mushy. Pass them through a mouli-légumes or a sieve into a bowl, then flavour the purée with a squeeze of lemon juice and the Calvados. Taste for sweetness and add a little more sugar if necessary. Leave to cool to room temperature.

To make the floating islands, fill a large frying or sauté pan with water and bring it to a simmer. The water should be at no more than a trembling boil. Whisk the egg whites in a bowl with the salt. Once they are risen, gradually sprinkle over the sugar, whisking well with each addition until you have a glossy meringue. To cook the floating islands, drop heaped tablespoons of the meringue mixture into the water using another spoon to help each 'island' slide off, you should have six in all. Turn after 30 seconds using a slotted spatula and cook for another 30 seconds. Remove and drain them on kitchen paper or a tea towel.

Spoon some of the purée (at room temperature) over the base of six shallow bowls or plates. Place a floating island on top, dollop on a spoonful of the crème fraîche, scatter over the raspberries or wild strawberries and accompany with a tuile or some other dessert biscuit.

Pistachio Kulfi

Indian kulfi isn't quite as rich as ice cream while not as austere as a sorbet, relying on milk that's reduced and thickened for its creamy body.

Serves 6

1.8 l full cream milk
1 level tsp cornflour
150 g caster sugar
1 tbsp rosewater
70 g raw shelled pistachios, plus a few extra

Pour the milk into a large saucepan, bring to the boil and simmer for about 45 minutes over a medium heat to reduce by half. Don't worry about the skin that forms during the cooking – simply lift this off at the end. Blend a tablespoon of the reduced milk with the cornflour, return it to the saucepan and simmer for several more minutes until it thickens a little. Remove from the heat, add the sugar and stir to dissolve, then add the rosewater. Pour through a sieve into a jug or bowl, cover the surface with clingfilm and leave to cool. Chill for a couple of hours or overnight.

Grind 50 g of the pistachios to a powder in an electric coffee grinder and finely chop the remaining 20 g. Stir the ground pistachios into the kulfi base, and then add the chopped ones. Freeze the mixture in your ice cream maker according to the instructions. Either serve it straightaway, or transfer it to a plastic container, cover and freeze. It is at its best eaten within about 3 hours; if keeping it any longer, take it out of the freezer 30 minutes before serving to allow it to soften a little. Finely chop a few more pistachios and sprinkle over the ice cream when you serve it.

Bottom-crust Pear and Gorgonzola Tart

An unlikely creation, which conveniently combines the cheese and sweet course and makes a deliciously dynamic end. The cheese melts over the sweetened pears, and as you cut into it the short crumbly pastry spills lots of syrupy juices. No call for cream.

Serves 6

PASTRY

350 g plain flour

½ tsp sea salt

1 tsp caster sugar

200 g unsalted butter, chilled and diced

2 medium egg yolks

FILLING

5 slightly under-ripe Comice pears, peeled, quartered and thickly sliced lengthwise

juice of ½ lemon

2 tbsp caster sugar

1 tbsp plain flour

130 g demerara sugar, plus 2 tsp

200 g Gorgonzola (weight excluding rind), diced

milk for brushing

To make the pastry, place the flour, salt, sugar and butter in the bowl of a food processor and whizz at a high speed until the mixture resembles fine crumbs. Incorporate the egg yolks, then with the motor running trickle in just enough cold water to bring the dough together in lumps. Transfer to a large bowl and gather into a ball using your hands. Wrap the dough in clingfilm and chill for at least 1 hour. It can be chilled for up to 2 days.

Toss the pears with the lemon juice in a bowl to prevent them from discolouring, then scatter over the caster sugar and set aside for 30 minutes. Drain the pears, discarding the juices, and dry on kitchen paper. Place in a large clean bowl and toss with the flour.

Heat the oven to 180°C fan oven/190°C electric oven/Gas 5. Knead the pastry until it's pliable, then thinly roll it out on a lightly floured worksurface and cut out a circle 35 cm in diameter. Carefully lift the pastry into a 23 cm pie plate or shallow-sided tart tin with a removeable base, on top of a baking sheet. You should have a 5 cm rim of pastry overhanging the sides. Sprinkle the 130 g demerara sugar over the pears and toss, then mix in half the cheese. Pile the filling into the tin, and fold the pastry sides up over the pears. Paint them with milk and dust with the remaining demerara sugar. Dot the remaining cheese over the exposed fruit (while this might appear crowded the cheese will melt down) and bake the tart for 45 minutes until the pastry and cheese are golden. Leave the tart to cool for at least 20 minutes. Loosen the collar with a knife, remove it and slip the tart on its base on to a plate. The tart is also delicious served at room temperature.

Raspberry Macaroon

A variation on the theme of a crumble, a crispy macaroon for a bed of raspberries, and apricots that are always so much better cooked than raw.

Serves 4–6

100 g self-raising flour

125 g desiccated coconut

150 g golden caster sugar

150 g unsalted butter, chilled and diced

8 apricots

200 g raspberries

Heat the oven to 170°C fan oven/180°C electric oven/Gas 4. Combine the flour, coconut and 120 g of the sugar in a bowl and rub in the butter until you have large crumbs. This can also be done in a food processor, but give it just a quick burst or two as it behaves in a slightly different fashion to a normal crumble, without reducing to very fine crumbs. It's ready as soon as the butter breaks down into little nibs, but if you do miss this point simply transfer the mixture to a large bowl and break up any large lumps with your fingers.

Quarter the apricots, removing the stones, and arrange them with the raspberries in the base of a shallow 1.7 l/30 cm oval gratin or ovenproof dish. Sprinkle over the remaining sugar, and then scatter over the crumble mixture. Bake the crumble for 40–45 minutes until golden and the juices are bubbling at the edges. The crumble is at its best eaten 20–30 minutes out of the oven.

Old-fashioned Rice Pudding

You can whisk this one together on a cold winter's afternoon, go out for a few hours and come back to the scent of vanilla filling the kitchen, and a golden-skinned pudding with a layer of creamy, sweetened milk below. It's in its element eaten with a spoonful of cherry jam, and you want the richest, yellowest milk you can find, with a good head of cream on it.

I favour risotto rice over the usual pudding variety, as it's that much better at retaining its texture and shape. They're both short grain, and belong to the Japonica family that includes sticky and sushi rice, but the starch is altogether different from that found in basmati and other long grain rice.

Serves 6

1 vanilla pod, slit
140 g arborio risotto rice
140 g golden caster sugar
1½ l whole milk
cherry jam to serve

Heat the oven to 120°C fan oven/130°C electric oven/Gas ½. Open out the vanilla pod and run a knife along its length to scrape out the seeds. Place these together with the rice, the sugar and a little milk in a small casserole or 1.8 l deep ovenproof dish (I use a china pie dish), and mess them up to distribute the vanilla seeds. Add the rest of the milk and stir, place the vanilla pod in the centre and cook in the oven for 3¾–4 hours by which time it should be sealed with a thin golden skin. Leave the pudding for 30 minutes to settle, then serve with a spoonful of cherry jam.

Spiced Peach Crumble

Sugar and spice and all things nice, the scent of peaches baking in a buttery cinnamon crumble. To accompany this, I'd think along the lines of some raw cream or crème fraîche, possibly flavoured with a drop of liqueur and a little icing sugar, or else vanilla ice cream. In Normandy ground hazelnuts are as common as ground almonds and equally good, easily mustered with a coffee grinder.

Serves 4–6

4 yellow or white peaches, stoned
  and sliced
juice of ½ lemon
2 tbsp golden caster sugar
50 g redcurrants
100 g plain flour
125 g ground almonds
125 g light muscovado sugar
¾ tsp ground cinnamon
150 g unsalted butter, chilled
  and diced

Place the peach slices in a bowl, pour over the lemon juice, scatter over the caster sugar, toss and set aside for 30 minutes. Drain them into a sieve, discarding the juices, and place in a shallow 1.7 l/30 cm oval gratin or ovenproof dish. Scatter over the redcurrants.

Heat the oven to 170°C fan oven/180°C electric oven/Gas 4. Combine the flour, ground almonds, muscovado sugar and cinnamon in a bowl and rub in the butter until you have large crumbs. This can also be done in a food processor, taking care to stop the motor before it turns into a dough. Scatter this mixture over the fruit, and bake for 45 minutes until the top is golden and crisp. Leave the crumble to cool for 20–30 minutes; it's also delicious cold.

Dark Chocolate Trifle

Lying halfway between a tiramisu and a trifle, this is suitably gorgeous. You could serve it with a bowl of raspberries or blackberries, both of which complement chocolate beautifully.

Serves 6

200 g dark chocolate (such as Menier), broken up

5 medium organic eggs, separated

250 ml strong fresh black coffee, cooled

125 ml Kahlua or Tia Maria

125 ml single cream

1 x 200 g packet of sponge fingers (boudoir biscuits)

70 g white chocolate, coarsely grated

raspberries to serve

Place the dark chocolate in a large bowl set over a pan of simmering water and heat gently until it melts. Remove from the heat and whisk in the egg yolks. Combine the cold coffee and Kahlua or Tia Maria in a shallow bowl. Stir a tablespoon of this into the chocolate mixture, and then add the single cream. Whisk the egg whites in another large bowl until they are stiff (I use an electric hand-held whisk for this), then fold them a third at a time into the chocolate mixture.

Smear a spoon or two of the chocolate mousse over the base of a 1.5 l, shallow dish (e.g. a 30 cm oval gratin dish). Dip the sponge fingers a few at a time into the coffee-liqueur mixture to soak them, and cover the base of the dish, using up half of them. Pour over half the chocolate mousse, then repeat with the remaining sponge fingers and mousse so you have two layers of each. You will probably use up all the liquor, but should you run out then make up a little more. Scatter over the white chocolate. Cover the trifle and chill for at least 2 hours, otherwise overnight. Serve scattered with raspberries.

Passionfruit and Mascarpone Roulade

There is something rather alluring about a sponge rolled with its filling into a snail-shell spiral. No need for extra sauce or cream here but a couple of physalis with their petals pulled back dusted with icing sugar look very pretty on the side. It is best eaten within a few hours of being made.

Serves 6–8

SPONGE

50 g plain flour

pinch of sea salt

3 large eggs

75 g caster sugar

½ tsp vanilla essence

icing sugar

FILLING

50 g icing sugar for dusting

350 g mascarpone

5 passionfruit, halved

To make the sponge, heat the oven to 180°C fan oven/190°C electric oven/Gas 5. Butter a 23 x 32 cm Swiss roll tin, line it with baking parchment and butter this also. Sift the flour into a bowl and add the salt. Place the eggs, sugar and vanilla essence in a bowl and whisk for 8–10 minutes using an electric whisk, until the mixture is almost white and mousse-like. You can also do this in a food processor using the whisking attachment, in which case reduce the time to about 5 minutes. Lightly fold in the flour in two goes. Pour the mixture into the prepared tin and smooth it using a palette knife. Give the tin a couple of sharp taps on the worksurface to eliminate any large bubbles and bake the sponge for 8–10 minutes until it is lightly golden and springy to the touch.

Lay out a clean tea towel and sift over a fine layer of icing sugar. Turn the cake out on to it and carefully roll it up with the tea towel leaving the paper in place, starting at the short end so you end up with a short fat roll. Leave this to cool for 40–60 minutes.

To fill the roulade, sift the icing sugar into a bowl, add the mascarpone and blend them. Carefully unroll the sponge and peel off the paper parchment. Spread with the mascarpone then scoop out and smooth the passionfruit seeds on top. Roll the sponge up again and tip it on to a long serving plate, seam downwards. Dust with icing sugar. Chill it uncovered if not serving straightaway, returning to room temperature 30 minutes before eating. Dust it with icing sugar at the last minute.

Chocolate Macaroni Pudding

A surprisingly good oddity, where the pasta acquires the texture of pancakes, coated in a creamy chocolate sauce.

Serves 4–6

1 l whole milk
150 ml double cream
80 g caster sugar
100 g high-percentage cocoa solids dark chocolate, broken into pieces
150 g macaroni

Heat the oven to 140°C fan oven/150°C electric oven/Gas 2. Place the milk, cream and sugar in a medium-sized saucepan and bring to the boil. Remove from the heat, add the chocolate and leave for several minutes, then whisk to blend it in. Bring back to the boil and scatter over the macaroni. Pour the mixture into a 1.5 l/ 30 cm gratin or other shallow ovenproof dish, evenly distributing the pasta over the base, and bake for 1½ hours. Allow to stand for 15 minutes before eating.

Panettone Pudding

Panettone contains an artful mix of dried fruits and candied peel that does away with the need for raisins and the like. Though for a traditional bread and butter pud you can scatter 50 g of sultanas and raisins over the base of the dish and replace the panettone with triangles of a coarse-textured white or rye bread with a good crust on it. A day's staling will provide just the right texture – nothing too fresh, as the aim is a crumb that can hold its custard.

After years of avoiding salted butter in favour of unsalted, I am doing a u-turn. The epiphany came in Normandy where salted butters are set with minute crystals of sea salt that crunch and dissolve on the tongue as you eat them.

Serves 6

3 medium eggs
150 g golden caster sugar
425 ml double cream
425 ml milk
salted butter
10–12 x 1 cm slices panettone, (cut from a 500 g loaf)
1 vanilla pod
90 g apricot jam, warmed and sieved (optional)

Heat the oven to 160°C fan oven/170°C electric oven/Gas 3. Whisk the eggs and sugar in a bowl, then whisk in the cream and milk. Butter the panettone and arrange in overlapping slices to cover the base of a 2.6 l/35 cm oval gratin or other shallow ovenproof dish. The centre may take two slices side by side, while the narrow ends will only hold one. Pour the custard through a sieve over and around the panettone, tuck the vanilla pod beneath the custard in the centre.

Place the gratin dish in a roasting pan with cold water that comes two thirds of the way up the sides. Bake for 1 hour until the custard is puffy and set and the bread golden. Brush the surface of the bread with the apricot jam; this bit is optional but it gives the pudding a lovely sticky glaze. Serve straightaway. The vanilla pod can be rinsed and used again.

INDEX

DEDICATION

For Jonnie, Rothko and Louis, with love

ACKNOWLEDGMENTS

With countless thanks to those who have assisted in the making of this book.
To my agent Rosemary Sandberg at Ed Victor, to Lorraine Dickey at Conran
Octopus for commissioning it, to the Art Director Chi Lam for designing it, and
to Katey Day as Senior Editor. Thanks also to Annie Lee for her painstaking copy
editing, Lisa Linder for the photographs, and Jacque Malouf for preparing the food
on shoot days. To Angela Mason, Food Editor on *YOU Magazine* in the *Mail on
Sunday*. And to Shona Crawford-Poole, Food Editor on *Country Living*. Lastly,
thanks to those friends who were game enough to have a camera pointed in their
direction, especially Louis's friends who were so beautifully behaved, and consumed
large quantities of jelly and cake without complaining.